ISBN 978-1-330-18418-9
PIBN 10046995

THE

NOVELS AND NOVELISTS

OF THE

EIGHTEENTH CENTURY,

IN ILLUSTRATION OF THE

Manners and Morals of the Age.

BY

WILLIAM FORSYTH, M.A., Q.C.,

AUTHOR OF 'THE LIFE OF CICERO,' 'CASES AND OPINIONS ON CONSTITUTIONAL LAW
ETC., ETC. ;
LATE FELLOW OF TRINITY COLLEGE, CAMBRIDGE.

LONDON :

JOHN MURRAY, ALBEMARLE STREET.

1871.

LONDON:
BRADBURY, EVANS, AND CO., PRINTERS, WHITEFRIARS.

PREFACE.

I BEGAN this work intending to amuse the idleness of a Long Vacation; but a severe and dangerous illness, caused by an accident, entirely baffled my design, and I was obliged to finish the task when I had much less leisure. I do not say this to deprecate criticism—if the work is to be criticised at all — but merely state the fact, which may account for shortcomings that are very likely to be discovered. But I hope that the book will be judged by what it professes to be, and not by what it is not. It is not a history of the works of Fiction of the last century, which would have required much more copious detail, but a view of the manners and morals of that century, as gathered principally from hints and descriptions in the novels of the period, corroborated by facts from other sources. But I have not thought it necessary to adhere strictly and formally to this programme, and have therefore introduced sketches of the plots and characters of some of the most interesting and once widely popular novels, which for various reasons remain practically unknown to the great mass of readers of the present day, and especially to the female part of them. To do this and give anything like a just idea of the originals, without offending against decorum, is no easy task, nor do I at all flatter myself that I have succeeded. But the very difficulty is in itself a proof of the difference, in one important respect, between the taste and manners of the last and the taste and manners of the present century. In these, I think, it cannot be denied that there has been a great improvement; but I hope it will not be supposed that I mean to imply that our more decorous sins are not morally quite as bad as the vices of our coarser and more free-spoken ancestors. We may be thankful that in many aspects the state of society is better now than then : but the luxury of the rich is still in startling contrast with the misery of the poor, and although vice may have lost its grossness, it still lurks like a canker in the Commonwealth. We shall have little cause to boast of our superior morality, if we

> Compound for sins we are inclined to,
> By damning those we have no mind to.

CONTENTS.

CHAPTER I.

PAGE

FICTION IN RELATION TO FACT.—INFORMATION TO BE GLEANED
FROM NOVELS.—GENERAL CHARACTERISTICS OF THE LAST
CENTURY.—ITS COARSENESS.—RELIGION.—LOVE.—INFLU-
ENCE OF THE AGE UPON WOMEN.—THE ESSAYISTS.—
HOGARTH.—PROGRESS OF REFINEMENT.—DANGER OF MIS-
TAKING SATIRE AND CARICATURE FOR TRUTH) . . . i

CHAPTER II.

DRESS. — MASQUERADES. — DRUMS. — 'PRETTY FELLOWS' AND
'MACCARONIES.'—CLUBS.—RANELAGH AND VAUXHALL.—
LONDON.—DANGERS OF THE STREETS — STATE OF THE
ROADS.—HIGHWAYMEN 54

CHAPTER III.

PRISONS. — DRUNKENNESS.—SWEARING. — GAMBLING. —DUEL-
LING.—JUSTICE OF THE PEACE.—COUNTRY SQUIRE . . 89

CHAPTER IV.

THE PARSON OF THE LAST CENTURY.—FLEET MARRIAGES . 121

CHAPTER V.

THE OLD ROMANCES—'THE FEMALE QUIXOTE.'—NOVELS OF
THE LAST CENTURY.—THEIR COARSENESS AND ITS APOLO-
GISTS.—'CHRYSAL, OR THE ADVENTURES OF A GUINEA.'
—'POMPEY.'—'THE FOOL OF QUALITY.'—TWO CLASSES
OF NOVELS.—'SIMPLE STORY.'—THE COMIC NOVELS . 149

CHAPTER VI.

PAGE

MRS. BEHN AND HER NOVELS. — 'OROONOKO.' — 'THE WANDERING BEAUTY.' — 'THE UNFORTUNATE HAPPY LADY.' — MRS. MANLEY AND 'THE NEW ATALANTIS.' — 'THE POWER OF LOVE IN SEVEN NOVELS.' — 'THE FAIR HYPOCRITE.' — MRS. HEYWOOD. — HER NOVEL, 'MISS BETSY THOUGHTLESS'. 174

CHAPTER VII.

RICHARDSON. — 'CLARISSA HARLOWE.' — 'PAMELA.' — 'SIR CHARLES GRANDISON.' — RICHARDSON'S CORRESPONDENCE. HIS PORTRAIT DRAWN BY HIMSELF 213

CHAPTER VIII.

FIELDING. — 'TOM JONES,' A FAVOURITE OF THE LADIES. — 'JOSEPH ANDREWS.' — 'AMELIA.' 258

CHAPTER IX.

SMOLLETT. — DIFFERENCE BETWEEN HIM AND FIELDING. — 'PEREGRINE PICKLE.' — 'HUMPHRY CLINKER.' — 'THE SPIRITUAL QUIXOTE' 278

CHAPTER X.

GOLDSMITH. — 'THE VICAR OF WAKEFIELD.' — CHARACTER OF LATER NOVELS AND ROMANCES. — MACKENZIE. — 'THE MAN OF FEELING,' 'THE MAN OF THE WORLD,' AND 'JULIA DE ROUBIGNÉ.' — MISS BURNEY. — 'EVELINA,' AND 'CECILIA.' — MISS EDGEWORTH. — 'BELINDA.' — JANE AUSTEN. — USES OF NOVELS. — RESPONSIBILITY OF THE NOVELIST . . 305

NOVELS AND NOVELISTS

OF THE

EIGHTEENTH CENTURY.

CHAPTER I.

FICTION IN RELATION TO FACT.—INFORMATION TO BE
GLEANED FROM NOVELS.—GENERAL CHARACTERISTICS
OF THE LAST CENTURY.—ITS COARSENESS.—RELIGION.
—LOVE.—INFLUENCE OF THE AGE UPON WOMEN.—THE
ESSAYISTS.—HOGARTH.—PROGRESS OF REFINEMENT.—
DANGER OF MISTAKING SATIRE AND CARICATURE FOR
TRUTH.

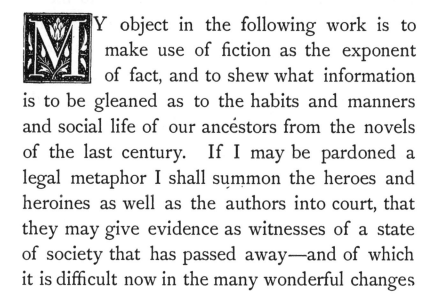

MY object in the following work is to make use of fiction as the exponent of fact, and to shew what information is to be gleaned as to the habits and manners and social life of our ancestors from the novels of the last century. If I may be pardoned a legal metaphor I shall summon the heroes and heroines as well as the authors into court, that they may give evidence as witnesses of a state of society that has passed away—and of which it is difficult now in the many wonderful changes

that have since taken place to form a right idea.
We may read Histories of England, and be
familiar with the pages of Cunningham, Belsham,
Adolphus, Hume and Smollett (I mean Smollett, as an historian), and yet be almost entirely
ignorant of the manners and habits and mode
of life of our forefathers : of their houses and
dress : their domestic arrangements and amusements : of the state of religion and morality and
all that goes to make up the character of a
people. As one of our greatest novelists has
said, " Out of the fictitious book I get the expression of the life, of the times, of the manners,
of the merriment, of the dress, the pleasures, the
laughter, the ridicules of society—the old times
live again, and I travel in the old country of
England. Can the heaviest historian do more
for me ? " *   I answer, not half so much.   The
historian tells us of Court factions and political
intrigues, and the struggles of an Oligarchy of
great families for power—of the Walpoles and
Newcastles, and Grenvilles and Pitts—of foreign
wars and domestic treason—but little of the
condition of the peasantry and life of the people,
and absolutely nothing of the state of society in
the period.   Paradoxical as it may seem, there
can be no doubt that fiction is often more truth-

* Thackeray, ' English Humourists,' p. 113.

ful than fact.   By this I mean that a more correct idea of a period may be formed from a story where the personages and many of the incidents are imaginary, than from a dry, dull, narrative of events.   The most lifelike account of the Civil Wars in England in the seventeenth century that I know is contained in De Foe's ' Memoirs of a Cavalier,' which it is impossible to read without believing that it is the work of a writer who had been himself an actor in the scenes which he describes—and which Lord Chatham indeed quoted as a genuine history. And yet it is as much a fiction as Waverley, with its picture of the Rebellion of 1745.

Without some such object in view, it would have been difficult to go through the task of reading what I have been obliged to read.   For as stories the novels of the last century, with the exception of some well-known names, are deplorably dull.   Their plots are contemptible, and the style is detestable.   But, however poor the incidents, or inartistic the construction, the writers unconsciously give us hints when they least intended it of the manners and customs of the time.   We may turn with disgust from the insipid narrative and stupid dialogue ; but we get from both little traits of habits and opinions which are valuable, as enabling us to form a just idea of the state of society around. We learn how our ancestors lived, how they amused themselves, and the conversation they indulged in ; how they travelled in lumbering coaches drawn by six Flanders mares ; the books they read, the hour at which they dined, and the dress they wore ; how the boys played at "tagg" and "thrush-a-thrush," and the girls at "draw-gloves" and "questions and commands." We are brought into contact with drums and ridottos, and masquerades ; with Ranelagh and Vauxhall, "Marybone Gardens" and the Pantheon ; with swords and periwigs, and *fontanges ;* dominoes and masques ; minuets, cotillons and Sir Roger de Coverleys ; ombre and quadrille, and lansquenet ; with Pope Joan, and "snip snap snorum ;" and we see pictured before us the "life of the fine old English gentleman— all of the olden time."

There is, indeed, no source from which so much information may be gleaned with respect to the social life of our ancestors as the Novels, supplemented by Diaries and Letters, such as those of Lady Cowper, Lady Mary Wortley Montague, and Mrs. Delany ; the Richardson correspondence, and that of the Malmesbury family and Horace Walpole. We find ourselves there living in a world strangely different from that of our own day. This difference is shown in a thousand ways, by which the writers unconsciously betray the existence of habits and manners which have now ceased to exist. We find there the loud swearing, the hard drinking, the loose talk, which were common even amongst those who called themselves gentlemen ; the swords drawn and the duels fought on the slightest provocation ; the stiffness of intercourse between parents and children, and the ceremonious coldness with which the latter addressed the former in their letters, beginning with " Sir" and " Madam," and ending with " Your dutiful child and humble servant." *

But there is a difficulty in the way. We have to face an amount of coarseness which is in the highest degree repulsive. It is like raking a dirt heap to discover grains of gold. And herein lies the specialty of the case. It is because the novels reflect, as in a mirror, the tone of thought and language of the age in which they were written, that the perusal of them even now is useful ; and we get from them a much more truthful idea of the state of society and morals than from pompous histories and laboured

* Dr. Johnson almost always ends his letters to Boswell with the subscription, " your affectionate and very humble servant", and Boswell does the same when he writes to the object of his idolatry.

essays. That 'Roderick Random,' 'Peregrine Pickle,' 'Tom Jones' and 'Tristram Shandy' could have been written and become popular, not only amongst men but amongst women, proves that society was accustomed to actions and language which would not be tolerated now.

It is beside my purpose to describe the intellectual characteristics of the century, and attempt to estimate its true value amongst the centuries of the world's history with reference to the greatness of the men it produced, and the works they left behind them. Whatever may be thought of the average, it is impossible to deny that the age was the parent of some of the most illustrious names of which England can boast. The general face of the sky might be dark, but there were stars in the firmament that shone with brilliant splendour. Butler and Clarke among Divines; Pope, Chatterton, and Cowper among Poets; Addison and Johnson, *magnum et venerabile nomen*, among Essayists; Wilson, Gainsborough, and Reynolds among Painters; Chatham and Burke among Statesmen; Hardwicke and Mansfield among Lawyers; Fielding, Smollett, and Goldsmith among Novelists; Marlborough among Generals; Bentley among Scholars; Gibbon among Historians; and

Erskine among Advocates ; — are names of which any period might be proud, and they redeem the eighteenth century from the reproach which has been cast upon it by a distinguished but eccentric writer of the present day, who says that "it lies massed up in our minds as a disastrous wrecked inanity not useful to dwell upon : a kind of dusky chaotic background, in which the figures that had some veracity in them — a small company, and ever growing smaller, as our demands rise in strictness—are delineated for us."*

As regards, however, the social aspect of the age, and the general tone of thought, it is, I think, impossible to deny that the bygone century is not an attractive period.

There was little of the earnestness of life and quick invention and active benevolence which are the characteristics of our own age. The questions that have stirred the hearts of the present generation then slumbered in the womb of time. Reform, Free Trade, Education, and Sanitary Laws, occupied no part of the thoughts of statesmen, and excited no interest in the people. The miracles of change which have been wrought by Steam, Electricity, Chloroform, Photography, and Breech-loading Artillery,

* Carlyle, ' Frederick the Great,' vol. i. p. 2.

revolutionising Mechanics and Science, and
Medicine, and Art and War, were not even
suspected as possible.   The state of our prisons
and workhouses and lunatic asylums was simply
a disgrace to humanity.   Our criminal law was
written in characters of blood.   To commit a
murder, or pick a pocket, or cut down a young
apple tree, was punished by the same penalty,
and that penalty was—death.   The lower classes
led the existence of animals and were brutal
even in their sports.   Cock-fighting, bull-baiting,
and the bear-garden were the ordinary amusements, diversified sometimes by the fun of duck-
ing an old woman in a horse-pond as a witch.
The country gentlemen, as a class, were boorish
and ignorant, devoted to the bottle and the
chase.   The country clergy frequented alehouses and intermarried with housemaids.   We
read in the 'Connoisseur' (A.D. 1755), that "the
kept-mistress is a constant part of the retinue of
a fine gentleman, and is indeed as indispensable
a part of his equipage as a French *valet-de-
chambre* or a four-wheeled post-chaise."

On the pleasant banks of the Thames, not far
from Marlow, may be seen the ruins of Med-
menham Abbey, which was formerly the scene
of the orgies of the Hell-Fire Club.   It was
here that the company of hard drinkers and

professed infidels were frightened out of their wits, one night, by the sudden appearance of a monkey, which in their tipsy confusion they mistook for the Devil. And yet they pretended not to believe in any devil at all !

A recent writer, who has attacked with unsparing severity the faults which, until our own day, disgraced English jurisprudence,* says of the period, " The upper classes were corrupt, without refinement ; the middle, gross without good humour ; and the lower, brutal without honesty."† I do not think it is fair to say that the middle classes had no good humour and the lower no honesty ; but it is certainly true, that grossness and brutality were their characteristics,‡ and beyond all doubt their condition was very lamentable.

---

* There was great truth in what a Justice of the Peace is made to say in Fielding's ' Amelia :'—" And to speak my opinion plainly, such are the laws, and such the method of proceeding, that one would almost think our laws were made for the protection of rogues rather than for the punishment of them." And as regards civil rights, those who wish to know how justice was sacrificed to chicane, even in our own day, may be amply satisfied by looking at the sixteen volumes of the ' Reports' of Meeson & Welsby.

† ' History of the Law of Evidence,' by J. G. Phillimore, p. 546.

‡ " The time when he (Fielding) wrote was remarkable for the low tone of manners and sentiment ; perhaps the lowest that ever prevailed in England : for it was precisely a juncture when the romantic spirit of the old chivalrous manners was extinguished

At the end of the century evidence was given that " the condition of the poor was every day made more wretched than ever."* The labourer was, in fact, almost as much *adscriptus glebæ* as a Russian serf before his late emancipation ; and the reason was, because if he removed from his parish in search of employment, he was likely to become chargeable to the new parish, township, or place to which he migrated. This evil was in some respect mitigated by an Act passed in 1795, 35 Geo. III. c. 101, the preamble of which states that industrious poor persons chargeable to the parish where they live, " are, for the most part, compelled to live in their own parishes and townships, and are not permitted to inhabit elsewhere, under pretence that they are likely to become chargeable to the parish " where they went for the purpose of getting employment.

The condition of the labourer, which from natural causes is generally bad, was made worse by vicious legislation. The Law of Settlement, which then, and indeed until recently prevailed, made it the interest of landowners to pull down cottages or build as few as possible, in order to diminish the pressure of the poor-rates. In

and before the modern standard of refinement was introduced."
—Shaw's ' History of English Literature,' p. 343.
  * Quoted in Pashley's ' Pauperism and the Poor Laws,' p. 252.

Burn's History of the Poor Laws, published in 1764, he says that "in practice the office of an overseer of the poor seems to be understood to be this . . . . . . to pull down cottages and to drive out as many inhabitants and admit as few as possibly they can ; that is, to depopulate the parish, in order to lessen the poor-rate."

> Where then, ah ! where shall poverty reside,
> To 'scape the pressure of contiguous pride ?

The price of wheat was no doubt much lower in the last century than it has been since, the average value between 1720 and 1750 being considerably below 40s. a quarter, and this might seem at first sight to indicate that the labourer had a greater command of the neces- saries of life. But it proves nothing unless we know its *exchangeable value*—that is, the pro- portion it bore to the value of other commodi- ties, and the price of labour, or, in other words, the rate of wages.*

As to the upper classes, I know few books that leave a more painful impression upon the reader than the volumes which contain the letters of Horace Walpole, in which we see all

---

* The average prices of wheat per quarter, from 1746 to 1765, was 32s. 3d., and from 1771 to 1774, was 45s. 8d. Even when the price was above 80s., towards the end of the century, the wages of the labourer did not exceed 8s. a week.

the froth and scum that floated to the surface
of what is called Good Society, and can form a
tolerable idea of what was fermenting in the
mass below.   With all his persiflage and cyni-
cism, he at all events may be trusted as a witness who does not invent, but retails the current
scandals of the day.   And what a picture he
gives us of the hollowness, the heartlessness, and
the vice of fashionable life !

The Rev. Charles Kingsley, in his preface to
Henry Brooke's 'Fool of Quality,' originally published in 1763, and republished by him in 1859,
asks, "Who, in looking round a family portrait
gallery, has not remarked the difference between
the heads of the seventeenth and those of the
eighteenth century ?   The former are of the
same type as our own, and with the same strong
and varied personality ; the latter painfully like
both to each other, and to an oil flask ; the jaw
round, weak, and sensual, the forehead narrow
and retreating.   Had the race really degene-
rated for a while, or was the lower type adopted
intentionally out of compliment to some great
personage ?"   I should be disposed to doubt
that the portraits of the seventeenth century
" are of the same type as our own."   It is impossible not to be struck with the greater
strength of face and feature—with the square,

massive forehead and resolute expression. And this we might expect of the heroes of the civil war and the grand theologians and poets of the century—of men like Cromwell and Hampden; Andrews and Jeremy Taylor; and Shakspeare and Milton.

What would be thought now but little more than a decent compliance with religious worship, such as attendance at the Sacrament and family prayers, was in the last century considered the badge of a Puritan and a Methodist. " Nothing is so sad," says a French writer in a recent work, " as the religious history of the eighteenth century. Piety languishes; science there is none, at least on the side of the defenders of Christianity. In England and Germany a parching wind blows over hearts and minds. There is preached in the Protestant pulpits a religion without grandeur, without mysteries, which has neither the boldness of philosophy nor that of faith." * The phraseology of the Evangelical School, with which we are so familiar, was deemed strange and unorthodox, and " the new birth and the operations of grace " were the standing jokes of

---

* Pressensé. L'Eglise et la Révolution Française. But we must not forget that in the eighteenth century appeared Bishop Butler's immortal work, ' The Analogy of Religion.'

novelists, who had, however, in the extravagance of Whitfield and his followers, too good
an excuse to ridicule doctrines which have since
been illustrated by some of the most exem-
plary men of whom the Church of England can
boast.

The laxity of the age is, I think, strongly
shown in the strange mixture of religion and
immorality which we see exhibited, not only in
the lives but in the writings of some of the most
distinguished men. It shows how little they
were able rightly to appreciate the requirements
of unworldliness and purity enjoined in the
Gospel. Their Christianity was in general only
skin deep ; and while they made a merit of pro-
fessing to believe the doctrines of Revelation,
they acted as if they had no higher code to
guide them than heathen Ethics. I am not
speaking of mere infirmities to which the best
of erring men are liable, of small blemishes
which detract from the purity of life—although
one is grieved to think that Addison had not
strength to resist the temptation of wine—but
of a general looseness of conduct and language
which would now be considered hardly com-
patible with anything like religious profession ;
but which was not thought so then. When one
thinks of the man, the sermons of Dean Swift,

although in themselves excellent, seem to be a mockery, and we can fancy them written by the author of a ' Tale of a Tub ' with a grin of derision on his face.* Defoe wrote religious tracts and sermons—' Religious Courtship ' and the ' Family Instructor '—as to the last of which he professes to have a firm belief that " he was not without a more than ordinary presence and assistance of the Divine Spirit in the perform-

---

* Swift's ' Sermon on the Trinity ' is one of the best I ever read on the subject. The following passage sums up the objections and the answer. " Since the world abounds with pestilent books written against the doctrine of the Trinity, it is fit to inform you that the authors of them proceed wholly upon a mistake ; they would show how impossible it is that three can be one, and one can be three ; whereas the Scripture saith no such thing, at least in that manner they would make it ; but only that there is some kind of unity and distinction in the Divine nature which mankind cannot possibly comprehend : thus the whole doctrine is short and plain, and in itself incapable of any controversy, since God himself hath pronounced the fact but wholly concealed the manner. And therefore many divines, who thought fit to answer those wicked books, have been mistaken too by answering fools in their folly, and endeavouring to explain a mystery which God intended to keep secret from us." The sermon concludes thus :—" May God of His infinite mercy inspire us with true faith in every article and mystery of our religion, so as to dispose us to do what is pleasing in His sight : and this we pray through Jesus Christ, to whom with the Father and the Holy Ghost be all honour and glory, now, and for evermore, Amen." There is an excellent sermon by Swift on the text, " The wisdom of this world is foolishness with God ;" and another upon ' Sleeping in Church.' In his ' Thoughts on Various Subjects,' he wittily asks, " Query, whether churches are not dormitories of the living, as well as of the dead ?"

ance;" but he is also the author of 'Moll
Flanders,' 'Roxana,' and 'Colonel Jack.' Most
certainly Steele was not a bad man—he was
amiable, affectionate and kindly—and the tone
of his papers in the 'Tatler' is unexceptionably
good.   But he was notoriously fond of the bottle, and constantly in debt.   Dr. Johnson said
leniently of him, " Steele, I believe, practises
the lighter vices."   He was not, therefore, the
kind of person from whom we should expect a
grave, religious treatise.   And yet Steele wrote
'The Christian Hero.'   If ever there was a free
liver, to say nothing of the loose morality of his
works—his genius and power are quite a different matter—it was Fielding : and yet no
writer could discourse in a more edifying manner about morality, virtue and religion.   What
shall we say of Sterne ?   He, like Swift, was by
profession a clergyman, and therefore, of course,
obliged to be a teacher of religion.   But his life
gave the lie to his profession, and he behaved
like a brute to his wife.   He seems to have
thought there was no inconsistency in preaching
and publishing sermons, and writing 'Tristram
Shandy.'

There is nothing in which the difference between the last century and the present is more
strikingly shown than in the delineation of love.

As a mere natural instinct, love, of course, is the same in all ages and in all climes, and fulfils the main object for which it was designed in the order of Providence, which is the preservation of the species. But the style and mode of its expression differ as widely as it is possible to conceive. In the whole range of Greek and Roman literature I hardly know a passage where love is described as a purifying passion of the soul.* And nothing can be more frigid than the language of love when lovers meet in the Greek tragedians, although its power as a Divinity is celebrated in chorus and in song. Among the Romans, if we except the exquisite description of the love of Dido for Æneas, it is almost always the language of desire. And to come to the eighteenth century, we find in its literature little, if anything, of the romance of love—such love as we read of in the ' Bride of Lammermoor' and ' Henrietta Temple'—and still less of its elevating influence on the heart.

> To an exact perfection they have brought
> The action love—the passion is forgot.

There is little trace of such an effect of love

---

* Let those who wish to see what Greek writers could say of Love, read the ' Deipnosophists' of Athenæus, Book xiii.

as is described in the beautiful lines of Dryden
in his 'Cimon and Iphigenia :'—

> Love taught him shame, and shame with love at strife
> Soon taught the sweet civilities of life—

No writer then thought of depicting love as
Coleridge has depicted and glorified it in the
following passage ;—

" That enduring personal attachment so beau-
tifully delineated by Erin's sweet Melodist, and
still more touchingly perhaps in the well-known
ballad 'John Anderson my Jo John,' in addi-
tion to a depth and constancy of character of no
every-day occurrence, supposes a peculiar sensibility and tenderness of nature, a constitutional
communicativeness and utterance of heart and
soul ; a delight in the detail of sympathy, in the
outward and visible signs of the sacrament
within,—to count, as it were, the pulses of the
life of love.   But above all, it supposes a soul
which even in the pride and summer-tide of life,
even in the lustihood of health and strength,
had felt oftenest and prized highest that which
age cannot take away, and which in all our
lovings is *the* love ; I mean that willing sense of
the unsufficingness of the self for itself, which
predisposes a generous nature to see in the
total being of another the supplement and com-
pletion of its own ; that quiet, perpetual seeking

which the presence of that beloved object modulates, not suspends; where the heart momently finds and finding again seeks on; lastly, when 'life's changeful orb has passed the full,' a confirmed faith in the nobleness of humanity thus brought home and pressed as it were to the very bosom of hourly experience; it supposes, I say, a heartfelt reverence for worth, not the less deep because divested of its solemnity by habit, by familiarity, by mutual infirmities, and even by a feeling of modesty which will arise in delicate minds when they are unconscious of possessing the same or the correspondent excellence in their own characters. In short, there must be a mind which, while it feels the beautiful and the excellent in the beloved as its own, and by the right of love appropriates it, can call goodness its playfellow; and dares make sport of time and infirmity while in the person of a thousandfoldly endeared partner we feel for aged virtue the caressing fondness that belongs to the innocence of childhood, and repeat the same attentions and tender courtesies which had been dictated by the same affection to the same object, when attired in feminine loveliness or in manly beauty." *

The term which best expresses the idea under

* Poetical Works, vol. ii. p. 120.

which the writers in the early part of the last
century expressed love, and indeed all the great
emotions of the human soul, is conventionality.
" One would like," says de Quincey,* " to see a
searching investigation into the state of society
in Anne's days—its extreme artificiality, its
sheepish reserve upon all the impassioned gran-
deurs, its shameless outrages upon all the decen-
cies of human nature.   Certain it is that Addison
(because everybody) was in the meanest of conditions which blushes at the very expression of
sympathy with the lovely, the noble, or the impassioned.   The wretches were ashamed of their
own nature, and perhaps with reason; for in
their own denaturalized hearts they read only a
degraded nature.   Addison, in particular, shrank
from every bold and every profound expression
as from an offence against good taste.   He
dared not for his life have used the word 'passion,' except in the vulgar sense of an angry
paroxysm.   He durst as soon have danced a
hornpipe on the top of the 'monument' as
have talked of 'rapturous emotion.'   What
would he have said?   Why, 'sentiments that
were of a nature to prove agreeable after an un-

---

* 'Essay on Schlosser's Literary History of the Eighteenth
Century'; one of the best and most amusing of this great writer's
essays.

usual rate.' In their odious verses the creatures of that age talk of love as something that 'burns' them.* You suppose at first that they are discoursing of tallow candles, though you cannot imagine by what impertinence they address *you*, that are not a tallow-chandler, upon such painful subjects. And when they apostrophise the woman of their heart (for you are to understand that they pretend to such an organ) they beseech her to ease their pain. Can human meanness descend lower? As if the man, being ill from pleurisy, had a right to take a lady for one of the dressers in a hospital, whose duty it would be to fix a burgundy pitch plaster between his shoulders."

* When a fellow-scholar brought to young Henry Brooke, the author of the 'Fool of Quality,' born in 1708, an Ode to the Moon, which broke off with the line—

"Ah, why doth Phœbe love to shine by night?"

—the precocious boy immediately wrote under it—

"Because the sex look best by candle light."

Richardson mentioned in one of his letters to Edwards, a forgotten sonneteer, that Miss Highmore had set herself on fire, and scorched herself with the curling irons. Upon which the poet, in answer, supposes that the accident must have happened, not from the heat of the irons, but from the love verses she used as curling papers ; and that the blaze happening on the left side was extinguished by the prevalent force of the cold about her heart.—' Correspondence of Richardson,' vol. iii. 35, 37. Such was sentiment in those days.

In an Essay in the 'Tatler' Steele says, "If
a man of any delicacy were to attend the dis-
courses of the young fellows of this age, he
would believe that there were none but prosti-
tutes to make the objects of passion .   .   .
But Cupid is not only blind at present, but dead
drunk; he has lost all his faculties: else how
could Clelia be so long a maid with that agreeable behaviour?   Corinna with that sprightly
wit?   Lesbia with that heavenly voice?   And
Sacharissa with all those excellencies in one
person, frequent the park, the play, and murder
those poor tits that drag her to public places,
and not a man turn pale at her appearance?"
In one of her letters in Richardson's novel of
'Sir Charles Grandison,' Harriet Byron says,
"And pray may I not ask if the taste of the age
among men is not dress, equipage, and foppery?
Is the cultivation of the mind any part of their
study?   The men in short are sunk, my dear,
and the women but barely swim."

Admiration of the sex was shewn not by deep
and respectful homage, but by extravagance of
conduct.   It was the fashion to inscribe the
names of reigning beauties on drinking glasses
with the point of a diamond.*   Goldsmith tells
us in his 'Life of Beau Nash' that in the days

* 'Tatler,' No. 24.

when his hero was young, a fellow would drink no wine but what was strained through his mistress's chemise, (nasty beast!) and he would eat a pair of her shoes tossed upon a fricassee. This last feat was repeated in the middle of the century. In a paper of the 'Connoisseur,' by the Earl of Cork (1754), we are told that he was present at an entertainment where a celebrated *fille de joie* was one of the party, and her shoe was pulled off by a young man who filled it with champagne and drank it off to her health. " In this delicious draught he was immediately pledged by the rest, and then, to carry the compliment still further, he ordered the shoe itself to be dressed and served up for supper. The cook set himself seriously to work upon it; he pulled the upper part of it (which was of damask) into fine shreds, and tossed it up in a ragout; minced the sole, cut the wooden heel into very thin slices, fried them in butter, and placed them round the dish for garnish. The company, you may be sure, testified their affection for the lady by eating very heartily of this exquisite impromptu."

For the difference between the past and present century in the mode of regarding the passion of love, two causes may be specially assigned. First, that the habits of the last age were libertine, and men acted upon the odious maxim,

And every woman is at heart a rake.

No one who is at all conversant with the literature of the age will deny this ; and nothing can be conceived which would have a more poisonous influence upon manners and morals than such a theory.   Men talked before women of things which one would have thought all decency and respect for the sex would have induced them to conceal.   They boasted of their intrigues, as if seduction and adultery were meritorious actions and titles of honour.   In ‘Sir Charles Grandison,’ Harriet Byron says, in one of her letters to Lucy Selby, “I am very much mistaken, if every woman would not find her account, if she wishes herself to be thought well of, in discouraging every reflection that may have a tendency to debase or expose the sex in general. How can a man be suffered to boast of his vileness to one woman in the presence of another, without a rebuke, that should put it to the proof whether the boaster was or was not past blushing ?”   Few women, in that age, had the courage and the sense of Stella, of whom Swift tells us in his ‘Character of Mrs. Johnson,’ that when “a coxcomb of the pert kind” began to utter some *doubles entendres* in the company of herself and several other ladies, and "the rest flapped their fans, and used the other common expedients practised in such cases, of appearing not to mind or comprehend whatever was said," she sternly rebuked him, and said, "Sir, all these ladies and I understand your meaning very well, having, in spite of our care, too often met with those of your sex who wanted manners and good sense. But, believe me, neither virtuous nor even vicious women love such kind of conversation. However, I will leave you, and report your behaviour, and whatever visit I make, I shall first inquire at the door whether you are in the house, that I may be sure to avoid you." And yet, strangely enough, in the short collection of 'Bons Mots de Stella,' which is given by Swift, there is one in which she made a joke of an intolerably vulgar and offensive expression, which Dr. Sheridan disgraced himself by uttering in her presence.*

We find the novelists introducing episodes which consist of stories told by women of their past lives, in which the most unblushing details of profligacy are given ; and the curious cir-

---

* The difference, however, between the two cases is this, and it serves as an illustration of the manners of the time. The language in the one case was licentious ; in the other, simply indecent. Stella had too much virtue to tolerate the one, and too little refinement to resent the other.

cumstance is, that they do so with apparently an utter unconsciousness that they offend against propriety by the narrative, however much they may have offended against it by their acts.

In the 'Spiritual Quixote,' published in the middle of the century, the author, who was a clergyman, makes every lady in whom he wishes the reader to take interest, give the history, or others tell the history of her past life—and, however modest and respectable she may have been, she has always been the object of libertine attempts. When she tells the story herself, she does it with a plainness of speech that is astonishing. Such is the narrative of Miss Townsend with whom Wildgoose, the hero, falls in love; and such is the story of Mrs. Rivers, the charming wife of Mr. Rivers, as told by her husband, who has settled down with her in an old country house, and taken to farming. One of the chapters is headed " Narrative of a Licentious Amour," and this narrative is supposed to be related by a gentleman in presence of several respectable unmarried ladies who make comments upon it as it proceeds.

Even in the 'Female Quixote,' written by a lady, which is as free as any of the old novels from licentiousness, we have the history of Miss Groves told with apparent unconsciousness of its impropriety. 'Peregrine Pickle' belongs to a different school, and in it, of course, we might expect anything. There is introduced a long episode called 'The Memoirs of a Lady of Quality,' or, in other words, the adventures of a kept mistress, who, in early life was married to a nobleman.* And the reason for mentioning them here is, that although they are the frankest possible confession of a life of profligacy, they are told by "her Ladyship" after she has become repentant and virtuous "in a select party," in hopes that they may perceive that however much her head might have erred, her heart had always been uncorrupted!

Lord Chesterfield says, speaking of the reign of Queen Anne, "No woman of fashion could receive any man at her morning toilet without alarming her husband and his friends." But this I do not believe. It is not likely that

---

* The lady of quality was Lady Vane, daughter of Mr. Hawes, a South-Sea director, first married to Lord William Hamilton, and secondly to Lord Vane. See 'Walpole's Letters,' edited by Cunningham, vol. i. p. 91. It was a not uncommon practice to make living persons figure in fiction, and describe their adventures and—*amours.* In 1780, Sir Herbert Croft, Bart., published a novel called 'Love and Madness, a Story too true, in a series of letters between parties whose names would perhaps be mentioned were they less known or less lamented.' This purported to be the correspondence between Miss Ray, the mistress of Lord Sandwich, and the Rev. Mr. Hackman, who shot her at the door of the opera, and was afterwards hanged.

women of fashion denied themselves in such
a case a liberty which women of the middle
classes were freely allowed to use.   In Mrs.
Heywood's novel of ' Miss Betsy Thoughtless,'
of which I shall speak more particularly hereafter, we find the heroine, a young unmarried
lady, receiving as a matter of course male
visitors in her dressing room while performing
her toilette.   At Bath ladies bathed in public,
and if we were to take literally the description
in Miss Burney's ' Evelina,' we might suppose
that the only part of the body that was covered
was the head—for Evelina says ; " As to the
pump-room I was amazed at the public exhi-
bition of the ladies in the bath ; it is true that
their heads are covered with bonnets, but the
very idea of being seen in such a situation by
whoever pleases to look is indelicate."   But we
can correct this impression from the account
given of the same scene by another young lady,
Miss Lydia Melford, in ' Humphry Clinker,'
" Right under the pump-room window is the
king's bath—a large cistern—where you see the
patients up to their neck in the hot water.   The
ladies wear jackets and petticoats of brown
linen with chip hats, in which they fix their
handkerchiefs to wipe the sweat from their
faces ; but . . . . they look so flushed and so

frightful, that I always turn my eyes another way."

No complaint was more common than that of insults offered to women when travelling in a .public conveyance, by the loose and indecent talk of their male companions. And they were not always so fortunate as to find an Ephraim the Quaker, who was in the stage-coach with the Spectator when a recruiting officer began to be impertinent to a young lady, and who was abashed by his rebuke : " Thy mirth, friend, savoureth of folly; thou art a person of a light mind ; thy drum is a type of thee, it soundeth because it is empty. Verily, it is not from thy fulness but thy emptiness that thou hast spoken this day." * And at places of public resort, like Ranelagh and Vauxhall, ladies were exposed to the grossest insults from " pretty fellows," and " fine gentlemen," as will be shown more fully hereafter.

A second cause was, that a woman was re-

* ' Spectator,' No. 132. I remember once in the old days of coaching, being on the top of a coach, when the driver told me that the day before there was a Quaker on the box, and a man behind him who was ridiculing the Bible. The Quaker remained silent until being addressed by the stranger thus : " Come, old square-toes, you say nothing : what do you think of the story of David and Goliath ? Do you believe that David killed the giant with a pebble ? " he replied, " I'll tell thee what, friend, if Goliath's forehead was as soft as thy pate, there could have been no difficulty in the matter."

garded chiefly for her beauty and accomplishments, and little honour was paid to her virtues and understanding. Steele was the author of those days, who seems to have regarded women with most respect, and to have been most disposed to look upon them as something better than playthings for amusement or instruments of desire. " The love of a woman," he says, in one of his papers in the ' Tatler,' " is inseparable from some esteem of her, and she is naturally the object of affection; the woman who has your esteem has also some degree of your love. A man that dotes on a woman for her beauty will whisper his friend, 'that creature has a great deal of wit when you are well acquainted with her.' And if you examine the bottom of your esteem for a woman you will find you have a greater opinion of her beauty than anybody else." This last sentence is certainly equivocal —for it may mean that esteem is founded upon admiration of the gift of beauty—but I think it has a nobler and profounder sense, that a man who esteems a woman finds in her a beauty which is unseen by others. The idea is the converse of that expressed by Withers in the two charming lines—

If she be not so to me,
What care I how fair she be?

A certain degree of licence must always be allowed to the stage, and it would not be fair to consider it an exact test of the modesty and decorum of a particular period. We ourselves should be sorry to be judged hereafter by such exhibitions as take place in the ballet, where decency is outraged without a blush before the eyes of wives, mothers and daughters. But if some future writer were to describe them, and then go on to say that they were patronised and applauded by English ladies, it would be very difficult to resist the inference that delicacy and purity amongst us had sunk to a very low ebb. And when we look at the plays which were acted at the theatres during the last century we are filled with astonishment. Grave matrons and young virgins listened to and laughed at jokes as broad and coarse as those of Aristophanes, and heard without a blush the language of the stables and the stews. "It is," says the 'Spectator' (A.D. 1712), " one of the most unaccountable things in our age, that the lewdness of our theatres should be so much complained of, so well exposed and so little redressed . . . . As matters stand at present multitudes are shut out from this noble diversion, by reason of those abuses and corruptions that accompany it. A father is often

afraid that his daughter should be ruined by
those entertainments which were invented for
the accomplishment and refining of human
nature . . . . Cuckoldom is the basis of most
of our modern plays. If an alderman appears
upon the stage you may be sure that it is in
order to be cuckolded — knights and baronets,
country squires, and justices of the quorum
come up to town for no other purpose . . . .
The accomplished gentleman upon the English
stage is the person that is familiar with other
men's wives and indifferent to his own, as the
fine woman is generally a composition of
sprightliness and falsehood."

Lady Cowper tells us in ·her 'Diary' (1715),
that she went with the Princess of Wales to
see the play of the 'Wanton Wife'—better
known as the 'Amorous Widow,' by Betterton,
a sort of free translation of Molière's 'George
Dandin,' and she says, "I had seen it once;
and I believe there were few in town had seen
it so seldom, for it used to be a favourite play
and often bespoke by the ladies . . . . Went to
the play with my mistress; and to my great
satisfaction she liked it as well as any play she
had seen; and it certainly is *not more obscene
than old comedies are.* It were to be wished
our stage was chaster." In a paper in the

'Connoisseur,' published in the middle of the century, the writer says, " I was present a few nights ago at the representation of the 'Chances,'" a most indecent play, "and when I looked round the boxes and observed the loose dress of all the ladies, and the great relish with which they received the high-seasoned jests in that comedy, I was almost apprehensive that the old story of the outrage of the Romans on the Sabine women would be inverted."

In a letter from Richardson, in 1748, to Lady Bradshaigh, who under the feigned name of Belfour carried on a correspondence with him, he says, " A good comedy is a fine perform- ance ; but how few are there which can be called good ? Even those that are tolerable, are so mixed with indecent levities (at which footmen have a right to insult by their roars their ladies in the boxes) that a modest young creature hardly knows how to bear the offence to her ears in the representation, joined with the insults given by the eyes of the young fel- lows she is surrounded by."

In Miss Burney's novel of ' Evelina ' the heroine says, " The play was ' Love for Love ; ' and, though it is fraught with wit and enter- tainment, I hope I shall never see it represented again ; for it is so extremely indelicate—to use the softest word I can—that Miss Mirvan and I were perpetually out of countenance, and could neither make any observations ourselves, nor venture to listen to those of others."

It must, however, be borne in mind that an age or period can only be described according to its leading features and general tendencies. The same is true of national character or national portraiture. And during the eighteenth century how many must have lived and died amongst our forefathers, to whom the general description of the age could have been by no means with truth applied.* When we speak of its laxity of morals and its indifference to religion we cannot doubt that there was piety both in the town and in the country—that there were gentle and loving souls who shrank from profanity and impurity, and were disgusted at the scenes of intemperance which they were too often obliged to witness. In the licentious periods of the reign of Charles II. in England and the Regency in France there were women like Mrs. Godolphin and Madame Louise, who,

* " In an age that prides itself on the careful rules of inductive reasoning, nothing is more surprising than the sweeping assertions with regard to national character, and the reckless way in which casual observations that may be true of one, two, three, or it may be ten or even a hundred individuals, are extended to millions."—' Chips from a German Workshop,' by Max Müller, vol. iii. p. 265.

amidst the corruptions of a court, devoted themselves to the service of God, and kept themselves unspotted from the world. We are not to suppose that all ladies spent their time in frivolous amusements or intrigues of gallantry—as the novelists too often represent them—and we may be sure that there were thousands who could give as innocent an account of their hours as Lady Bradshaigh does in one of her letters to Richardson : " I rise about seven, sometimes sooner ; after my private duties, I read or write till nine ; then breakfast ; work and converse with my company till about twelve ; then, if the weather permit, walk a mile in the garden ; dress and read till dinner ; after which sit and chat till four ; from that till the hour of tea-drinking each day variety of employments. You know what the men say enters with the tea-table ; though I will venture to say, if mine is not an exception, it is as near one as you can imagine." *

And when we visit an old mansion-house in the country, with its oriel windows and deep red brick, mellowed by time ; its terrace walks and trim gardens shaded by venerable yews, it is pleasing to think of our great-grandmothers, then young and lovely women,

* ' Correspondence of Richardson,' vol. vi. pp. 54-5.

quietly and happily passing their time there. We can fancy the scene of some fair girl whose face Gainsborough has painted, immersed in the volumes of 'Amadis de Gaul' or perhaps 'Clarissa.'

> Gracefully o'er some volume bending,
>   While by her side the youthful sage
> Held back her ringlets, lest descending
>   They should o'ershadow all the page.

And we are not to suppose that there were not in England many others besides Cowper who, although not gifted with a genius like his, and the power of expressing their thoughts in prose or verse like him, did not equally with him mourn over the degeneracy of the age, and pour out their hearts in prayer to God for a reformation in the habits of the people, and that Christianity might be more than a name. We know few of their names now; they are only chronicled on the tombstone—the silent witnesses have passed away, and we must judge the century by its works and the records it has left.

We find in the Essayists much useful matter that throws light upon manners and social usages, and they form a valuable supplement to the novels; or, rather I should say, as the essays go more fully and directly to the point, the novels form a supplement to them. But it

we attempt to appreciate their worth, I fear I
shall be thought to broach a heresy when I say
that, in my opinion, the great body of the
Essayists are very dull. Of course I except
many papers by Addison, such as those that
relate to the delightful Sir Roger de Coverley,
the 'Visions of Mirza,' and the criticisms on
Virgil and Milton ; and some by Steele, Goldsmith, Johnson, and Hawkesworth. But, taking
them as a whole, it is difficult to feel interest in
them now, except so far as they tend to illustrate
the condition of society at the time. What strikes
one most is the frivolity of many of the subjects
about which men of mark and genius thought
it worth while to write. The wit is generally
of the mildest kind, and the good-natured public
seems to have been very easily amused. We
have essays and letters about the size of petticoats and hoops, and the mode of flirting with
fans—about patches and the love of women
for puppet-shows, about riding-habits and com-
modes : accounts of the She-romp Club, the
Ugly Club, the Lazy Club, and the Amorous
Club ; of female " salamanders," and all the
fashions, follies, and nonsense of the age.
Women of the town, like Rebecca Nettletop,
recite their adventures, and modest women,
like Belvidera, write to complain of female

panders.   Betty Saunter sends a letter to
ask whether "dimple" is spelt with a single or
double "P," and Benjamin Easy writes to warn
the public against the danger caused by the fan-
exercise.   "Last Sunday," he says, "he met
with a soldier of your own training; she
furls a fan, recovers a fan, and goes through
the whole exercise of it to admiration : this
well-managed officering of yours has, to my
knowledge, been the ruin of above five young
gentlemen, besides myself, and still goes on
laying waste wheresoever she comes, whereby
the whole village is in great danger."   And he
goes on to suggest that the management of the
fan should be met with the management of the
snuff-box, which hint is accordingly taken up;
and in a subsequent number appears an advertisement stating where "the exercise of the
snuff-box, according to the most fashionable
airs and motions," will be taught.

The grave Dr. Johnson gives us letters in
the 'Idler' from Betty Brown and Molly Quick
and Deborah Singer : and an imaginary complaint from a grocer's wife, whose husband,
instead of attending to the shop, spent his time
in a nine-pin alley, and on Sunday in an ale-
house.   Also another from Peggy Heartless,
whose peace of mind is disturbed because her

husband cannot find lodgings in London to suit his fancy.

In one of Jane Austen's novels, ' Northanger Abbey,' where she is defending the reading of novels, she contrasts the conduct of a young lady who might be caught with a novel in her hand, and "lays it down with affected indifference or momentary shame—although it were perhaps ' Cecilia,' or ' Camilla,' or ' Belinda ' "— with her conduct if discovered reading the ' Spectator.' " Now, had the same young lady been engaged with a volume of the ' Spectator ' instead of such a work, how proudly would she have produced the book and told its name! though the chances must be against her being occupied with any part of that voluminous publication of which either the matter or manner would not disgust a young person of taste; the substance of its papers so often consisting in the statement of improbable circumstances, unnatural characters, and topics of conversation which no longer concern any one living; and their language frequently so coarse as to give no very favourable idea of the age that could endure it."

The object of the writers was no doubt good —to reform manners and morals by irony and satire; but Lord Macaulay certainly attributes

too much influence to the satire of Addison
when he says that he so effectually retorted on
vice the mockery which had recently been
directed against virtue, that since his time the
open violation of decency has always been considered as the mark of a fool.   This, I suppose,
was suggested by the well-known lines—

> Immodest words admit of no defence,
> For want of decency is want of sense.

But the aphorism is not true in itself, and it
was long after Addison before indecency of
conduct, and indecency of talk, even before
women, were banished from society.   The
change was due to that silent revolution in
opinions and manners which is brought about
by time, and the effect of which is so well
described by Mr. Lecky in his 'History of
Rationalism.'   The strange thing, however, is
—and it is a remarkable proof of the manners
of the century—that in works seriously and
sincerely devoted to the cause of morality and
religion, and intended to be read at every breakfast table in the kingdom, letters should be
printed which exhibited vice in its most naked
form.   The same, indeed, may be said of the
reports of cases in our newspapers at the present day, and it is, I think, deeply to be regretted that they give at full length such

polluting details as often fill their columns. It will generally be found that the minuteness of the narrative, or the fidelity of the report of the evidence, is in proportion to the objectionable nature of the subject-matter; and attention is called by leaded type to conversations and actions in real life which, if dressed up as fiction, and sold as novels, would lead to a prosecution by the Society for the Suppression of Vice, or a seizure under Lord Campbell's Act. I know the sort of apology which is made for this; namely, that publicity is the most effectual punishment of vice and crime. But the answer is twofold — First, publicity may be given without revelling in the details of indecency— a picture may be a sketch instead of being a photograph—and, secondly, the object of the proprietors in so doing is *not* to advance the cause of morality, but to put money into their pockets. The sale of a newspaper increases with the enormity of the scandal it reports, and the simple reason why the report is so disgustingly minute is that it *pays*. Of course there is the difference between the two cases— the modern newspapers detail facts that have actually occurred, and evidence that has been given in a court of justice, while the objectionable letters in the 'Tatler,' and 'Spectator,' and 'Guardian,' are purely imaginary.　But the effect is the same, or rather, I should say, the effect of the modern practice is infinitely worse, for the interest of the readers is more engaged, and the mind realises more vividly the scenes that are described.

Another source of information as to the manners of the age, is Painting.　The pictures of Hogarth, so well known to all of us by the engravings, are of excellent use in conveying a truthful idea of these, and the costume of the time.　But this has been so admirably drawn by a master hand, that I shall not attempt to give an analysis of my own, but merely quote two or three sentences from Thackeray.*　"We look and see pass before us the England of a hundred years ago—the peer in his drawing-room, the lady of fashion in her apartment, foreign singers surrounding her, and the chamber filled with gewgaws in the mode of that day; the church, with its quaint florid architecture and singing congregation; the parson with his great wig, and the beadle with his cane,—all these are represented before us, and we are sure of the truth of the portrait. . . . . The Yorkshire waggon rolls into the inn yard; the country parson, in his jack-

* 'English Humourists,' pp. 244-5.

boots, and his bands, and short cassock, comes trotting into town, and we fancy it is Parson Adams with his sermons in his pocket. The Salisbury fly sets forth from the old Angel. You see the passengers entering the great heavy vehicle, and up the wooden steps, their hats tied down with handkerchiefs over their faces, and under their arms sword-hanger and case-bottle; the landlady, apoplectic with the liquors in her own bar, is tugging at the bell; the hunchbacked postillion—he may have ridden the leaders to Humphry Clinker—is begging a gratuity; the miser is grumbling at the bill; Jack of the Centurion lies on the top of the clumsy vehicle with a soldier by his side—it may be Smollett's Jack Hatchway, it has a likeness to his make-up."

Before, however, entering more into detail as to the manners and habits of our forefathers, I wish to make one remark on which I shall have occasion to insist hereafter, when I come to speak more particularly of the novels of the last century. It must not be supposed that in describing its vices and failings, I mean to imply that we at the present day have any right to sit with Pecksniff complacency in judgment upon the past, and congratulate ourselves, as if we had nothing to be ashamed of in our

morals and conduct.   In some respects we may
be thankful for a vast improvement, and it
would be lamentable indeed if it were not so.
There can be no doubt that in language, and
manners, and taste, we are much more refined
than our ancestors of a hundred or a hundred
and fifty years ago.   Drinking, swearing, and
duelling are no longer the accomplishments of
gentlemen.   Coarse jests and improper allusions are no longer permitted in the presence
of women, and even amongst men an habitual
offender in those respects would soon find that his
society was shunned.   Women may be treated
with less ceremony, but they are certainly treated
with more respect.   In our houses, our furniture,
and our sanitary arrangements, there is far more
comfort and attention to cleanliness and health.*

---

* " It is not necessary to go back much beyond half-a-century
to arrive at the time when prosperous shop-keepers, in the
leading thoroughfares of London, were without that necessary
article of furniture, a carpet, in their ordinary sitting rooms :
luxury in this particular seldom went further with them than a
well-scoured floor strewed with sand."—' Porter's Progress of the
Nation,' p. 522. In his ' Life of Beau Nash,' Goldsmith thus speaks
of Bath at the beginning of the last century :—" The lodgings for
visitants were paltry though expensive ; the dining-rooms and
other chambers were floored with boards coloured brown with
soot and small beer to hide the dirt ; the walls were covered
with unpainted wainscot : the furniture corresponded with the
meanness of the architecture ; a few oak chairs, a small looking-
glass, with a fender and tongs, composed the magnificence of
their temporary habitations." I do not believe that from the

But the real progress made, beside the improvement in manners and refinement (I say nothing of politics), is in the enlarged scope of modern legislation and consideration for the wants of the poor.

We are not, however, to suppose that the age was without manly virtues and womanly decorum, still less that the minds of the men of former generations were unfeeling or corrupt, because they tolerated things which we should now regard with pity or disgust. We must cautiously discriminate between the outward act and the inward sentiment. Take the case of religious persecution in former times. As has been forcibly remarked by Mr. Lecky, " The burnings, the tortures, the imprisonments, the confiscations, the disabilities, the long wars and still longer animosities, that for so many centuries marked the conflicts of great theological bodies, are chiefly due to men whose lives were spent in absolute devotion to what they believed to be true, and whose characters have passed unscathed through the most hostile and searching criticism. In their worst acts

beginning to the end of the century there could be found in any house, in town or country, a really easy arm-chair. We all know the stiff, hard, upright things on which our great-grandfathers and great-grandmothers used to sit, and which we can hardly look upon without feeling a pain in the back."

the persecutors were but the exponents and
representatives of the wishes of a large section
of the community, and that section was commonly the most earnest and the most un-
selfish."*

So, again, with regard to the state of our
criminal law. The frequency of capital punish-
ments, when miserable wretches were hanged
by the dozen for picking pockets, or stealing
sheep, or cutting down apple-trees, did not
shock the moral sense of the public, and excited
remonstrance only in the minds of a few
thoughtful men,—not because the public was
more cruel, and took pleasure in human suffer-
ing, but because they were thought indispensable to the safety of the community ; and the
idea of the necessity of protecting property
outweighed considerations of the value of
human life. In old times, indeed, the number
of executions was thought a proof of the superiority of our countrymen, as indicating the
existence of valiant crime. Chief Justice For-
tescue, in the reign of Henry VI., wrote almost
with a kind of pride, that "more men are
hanged in Englande in one year, than in France
in seven, because the English have better

* 'The Rise and Influence of Rationalism in Europe,' vol. i.
p. 387.

partes. The Scotchmenne likewise never dare rob, but only commit larcenies."* Bull-baiting and bear-baiting were defended by Canning and Windham, and yet no one has ever brought against those eminent men the charge of cruelty. The Puritans were not cruel, and yet Macaulay says of them, " If the Puritans suppressed bull-baiting, it was not because it gave pain to the bull, but because it gave pleasure to the spectators." And then again with respect to the Slave Trade, how long it was before public opinion was effectually brought round to second the efforts of Clarkson and Wilberforce for its abolition. But it would be most untrue to say that the men and women who defended it—some within living memory,—were in their dispositions and characters, more inhuman than ourselves.

Nor while we congratulate ourselves upon the progress made in civilization and refinement, must we forget "the beam that is in our own eye." We may turn with disgust from the coarseness that sullies the pages of the literature of the eighteenth century, but what shall we say of the sensational novels of the present day, with their tales of murder, seduc-

---

* Quoted by Mr. Lecky in his ' Rise and Influence of Rationalism in Europe,' vol. i. p. 381.

tion, adultery, and intrigue, the writers of which seem to have studied nothing but the morbid anatomy of the human heart.

" Those were times," says the Rev. Charles Kingsley, speaking of the last century, in his preface to Brooke's 'Fool of Quality,' "in which men were coarser and more ignorant, but yet heartier and healthier than now. Those ' intricacies of the human heart,' which (as unravelled by profligate Frenchmen or pious Englishwomen) are now in such high and all but sole demand, were then looked on chiefly as indigestions of the human stomach or other physical organs ; and the public wanted, over and above the perennial subject of love, some talk at least about valour, patriotism, loyalty, chivalry, generosity, the protection of the oppressed, the vindication of the innocent, and other like matters, which are now banished alike from pulpit and from stage, and only call forth applause (so I am informed) from the sluts and roughs in the gallery of the Victoria theatre." In so far as the miserable trash of a certain school of fiction prevalent among us, is here condemned, I entirely agree with Mr. Kingsley, although happily the writers usurp only a part of the domain of fiction, and we can point to authors still living, or only recently departed, who are as hearty and healthy as Fielding or Smollett, without any of their coarseness or scenes of prurient vice.

There is another danger to guard against in forming an opinion with regard to the manners and morals of a bygone age, and that is, lest we should mistake satire for truth and caricature for likeness. In making use of the novels for this purpose some caution is no doubt necessary.

But here an important distinction must be made. It would be very wrong to consider that particular characters in the hands of novelists truthfully represent a class, where it is obvious that the object is to indulge in exaggeration and provoke a laugh. Nobody believes that the grotesque personages who figure in the pages of Dickens are anywhere to be found in real life. His plan was to seize upon some oddity of human nature, and invest his puppets with it so completely that they can never open their lips without betraying it. Who ever met with such a compound of impudence and wit in a shoe-black, or a groom, as we find in the immortal Sam Weller? It may have been our lot to know " a great man struggling with the storms of fate," but where shall we look for a man who is jolly in proportion as he is un-

fortunate, like Mark Tapley? Who can believe
in the actual existence of such persons as Miss
Flite and Miss Mowcher and Toots? Grad-
grind is so practical that he ceases to be human;
Micawber is full of maudlin sentiment and
emphatic nonsense; Mrs. Nickleby is always
parenthetical and incoherent; Boythorn never
opens his lips without being intensely and
boisterously energetic; and Major Bagstock
always describes himself as "tough old Joe;"
"Joe is rough and tough, sir! blunt, sir, blunt
is Joe." It would be in the last degree absurd
for a future writer to take these characters as
types of English society in the middle of the
nineteenth century; and, to a certain extent,
the same kind of allowance must be made for
the characters in the novels of the last century.
For it is impossible to believe that the portrait
of Squire Western represented in all its brutal
details the country gentleman of England; that
Parson Adams and Parson Trulliber give us
a just idea of the clergy, or that the Roxana of
Defoe, the Mrs. Waters and Lady Bellaston of
Fielding, the Miss Grizzle Pickle and Miss
Tabitha Bramble of Smollett, the Mrs. Harriet
Freke of Miss Edgeworth, and the Mrs. Ben-
nett of Jane Austen, are true types of the
modesty, education, refinement and intelligence

of Englishwomen of the time. I say that this allowance should be made only to "a certain extent," for I believe that the characters drawn by the old novelists are, with a few exceptions, intended to be less imaginary than the creations of fiction in our own day, and have a substratum of reality which is wanting in many of the amusing characters of Dickens. But, at all events, we may use the novels as evidence of a state of society and manners on two grounds, which are independent of the question whether particular characters truthfully represent a class. First, we may be sure that in the *general* tone of conversation and description, and the unconscious introduction of little incidents of every-day life, the writers hold the mirror up to nature and reflect the image they themselves received from the world around them. And next the degree of popularity which their works enjoyed is evidence that their coarseness did not disgust nor their licentiousness repel the public taste. Such scenes as they described, and such language as they put into the mouths of their heroes, would now make a book unsaleable—whereas, then, 'Clarissa Harlowe' was thought to teach lessons of virtue, and young ladies were not ashamed to avow their familiarity with ' Tom Jones.'

We are not therefore to conclude that they
were rakes and ready to throw themselves into
the arms of the first adventurer they met; but
we must infer that their delicacy was less sus-
ceptible and their modesty less sensitive than
now.   In Lockhart's 'Life of Scott'* there is
an instructive anecdote told by Sir Walter, which
remarkably illustrates this change in the public
taste.   A grand-aunt of his, Mrs. Keith of
Ravelstone, when a very old lady, once asked
him whether he had ever seen Mrs. Behn's
novels. Sir Walter confessed that he had. She
then asked him whether he could get her a
sight of them, and, "with some hesitation," he
said he believed he could, but he did not think
that she would like either the manners or language. "Nevertheless," said the good old lady,
"I remember their being so much admired, and
being so much interested in them myself, that
I wish to look at them again." "So," says Sir
Walter, "I sent Mrs. Aphra Behn, curiously
sealed up, with 'private and confidential' on
the packet, to my gay old grand-aunt. The
next time I saw her afterwards she gave me
back Aphra, properly wrapped up, with nearly
these words—'Take back your bonny Mrs.
Behn, and, if you will take my advice, put

* Vol. v. pp. 136-7.

her in the fire, for I find it impossible to get
through the very first novel. But is it not,' she
said, 'a very odd thing that I, an old woman of
eighty and upwards, sitting alone, feel myself
ashamed to read a book which sixty years ago
I have heard read aloud for the amusement of
large circles, consisting of the first and most
creditable society in London ?'"

CHAPTER II.

DRESS.—MASQUERADES.—DRUMS.—" PRETTY FELLOWS" AND
"MACCARONIES."—CLUBS.—RANELAGH AND VAUXHALL.—
LONDON.—DANGERS OF THE STREETS.—STATE OF THE
ROADS.—HIGHWAYMEN.

ET us now go a little more into detail,
and consider some of the aspects of
the social life and habits of our
great-great-grandfathers and great-great-grandmothers.

And first as to the dress of the ladies. At
the beginning of the last century the fashionable head-dress was the *commode*, or *fontage*,
by which the hair was piled up on wires to a
prodigious height. Then there came a sudden
fall, so that women who were more than seven
feet high were reduced to five. In a letter in
the 'Spectator,' from a barrister of the Middle
Temple who "rode" the Western Circuit, he
says that one of the most fashionable women
he met with in all the circuit was the landlady
at Staines, and her *commode* was not half a foot
high, and her petticoat "within some yards of a

modish circumference." The writer of a letter in the 'London Magazine' of August, 1768, says, "I went the other morning to make a visit to an elderly aunt of mine, when I found her pulling off her cap and tendering her head to the ingenious Mr. Gilchrist, who has lately obliged the public with a most excellent essay on hair. He asked her how long it was since *her head had been opened or repaired.* She answered, *not above nine weeks.* To which he replied, that it was as long as a head could well go in summer, and that therefore it was proper to deliver it now; for he confessed that it began to be a little *hazardé.*" * And to show how the follies of fashion repeat themselves, I may mention that the satirists of the last century used to mourn over the nakedness of the birds which had been robbed of their plumage to deck the heads of the ladies.

When Lydia Melford, in 'Humphry Clinker,' dresses for an assembly, she says, "I was not six hours in the hands of the hair-dresser, who stuffed my head with as much black wool as would have made a quilted petticoat, and after all it was the smallest head in the assembly except my aunt's." In Miss Burney's 'Evelina' the heroine says, "I have just had my hair

* Quoted in 'Wright's Caricature History of the Georges.'

dressed. You cannot think how oddly my head feels; full of powder and black pins, and a great cushion on the top of it . . . . . When I shall be able to make use of a comb for myself I cannot tell; for my hair is so much entangled, frizzled they call it, that I fear it will be very difficult."

In the reigns of George I. and George II. the petticoats of the ladies attained such a monstrous and extravagant size as to become the favourite subjects of satire and caricature. Mrs. Delany says in one of her letters, written in 1738—" The fashionable hoops are made of the richest damask with gold and silver, fourteen guineas a hoop."* There is in the 'Tatler,'† a paper which gives an account of a mock trial of a pretty young woman for wearing a monstrous petticoat, which when taken off the judge ordered to be drawn up by a pulley, and it formed "a very vast and splendid canopy, and covered the whole court of judicature with a kind of silken rotunda, in its form not unlike the cupola of St. Paul's." Counsel was heard in defence of the petticoat, and amongst other arguments they insinuated that its weight and unwieldiness might be of great use to preserve

* Mrs. Delany's 'Autobiography,' vol. ii. p. 25.
† No. 116.

the honour of families. The *corpus delicti* was, however, condemned, and sentence of forfeiture pronounced. And in the letter of the lawyer of the Western Circuit, which I have already quoted, he says, " As I proceeded on my journey, I observed the petticoat grew scantier and scantier, and about three-score miles from London was so very unfashionable that a woman might walk in it without any manner of inconvenience." They disappeared in the early part of the reign of George III., but we all know that they were revived in a slightly modified form in the reign of Queen Victoria.

What Goldsmith says of the tyranny of female fashion in his day is equally true now. " Our ladies seem to have no other standard for grace but the run of the town. If fashion gives the word, every distinction of beauty, complexion, or stature ceases. Sweeping trains, Prussian bonnets, and trollopees, as like each other as if cut from the same piece, level all to one standard."*

But those who wish to have an accurate idea of the dress of their female ancestors in the last century, had better consult the pages of the diary of the first Earl of Malmesbury, recently published, where they will find full

* 'Bee,' October, 1759.

details of their gowns, ribbons, laces, and ornaments.

As to the dress of the men, the chief thing to notice in contrast with our present apparel was its extreme gaiety. Velvet with lace for coats, embroidered waistcoats with deep pockets and low flaps, satin breeches and buckled shoes, were the attire of our great-great-grandfathers ; and it is difficult to understand how they could support the expense. Thackeray says of Steele, with a delightful touch of sarcasm, " He paid, or promised to pay, his barber fifty pounds a-year, and always went abroad in a laced coat and large black-buckled periwig that must have cost somebody fifty guineas."

When Goldsmith resolved to try to better his fortune by practising as a physician, in 1765, he came out,—according to the account books of Filby, the tailor,—in purple silk small-clothes and a scarlet roquelaire, with a wig, a sword, and a gold-headed cane. And the same minute record shows that he had a blue velvet suit which cost twenty guineas, and a rich straw silk tamboured waistcoat, which cost four guineas, to say nothing of the " Tyrian bloom, satin grain, and garter blue silk breeches." He was, as we know from Boswell, rather vain of his bloom-coloured coat, notwithstanding the surly remark of Johnson that his tailor hoped that people would stare at it and see how well he could make a coat of so absurd a colour.

In 1746, Lord Derwentwater ascended the scaffold dressed in scarlet, faced with black velvet trimmed with gold, a gold-laced waistcoat, and a white feather in his hat.* But he certainly did not show the white feather in his conduct, for he met death with the utmost bravery. In 1753 Dr. Cameron went to execution in a light coloured coat, red waistcoat and breeches, and a new bag wig.†

It was in the following guise that Commodore Trunnion in 'Peregrine Pickle,' one of Smollett's most amusing characters, was dressed on the morning of his intended marriage with Miss Grizzy Pickle. "He had put on, in honour of his nuptials, his best coat of blue broadcloth, cut by a tailor of Ramsgate, and trimmed with five dozen of brass buttons, large and small. His breeches were of the same piece, fastened at the knees with large bunches of tape; his waistcoat was of red plush, lap-

---

* 'Gentleman's Magazine,' vol. xvi. 666.

† Ibid. vol. xxiii. 292. The size of watcnes may be imagined from the fact mentioned by Lady Cowper in her Diary (A.D. 1716) that Lord Winton, when a prisoner in the Tower, had sawed an iron bar very near in two with the spring of his watch, in order to try and make his escape.

pelled with green velvet and garnished with
vellum holes; his boots bore an infinite re-
semblance, both in colour and shape, to a pair
of leather buckets; his shoulder was graced
with a broad buff belt, from whence depended a
huge hanger, with a hilt like that of a back
sword; and on each side of his pommel appeared a rusty pistol rammed in a case covered
with a bear skin. The loss of his tie periwig
and laced hat, which were curiosities of the
kind, did not at all contribute to the improvement of the picture; but, on the contrary, by
exhibiting his bald pate and the natural exten-
sion of his lantern jaws, added to the pecu-
liarity and extravagance of the whole."

The most important and conspicuous part of
the dress was the wig. In 1765 the peruke
makers presented a petition to the King,
praying that their distressed condition might
be taken into consideration on account of so
many persons wearing their own hair; upon
which his Majesty was graciously pleased to
declare that he held nothing dearer to his heart
than the happiness of his people, and he would
at all times use his endeavours to promote their
welfare. It seems that on this occasion some of
the wig-makers who attended the deputation
were so inconsistent as to wear their own hair,

which was cut off by the mob that attacked them.* In Graves's 'Spiritual Quixote' there is a chapter headed " A Dissertation on Periwigs," where a history of these cauliflowers for the head is given, and we are told that " of late years any man that has a mind to look more considerable or more wise than his neighbours goes to a barber's and purchases fifty shillings' worth of false hair (white, black, or grey) and hangs it upon his head, without the least regard to his complexion, his age, or his person, or his station in life ; and certainly if an inhabitant of the Cape of Good Hope were to behold the stiff horsehair buckles or the tied wigs of our lawyers, physicians, tradesmen, or divines, they would appear as barbarous and extraordinary to them as the sheep's tripe and chitterlings about the neck of a Hottentot do to us." And these wigs were not confined to the men. " I heard lately of an old baronet," says the same authority, " that fell in love with a young lady of small fortune at some public place for her *beautiful brown locks*. He married her on a sudden, but was greatly disappointed upon seeing her wig, or *tête*, the next morning, thrown carelessly upon her toilette, and her ladyship appearing at breakfast in very bright *red hair*, which was a

* 'Ann. Reg. Chron.' Feb. 1765.

colour the old gentleman happened to have a particular aversion to." *   If we substitute *chignon* for wig are we quite sure that the same misadventure might not happen now ?

Wesley, when a young man, was distinguished for his long flowing hair, which he wore to save the expense of a periwig that he might give the money to the poor.†   I do not know the exact period when the fashion of wearing periwigs went out ; but in Miss Burney's ' Cecilia,' published at the latter end of the century, the vulgar old miser, Mr. Briggs, is represented as taking off his wig at a masquerade and wiping his head with it.

A favourite form of public amusements was masquerades, which, however, led to great abuse.   In 1749 Elizabeth Chudleigh, afterwards Duchess of Kingston, who was tried for bigamy and sentenced to be burnt in the hand, but praying " her clergy " as a peeress, escaped the punishment, appeared when she was one of the maids of honour of the Princess of Wales

---

* In one of Walpole's letters he says, " You must know that the ladies of Norfolk universally wear periwigs and affirm that is the fashion in London," vol. i. p. 272.

† Horace Walpole heard him preach at Bath in 1766, and describes him as "a lean elderly man, fresh coloured, his hair smoothly combed, but with a *soupçon* of curls at the ends, wondrous clean, but as evidently an actor as Garrick."—' Walpole's Letters,' edited by Cunningham, vol. v. p. 16.

at a masquerade, in the character of Iphigenia ready for sacrifice, in a close dress of flesh-
coloured silk. The Princess, by way of rebuke,
threw her own veil over her. And in 1771,
Col. Luttrell, the opponent of Wilkes, in the
Middlesex election, came to a masquerade as a
dead corpse in a shroud with his coffin. These
exhibitions became at last, however, so offensive,
that they were put down after public opinion had
become disgusted.* It is from a masquerade
that Harriet Byron, in Richardson's novel of
'Sir Charles Grandison,' is carried off by Sir Hargrave Pollexfen; at a masquerade Tom Jones
and Lady Bellaston meet; and it is at a masquerade that Captain Booth, in Fielding's
'Amelia,' is tortured with jealousy, having
mistaken another woman who was there for
his wife.

Private parties given by ladies were called
drums. In the novel of 'Amelia' the heroine
is asked to go to Lady Betty Castleton's, but
excuses herself on the ground that she does

* A writer in the 'Westminster Magazine,' in May, 1774,
describing a masquerade at the Pantheon says, "I saw ladies
and gentlemen together in attitudes and positions that would
have disgraced the Court of Comus. In short, I am so
thoroughly sick of masquerading, from what I beheld there,
that I do seriously decry them, as subversive of virtue and
every noble and domestic point of honour."

not know her. " Not know Lady Betty ? How is that possible ? But no matter, I will introduce you. She keeps a morning rout, indeed ; a little bit of a drum ; only four or five tables. Come, take your capuchin ; you positively shall go." And in one of Daniel Wray's letters, dated Nov. 4, 1766, he thus speaks of a party given by his wife—" Mrs. W., like a miser who gives a dinner but once a year, determined to be magnificent, and peopled her drum so well, that her fire was put out ; and had the company been less chosen it would have been a most insufferable crowd. We amounted in common arithmetic to forty-four souls ; but as one lady was near her time, and as the number is fashionable, we counted forty-five." *

At the beginning of the century, men who affected the extreme of fashion were called " bucks," or " pretty fellows." This name was changed in the early part of the reign of George II. to " beaux" ; then came the " fribbles," and after them the " maccaronies."

> With little hat and hair dressed high
>   And whip to ride a pony,
> If you but take a right survey,
>   Denotes a maccaroni.

---

* I suppose that this refers to No. 45 of the 'North Briton,' for which Wilkes was imprisoned, but afterwards discharged on *habeas corpus*.

These were followed by the 'dandies,' who continued down to our own day; and perhaps are not yet wholly extinct.

In Richardson's correspondence there is a letter from Miss Westcourt, in which she speaks of the celebrated Miss Gunnings, one of whom afterwards married the Duke of Hamilton with the ring of a bed curtain for a wedding-ring, and the other the Earl of Coventry.* They had just left Enfield, (where Miss Westcourt resided,) as not being gay enough. And she says, " May toupees, powder, lace, and essence (the composition of the modern pretty fellows) follow them in troops to stare and be stared at, till the more bashful youths give the first blush." The bucks were fond of practical jokes, and anticipated the famous one of Theodore Hook in Berner's Street. " Once I remember," says a writer in the 'Connoisseur,'† " it was a frolic to call together all the wet nurses that wanted a place; at another time to summon several old women to bring their male tabby cats, for which they were to expect a considerable price; and, not long ago, by the

---

* Richardson thoroughly reciprocated this lady's dislike of the Miss Gunnings, and expressed a wish " and—that in charity —that they may catch the small-pox and have their faces scarred with it " !—'Correspondence of Richardson,' vol. iii. p. 273.

† No. 54. 1755.

proffer of a curacy, they drew all the poor parsons to St. Paul's Coffee House, where the bucks themselves sat in another box to smoke (that is, laugh at) their rusty wigs and brown cassocks." Sometimes they outwitted themselves in their mad merriment, as when a party of tipsy Templars set out at midnight on a voyage to Lisbon to get good port. "They took boat at Temple Stairs and prudently laid in by way of provisions a cold venison pasty and two bottles of raspberry brandy; but when they imagined themselves just arrived at Gravesend, they found themselves suddenly overset in Chelsea Reach, and very narrowly escaped · being drowned." They must have been as drunk as the Greek revellers at Corinth, described by Athenæus, who seeing the room appear to move up and down, fancied that they were at sea in a storm on board a trireme, and began to throw the tables and couches out of window, in order to lighten the vessel. These were certainly at least half-seas over.

The Clubs—very different from the palaces of Pall Mall—and Coffee-houses were the great resort of politicians and literary men —and, indeed, of everybody who liked to pick up news and retail it over a cup of sack or beer and pipe of tobacco. There were White's Chocolate-house in St. James's Street; Willis's Coffee-house, called also Button's, on the north side of Russell Street in Covent Garden; the Cocoa Tree in St. James's Street; the Grecian, in Devereux Court in the Strand; Child's Coffee-house in St. Paul's Churchyard, where the clergy resorted; the Rose, by Temple Bar, close beside which was the barber's shop, where the young Templar used to have "his shoes rubbed and his periwig powdered" before he went to the play; the Devil Tavern, not far off Jonathan's in Change Alley, frequented by merchants and brokers, and several others. And the sort of club-life which men of letters led then is pleasantly described by Addison in the first number of the 'Spectator.' "Sometimes I smoke a pipe at Child's, and while I seem attentive to nothing but the 'Postman,' overhear the conversation of every table in the room. I appear on Tuesday night at St. James's Coffee-house, and sometimes join the little committee of politics in the inner room as one who comes to hear and improve. My face is likewise very well known at the Grecian, the Cocoa Tree, and in the theatres both of Drury Lane and the Haymarket. I have been taken for a merchant

F 2

upon the Exchange for above three years, and
sometimes pass for a Jew in the assembly of
stockjobbers at Jonathan's.   In short, wherever
I see a cluster of people I mix with them,
though I never open my lips but in my own
club."   Dr. Johnson tells us that when Addison
had suffered any vexation in his ill-assorted
marriage with the Countess of Warwick—
which was often enough—he withdrew the
company from Button's house, and " from
the coffee-house he went again to a tavern,
where he often sat late and drank too much
wine."   Button had been a servant in the
Countess's family.

Whatever may be said against clubs now-
a-days, as interfering with domestic life and
preventing matrimony, the attractions of the
old coffee-houses seem to have been more
injurious to the supremacy of the wife.   Here
are one or two short notes written by Steele
to his second wife Miss Scurlock, "his dear
Prue," shortly after their marriage in 1707.

"DEVIL TAVERN, TEMPLE BAR.
Jan. 3, 1707-8.

" DEAR PRUE,

"I have partly succeeded in my business to-day, and enclose two guineas as earnest
of more.   Dear Prue, I cannot come home to

dinner. I languish for your welfare, and will never be a moment careless more.

"Your faithful husband,

"RICH. STEELE."

How cunningly he tried to bribe her into good humour with the two guineas! But, alas, for his promises. A few days afterwards he writes—

"DEAR WIFE,

"Mr. Edgcombe, Ned Ask, and Mr. Lumley have desired me to sit an hour with them at the George in Pall Mall, for which I desire your patience till twelve o'clock, or that you will go to bed. . . . ."

On another occasion he begs her not to send for him, lest he should seem to be a hen-pecked husband. "Dear Prue, don't send after me, for I shall be ridiculous." But he was, I fear, incorrigible, and must have tried Prue's patience not a little by such letters as the following—

"TENNIS-COURT COFFEE-HOUSE.
May 5, 1708.

"DEAR WIFE,

"I hope I have done this day what will be pleasing to you; in the meantime, shall lie this night at a baker's, one Leg, over against the Devil Tavern, at Charing Cross. . . . . If the printer's boy be at home, send him hither; and let Mrs. Todd send by the boy my night-gown, slippers, and clean linen. You shall hear from me early in the morning."

And yet he tells her in another letter, that he "knows no happiness in this life comparable to the pleasure he has in her society," although he adds a bit of advice which may, perhaps, have somewhat dashed the compliment. "Rising a little in the morning, and being disposed to a cheerfulness . . . . would not be amiss."

It seems that the complaint so often heard that young men will not marry, and therefore that young women are not married, is as old as the times of Richardson, and the causes assigned are nearly the same. Miss Byron, in one of her letters in 'Sir Charles Grandison,' says, "I believe there are more bachelors now in England by many thousands than were a few years ago; and probably the number of them (and of single women of course) will every year increase. The luxury of the age will account a good deal for this, and the turn our sex take in *un*-domesticating themselves, for a good deal more. But let not those worthy young women who may think themselves destined to a single life, repine over-much at their lot; since possibly if they have had no lovers, or having had one, two, or three, have not found a husband, they have had rather a miss than a loss, as men go. And let me here add, that I think as matters stand in this age, or, indeed, ever did stand, that those women who have joined with the men in their insolent ridicule of old maids, ought never to be forgiven ; no, though Miss Grandison should be one of the ridiculers. An old maid *may be* an odious character, if they will tell us that the bad qualities of the persons, not the maiden state, are what they mean to expose ; but then they must allow that there are old maids of twenty, and even that there are widows and wives of all ages and complexions, who, in the abusive sense of the words, are as much old maids as the most particular of that class of females."

The favourite places of public resort were Ranelagh and Vauxhall, and at a later period Marylebone or " Marybone " Gardens, as they were called, and the Pantheon. Ranelagh was on the south side of Hans Place, and was so named from its site being that of a villa of Viscount Ranelagh. The last entertainment given there was the installation of the Knights of the Bath, in 1802. In one of his letters, Walpole says—" I have been breakfasting this

morning (1742), at Ranelagh Garden: they
have built an immense amphitheatre full of
little alehouses; it is in rivalry of Vauxhall,
and costs above twelve thousand pounds."* In
another letter he describes it as " a vast amphitheatre, finely gilt, painted and illuminated, into
which everybody that loves eating, drinking,
staring, or crowding, is admitted for twelve
pence."† It was frequently visited by the king
and the royal family, and was apparently very
much like the Cremorne Gardens of the present
day, which, however, royalty does *not* visit.
We have a description of the place in several
of the old novels.

Horace Walpole mentions, in a letter to
George Montague, dated June 23, 1750, a
party of pleasure of ladies and gentlemen, of
which he made one, at Vauxhall: " We got
into the best order we could, and marched to
our barge, with a boat of French horns attending, and little Ashe singing. We paraded
some time up the river, and at last debarked
at Vauxhall; there, if we had so pleased, we
might have had the vivacity of our party in-

* ' Walpole's Letters, edited by Cunningham,' vol. i. p. 158.
† When Dr. Johnson visited Ranelagh he said that " the
coup d'œil was the finest thing he had ever seen."—' Boswell's
Life of Johnson.'

creased by a quarrel. . . . . Miss Spurre, who
desired nothing so much as the fun of seeing a
duel—a thing which, though she is fifteen, she
has never been so lucky to see—took due pains
to make Lord March resent this, but he, who is
very lively and agreeable, laughed her out of
this charming frolic with a great deal of
humour. Here we picked up Lord Granby,
arrived very drunk from Jenny's (a well-known
tavern at Chelsea) where, instead of going to
old Strafford's catacombs to make honourable
love, he had dined with Lady Fanny, and left
her, and eight women, and four other men,
playing at Brag." The party then enjoyed themselves mincing chickens in a china dish, which
Lady Caroline Petersham stewed over a lamp,
with pats of butter, and eating strawberries and
cherries brought by Betty, the fruit-girl.*

There is an amusing account in the 'Connoisseur' (1755), of the surprise of an honest
citizen, whose wife and two daughters had
persuaded him to take them to Vauxhall, when
he found how thin were the slices of ham, and
how heavy was the reckoning. His daughters
ask him when they shall come again to the
Gardens, but he retorts by asking them if they
mean to ruin him. " Once in one's life is

* 'Walpole's Letters, edited by Cunningham,' vol. ii. p. 211.

enough, and I think I have done very handsome. Why it would not have cost me above
fourpence-halfpenny to have spent my evening
at Lot's Hole ; and what with the cursed coach-
hire, and all together, here's almost a pound
gone, and nothing to show for it." And so he
flapped his hat, and tied his pocket-handker-
chief over it, to save his wig, as it began to
rain, and shook the dust of Vauxhall from off
his feet.

In 'Humphry Clinker,' Mr. Matthew Bramble asks, what are the amusements of Vauxhall ?
"One half of the company are following one
another's tails in an eternal circle ; like so many
blessed asses in an olive-mill, where they can
neither discourse, distinguish, nor be distinguished ; while the other half are drinking hot
water, under the denomination of tea. . . . .
Vauxhall is a composition of baubles, over-
charged with paltry ornaments." But Lydia
Melford speaks in raptures of Ranelagh, which
she says, " looks like the enchanted palace of a
genio," and as to Vauxhall, she is " dazzled and
confounded with the variety of beauties that
rushed all at once upon my eye."

No account, however, that I have read of
Ranelagh or Vauxhall, is so life-like and spirited
as that by Thackeray, of Vauxhall, in ' Vanity

Fair.' He could speak from experience, for Vauxhall existed in his youth, and he vouches for the truth of the fact there was no headache in the world like that caused by Vauxhall punch. He tells us of all the delights of the Gardens ; of the hundred thousand *extra* lamps which were always lighted, the fiddlers in cocked hats, who played ravishing melodies under the gilded cockle-shell in the midst of the gardens ; the singers, both of comic and sentimental ballads, who charmed the ears there ; the country dances formed by bouncing cockneys and cockneyesses, and executed amidst jumping, thumping, and laughter ; the signal that announced that Madame Saqui was about to mount skyward on a slack rope, ascending to the stars ; the hermit that always sat in the illuminated hermitage ; the dark walks so favourable to the interviews of young lovers ; the pots of stout handed about by the people in the shabby old liveries ; and the twinkling boxes in which the happy feasters made believe to eat slices of almost invisible ham.

But there is hardly a scene at Ranelagh described by the old novelists, where some insult is not offered to ladies by men calling themselves gentlemen, although they did not always attack them quite as openly as the

young nobleman, who, in Fielding's ' Amelia,'
meets the heroine at Vauxhall, and cries out,
" Let the devil come as soon as he will;
d——n me if I have not a kiss."

We find in the novels of the last century,
several incidental notices of London, which give
us some idea of the difference between the metropolis then and as it exists now. We are told in
' Humphry Clinker,' that " Pimlico and Knights-
bridge are now almost joined to Chelsea and
Kensington, and if this infatuation continues
for half a century, I suppose the whole county
of Middlesex will be covered with brick."*

In Mrs. Heywood's novel of ' Miss Betsy
Thoughtless,' a gentleman mentions in a letter
that he wants a house, and says, " I should
approve of St. James's Square if rents are not
exorbitant, for in that case a house in any of
the adjoining streets must content me ; I would
not willingly exceed 100*l.* or 110*l.* per annum ;
but I should be as near the Park and Palace as
possible." The idea of a house in St. James's
Square at a rent of a hundred a-year is rather

---

* The sights of London are described by Mrs. Winifred
Jenkins in the same veracious work. " And I have seen the
park and the paleass of St. Gimses, and the king's and the
queen's magisterial pursing, and the sweet young princes, and
the hillyfents and pye-bald ass, and all the rest of the royal
family."

startling, and is probably a mistake on the part of the authoress.

Let those who wish to understand what might happen in the streets of London in the reign of Queen Anne, read the attempt of Captain Hill to seize and run away with the beautiful actress, Mrs. Bracegirdle, as the story was told upon sworn evidence in the House of Lords, and is chronicled in the pages of the State Trials. The gallant lover, assisted by Lord Mohun, lay in wait for his mistress in Drury Lane, with a hackney-coach and six horses and half-a-dozen soldiers. He caught hold of her hand and tried to force her into the carriage, while the soldiers attacked with their swords Mr. Page, a friend who accompanied her. But a hubbub arose, and the bystanders came to the rescue, so that his Lordship and Captain Hill were obliged to let the fair Bracegirdle go, and in revenge for their disappointment they afterwards attacked Mountford the comedian—of whom Hill was jealous—as he was coming out of a house in Norfolk Street in the Strand, and killed him. For this murder Lord Mohun was tried by his peers, but found not guilty, as the actual blow was struck by Hill, while the attention of Mountford was engaged in conversation by his Lordship.

In the early part of the century the streets
of London were infested by a body of wild
young men, who called themselves members
of the Mohock Club.   Their exploits consisted
in knocking down watchmen, assaulting the
citizens, and rolling women in tubs.*

> Who has not heard the scourer's midnight fame?
> Who has not trembled at the Mohock's name?
> Was there a watchman took his nightly rounds,
> Safe from their blows, or new-invented wounds?
> I pass these desperate deeds, and mischiefs done,
> Where from Snow-hill black steepy torrents run;
> How matrons, hooped within the hogshead's womb,
> Were tumbled furious thence; the rolling tomb
> O'er the stone thunders, bounds from side to side;
> So Regulus, to save his country, died.†

The dangers of the streets, from Mohocks
and other ruffians, was such that to go to the
theatre was like going to Donnybrook Fair.
When Sir Roger de Coverley wished to see a
play Captain Sentry came to accompany him,
after putting on his sword, and, in the words
of the 'Spectator,' "Sir Roger's servants, and
amongst the rest my old friend the butler, had
I found, provided themselves with good oaken
plants, to attend their master on this occasion.
When we had placed him in his coach, with
myself at the left hand, the captain before him,

* 'Spectator,' No. 324.
† Gay's 'Trivia,' published in 1711.

and his butler at the head of the footmen in the rear, we conveyed him in safety to the play-house."

The roads were everywhere in an abominable state. In the country they were merely green lanes, with deep ruts, almost impassable from mud in winter, or after rain; and coaches drawn by six horses stuck in them as in an impervious morass. The average speed of a stage-coach was about three miles an hour. It took a week to travel from York to London, and between London and Edinburgh the time allowed, in 1763, was a fortnight.* But this was by the ordinary coach, for we learn from Richardson's Correspondence that the "fast coaches" actually performed the journey between London and York in three days! In the metropolis the gutters flowed in the middle of the streets, and there was no side pavement, or *trottoir*, for pedestrians.

Describing his journey between Chester and London in a stage-coach in 1740, Pennant says, "The strain and labour of six good horses, sometimes eight, drew us through the sloughs

---

* On Monday, April 26, 1669, the "Flying Coach" went from Oxford to London for the first time in one day. It had a boot on each side. Amongst the passengers, we are told, was Mr. Holloway, "a Counsellor of Oxon, afterwards a Judge."

of Mireden and many other places.   We were
constantly out two hours before day, and as
late at night, and in the depth of winter pro-
portionately greater."   And he draws an un-
favourable contrast between the single gentleman of former times—who equipped in jack-
boots rode post through thick and thin, and
guarded against the mire, defied the frequent
stumble and fall—and "their enervated posterity, who sleep away their rapid journeys in
easy chairs!"

The same author speaks of the Chester stage
as " no despicable vehicle for country gentlemen."   He reached London from Chester, " as
a wondrous effort," on the sixth day before
nightfall.   " Families who travelled in their own
carriages contracted with Benson & Co., and
were dragged up in the same number of days,
by three sets of able horses." *   We need not,
therefore, be surprised that the old novelists so
frequently introduce the family coach and six,
although it is difficult to understand how
country gentlemen of moderate means could
bear the expense.

When Mrs. Delany travelled from London to
"the Farm" in Gloucestershire in her father's
coach and six, the journey occupied five days,

* Journey from Chester to London, p. 187.

"through miserable roads." Writing to her sister, in 1728, she says, "At the end of the town some part of the coach broke and we were obliged to get out, and took shelter in an ale-house; in half-an-hour we jogged on, and about an hour after that, flop we went into a slough, not overturned, but stuck. Well! out we were hauled again, and the coach with much difficulty was heaved out." * Horace Walpole, writing in 1752, describes the roads in the neighbourhood of Tunbridge Wells as "bad beyond all badness," where young gentlemen were forced to drive their curricles with a pair of oxen.† Mrs. Scudamore says, in a letter to Richardson the novelist, written from Kent Church in 1757, "Thank God, we have met with no ill accident; all arrived in health. We now and then stuck a little by the way from the narrowness of the roads, which we were obliged to make wider in places by a spade." ‡

In a letter written by Lord Hervey from Kensington, in 1763, he says, "The road between this place and London is grown so infamously bad, that we live here in the same solitude as we would do if cast upon a rock in

---

* 'Mrs. Delany's Autobiography,' vol. i. p. 12, 17.
† 'Walpole's Letters,' edited by Cunningham, vol. ii. p. 281.
‡ 'Correspondence of Richardson,' vol. iii. p. 327.

the middle of the ocean, and all the Londoners tell us that there is between them and us an impassable gulf of mud."

In Arthur Young's ' Tour in the North of England,' published 1770, he describes a *turnpike* road between Preston and Wigan, and cautions travellers to avoid it "as they would the devil;" saying, "they will here meet with ruts, which I actually measured, four feet deep, and floating with mud, only from a wet summer—what, therefore, must it be after a winter? The only mending it receives in places is the tumbling in some loose stones, which serve no other purpose but jolting a carriage in the most intolerable manner."

In his sketch of the life of Jane Austen, the Rev. Mr. Leigh describes the road between the villages of Deane and Steventon, of which successively her father was incumbent, as being, in the year 1771, "a mere cart-track, so cut up by deep ruts as to be impassable for a light carriage. Mrs. Austen, who was not then in strong health, performed the short journey on a feather-bed placed upon some soft articles of furniture in the waggon which held their household goods. In those days it was not unusual to set men to work with shovel and pickaxe to fill up ruts and holes in roads seldom used by carriages, on such special occasions as a funeral or a wedding."

But besides the danger of an upset from holes and mud, there was the more serious danger of an attack from highwaymen, who infested all the great roads. No wonder, then, that pious Ralph Thoresby, when travelling by coach from Leeds to London in 1708 records in his diary—" Evening : I got an opportunity in secret to bless God for mercies vouchsafed, and implore further protection, though I had a Scotch physician for my chamber-fellow"! When a family of even moderate wealth travelled to Tunbridge, or Bath, or Harrogate, or Scarborough, they set out in a coach and six, attended by servants on horseback, armed with pistols, to guard them against robbers.* To be attacked on the road by highwaymen was indeed one of the commonest incidents of travel, and there is hardly a novel of the last century which does not introduce some such a scene as the most natural thing in the world.

Lady Cowper has the following entry in her diary, under date 1716 : " Friday night Mr.

* Beau Nash, at the beginning of the century, used to travel from Bath to Tunbridge in a post-chariot and six greys, with outriders, footmen, French horns, and—a white hat ; which last he said he wore to prevent it from being stolen.—Goldsmith's ' Life of Beau Nash.'

Micklethwaite was set upon by nine footpads, who fired at his postilion, without bidding him stand, just at the end of Bedford Row, in the road that goes there from Pancras Church to Gray's Inn Lane. His servants and he fired at them again, and the pads did the same till all the fire was spent."

This was at the beginning of the century; but towards its close Horace Walpole tells us in one of his letters, written in 1781, that he and Lady Browne were robbed by a highwayman as they were going to an evening party at the Duchess of Montrose's, near Twickenham Park, and after Lady Browne had given the thief her purse and he had ridden away, she said, "I am in terror lest he should return, for I have given him a purse with only bad money *that I carry on purpose.*"* And when Mrs. Calderwood of Coltness went from Edinburgh to London in 1756, she says in her diary that she travelled in her own post-chaise, attended by John Rattray, her stout serving-man, on horseback, with pistols at his holsters and a good broadsword by his side. She had also with her in the carriage a case of pistols for use upon an emergency.†

* 'Walpole's Letters,' vol. viii. p. 89.
† Quoted in Smiles's 'Lives of the Engineers,' vol. i. p. 176.

In a letter written by Mrs. Harris, the
mother of the first Lord Malmesbury, to her
son, dated Feb. 16, 1773, she says,* "A most
audacious fellow robbed Sir Francis Holburne
and his sisters in their coach in St. James's
Square, coming from the opera. He was on
horseback, and held a pistol close to the breast
of one of the Miss Holburnes for a considerable time. She had left her purse at home,
which he would not believe. He has since
robbed a coach in Park Lane." "It is shocking
to think," writes Walpole, in 1752, "what a
shambles this country has grown! Seventeen
were executed this morning after having mur-
dered the turnkey on Friday night, and almost
forced open Newgate. One is forced to travel,
even at noon, as if one was going to battle."†

In his introduction to a 'Voyage to Lisbon,'
Fielding congratulates himself on having broken
up, in 1753, the gang of cut-throats and street-
robbers, who had been the terror of the
metropolis, so that "instead," he says, "of
reading of murders and street-robberies in the
news almost every morning, there was in the
remaining part of the month of November, and
in all December, not only no such thing as a

* 'The Letters of the First Earl of Malmesbury,' vol. i. p. 258.
† 'Walpole's Letters,' vol. ii. p. 281.

murder, but not even a street robbery committed." In his 'Amelia,' he describes the watchmen of London as " poor, old, decrepit people, from their want of bodily strength rendered incapable of getting their livelihood by work." And we must remember that Fielding was a London magistrate and sat in Bow Street, so that his testimony is unexceptionable. He says in his 'Inquiry into the Causes of the Increase of Robberies,' that he makes no doubt that the streets of London and the roads leading to it will shortly be impassable without the utmost hazard, and speaks of a great gang of rogues who were incorporated into one body, had officers and a treasury, and reduced theft and robbery to a regular system. The first cause to which he attributes the evils he complains of is the too frequent and expensive dressiness amongst the lower kind of people. Amongst them he instances masquerades, which were by no means confined to places of fashionable resort, like Ranelagh and Vauxhall, but were scattered over the metropolis and its neighbourhood, " where the places of pleasure have almost become numberless." The next cause is drunkenness, for the cure of which he proposes that all spirituous liquors should be locked up in the chemists' and apothecaries' shops, "thence never to be drawn till some excellent physician call them forth for the cure of nervous distempers." The third cause is gaming, and the fourth the state of the poor-law. Fielding was, in the matter of law-reform, far in advance of his age; and he points out with great force and acuteness the defects of our boasted system of jurisprudence. " There is," he says, "no branch of the law more bulky, more full of confusion and contradiction, I had almost said of absurdity, than the law of evidence as it now stands." And yet that law was suffered to remain unchanged until a few years ago! He had the good sense to suggest the improvement, which has only just been sanctioned by Parliament, of private instead of public executions, and he exhausts the argument for it in a few words, when he says, " If executions, therefore, could be so contrived that few could be present at them, they would be much more shocking and terrible to the crowd without doors than at present, as well as much more dreadful to the criminals themselves, who would thus die only in the presence of their enemies; and thus the boldest of them would find no cordial to keep up his spirits, nor any breath to flatter his ambition."

The subject of executions in the last century

and during a great part of the present, is really almost too dreadful to dwell upon. It is sickening to turn over the pages of the Annual Register and see what a holocaust of victims was given over to the hangman for offences which now would be punished by a few months' imprisonment. There was quite a trade in " last dying speeches." " I continued," says Thomas Gent, printer of York, in his autobiography, speaking of 1733, " working for Mr. Woodfall until the execution of Counsellor Layer, on whose few dying words I formed observations in the nature of a large speech, and had a run of sale for about three days successively, which obliged me to keep in my own apartments, the unruly hawkers being ready to pull my press in pieces for the goods."

CHAPTER III.

PRISONS.—DRUNKENNESS.—SWEARING.—GAMBLING.—DUEL-
LING.—JUSTICE OF THE PEACE.—COUNTRY SQUIRE.

THE mention of robberies leads naturally to speak of prisons, and it is
shocking to think of what they were.
They were more like dens of wild beasts than
habitations of men. Some idea of the condition of the Fleet may be obtained from the
perusal of a report of a Committee of the House
of Commons in 1729, when the House resolved
that several of the officers of the prison should
be committed to Newgate, and some of them
were afterwards tried for murder, but acquitted.
Nothing in fiction exceeds the reality of the
horrible disclosures which these trials brought
to light. The following is a description of the
dungeon called the strong room.*

"This place is like a vault, like those in
which the dead are interred, and wherein the
bodies of persons dying in the said prison are

* Howell's ' State Trials,' vol. xvii. p. 298.

usually deposited till the coroner's inquest hath passed upon them : it has no chimney nor fire-place, nor any light but what comes over the door, or through a hole of about eight inches square. It is neither paved nor boarded ; and the rough bricks appear both on the sides and top, being neither wainscotted nor plastered. What adds to the dampness and stench of the place is its being built over the common sewer, and adjoining to the sink and dunghill, where all the nastiness of the prison is cast. In this miserable place, the poor wretch was kept by the said Bambridge, manacled and shackled for near two months."

At one of the trials the following evidence was given*—

Mr. Ward.—Was Acton there ?

Demotet.—Acton came and saw Newton locked into the strong room. When he was first put in, Captain Delagol was confined there at the same time.

Mr. Ward.—Was Newton sick in the strong room ?

Demotet.—He fell sick there ; both of them were lousy ; his wife and young child came to take care of her husband, and petitioned to Mr. John Darrell to have him released ; he was put

---

* Howell's ' State Trials,' vol. xvii. p. 531.

in the sick room, and there died in four or five days after. His wife broke her heart, and she and the little child died in the same week.

Mr. Ward.—What was the occasion of his being sick?

Demotet.—That he was on the ground; he had no bed to lie on, and the water came in on the top.

Mr. Ward.—What kind of place is the strong room?

Demotet.—It is not fit to put a man in; the rain comes in.

Mr. Baron Carter.—Were you ever in it?

Demotet.—I was in it myself; Grace put me in there.

Mr. Baron Carter.—How long were you in the strong room?

Demotet.—I was in there for ten minutes, and there were two dead men in at the same time, and I fell sick for five months.

Mr. Marsh.—Was it infested with rats?

Demotet.—It was very much infested with rats and vermin.

Large sums were extorted from the wretched prisoners in the shape of fees. In the case of Huggins and Bambridge, reported on by the same Committee of the House of Commons, in 1729, the Judges reprimanded them, and de-

clared that " a gaoler could not answer the iron-
ing of a man before he was found guilty of
crime ; but *it being out of term*, they could not
give the prisoner any relief or satisfaction."
Notwithstanding this opinion of the judges, the
said Bambridge continued to keep the prisoner
in irons till he had paid him six guineas.*   So
that there is no exaggeration in the story told
by Fielding in his ' Amelia,' of a prisoner in
Bridewell.   " The case of this poor man is
unhappy enough.   He served his country, lost
his limb, and was wounded at the siege of
Gibraltar ; he was apprehended and committed
here on a charge of stealing ; he was tried and
acquitted — indeed his innocence manifestly
appeared at the trial—*but he was brought back
here for his fees*, and here he has lain ever
since."   The same author gives us a picture
of the interior of this prison, in which Captain
Booth was incarcerated, but it is by no means
so revolting as many others that might be
quoted from the writers of the time.   " The
first persons he met were three men in fetters,
who were enjoying themselves very merrily
over a bottle of wine and a pipe of tobacco.
They were street-robbers, who were to be tried
for a capital felony, and certain to be hanged.

* Howell's ' State Trials,' vol. xvii. p. 304.

The next was a man prostrate on the ground, whose groans and frantic actions showed that his mind was disordered. He had been committed for a small felony, and his wife, who was then in her confinement, had thrown herself from a window two stories high. A pretty innocent-looking girl came up and uttered a volley of oaths and indecent ribaldry, while not far off was a young woman in rags, supporting the head of an old man, her father, who appeared to be dying. She had been committed for stealing a loaf in order to support him, and he for receiving it knowing it to be stolen."

In the 'Fool of Quality,' a novel written by Henry Brooke, in 1763, of which more hereafter, we find terrible complaints of the severity of the law against debtors, and arguments against imprisonment for debt, to which it took more than a hundred years afterwards to give practical effect. I do not know any book, or report, or speech, where the case is stated more strongly and concisely for a change in the law, than in the following passage :—

" As all the members of a community are interested in the life, liberty, and labours of each other, he who puts the rigour of our laws in execution, by detaining an insolvent brother in jail, is guilty of a fourfold injury ; first he robs the community of the labours of their brother; secondly, he robs his brother of all means of retrieving his shattered fortune; thirdly, he deprives himself of the possibility of payment; and lastly, he lays an unnecessary burden on the public, who, in charity, must maintain the member whom he in his cruelty confines." In the same work, speaking of the prisons in which debtors were confined, he describes them as driven to kennel together in a hovel fit only to stable a pair of horses; and huddled into windowless rooms, with naked walls, while they were squeezed by exorbitant charges and illicit demands "as grapes are squeezed in a wine-press, so long as a drop remains." There is, however, not a single novel of the last century, which describes the interior of a prison, at whatever time it was written, whether in the middle of the period by Fielding, or towards its close, by Godwin and Mackenzie, where the same testimony is not borne to its revolting horrors.*

As to the almost universal prevalence of one vice in the last century, there can be no dif-

* In a paper in the ' Idler' (A.D. 1759), Dr. Johnson computes that there were 20,000 debtors in England in prison, and that one in four of them died every year in consequence of their treatment there, "the corruption of confined air, the want of exercise, and sometimes of food, the contagion of diseases, and the severity of tyrants."

ference of opinion—I mean the vice of drunkenness. The preamble to the Act 9 Geo. II.
c. 23, recites that "the drinking of spirituous
liquors, or strong waters, is become very common, especially among the people of lower and
inferior rank, the constant and excessive use
whereof tends greatly to the destruction of
their healths, rendering them unfit for useful
labour and business, debauching their morals,
and exciting them to perpetrate all manner of
vices." I fear that as regards the lower classes,
it cannot be said that this recital would be
wholly inapplicable now, but the reformation
that has taken place amongst the gentry and
middle classes generally is wonderful. It is
difficult for us to realise the extent to which
our forefathers carried their potations.* Mrs.

---

* This of course does not apply to the other sex ; and I do not
find in the literature of the century any hint that women were
given to excess. There is a passage in Thoresby's ' Diary,' vol.
ii. p. 207, under date 1714, which we must interpret charitably :
"Had other passengers which, though females, were more chargeable with wine and brandy than the former part of the journey,
wherein we had neither." I once was asked by an English-
woman, with two or three daughters, at an hotel in Germany, to
explain to her an item in her bill, which being written in German,
she did not understand. "Madam," I said, "that is a charge
for brandy." "Oh !" she answered, getting rather red in the
face, "one of my daughters was taken ill in the night." Let us
hope that the brandy alluded to by Thoresby was required for a
similar reason.

Delany, writing in 1719, says that Sir William
Pendarves had a copper *coffin* placed in the
middle of his hall, which was filled with punch,
and he and his boon companions used to sit
beside it and get drunk.* Lady Cowper, in
her Diary, under date 1716, says, "At the
drawing-room, George Mayo turned out for
being drunk and saucy. He fell out with Sir
James Baker, and in the fray had pulled him by
the nose."† And again, in 1720, on the King's
birthday, at Court, "the Duke of Newcastle
(then Lord Chamberlain) had got drunk for our
sins ; so the Princess's ladies had no places, but
stood in the heat and the crowd all the night."
And the servants were not behind their
masters, for immediately afterwards she makes
the following entry. "Dined with Aunt Alla-
vern. Go to the Master of the Rolls. The
servants got so drunk I was forced to send one
of them home." Again, "I dine with Mrs. Clay-
ton. Left by chairmen and servants all drunk.
I can hardly get to the Princess." In one of the

---

* 'Autobiography,' vol. i. p. 66.

† An old German writer, Paul Hentzner, who visited England
in 1598, says : "In London, persons who have got drunk, are
wont to mount a church tower, *for the sake of exercise*, and to
ring the bells for several hours."—Quoted by Max Müller in his
'Chips from a German Workshop,' vol. iii. p. 247. It would be
curious to find out the source of information from which Hentzner got this strange story.

essays in the 'Tatler,' Steele says, "I will undertake, were the butler and swineherd, at any true enquiries in Great Britain, to keep and compare accounts of what wash is drunk up in so many hours in the parlour and pigsty, it would appear the gentleman of the house gives much more to his friends than his hogs." *

This wretched habit continued with little diminution to the end of the century. In Miss Edgeworth's 'Belinda,' written about that time, on the first occasion when the heroine saw Lord Delacour, he was dead drunk in the arms of two footmen, who were carrying him upstairs to his bed-chamber, while his lady, who had just returned from Ranelagh, passed by him on the landing-place with a look of sovereign contempt. "Don't look so shocked and amazed," said Lady Delacour to Belinda, "don't look so *new*, child; this funeral of my lord's intellects is to me a nightly, or," added her ladyship, looking at her watch and yawning, "I believe I should say a *daily* ceremony. Six o'clock, I protest!"

* In a touching paper in the 'Tatler,' in which he describes his father's death and his mother's grief, Steele says he is interrupted by the arrival of a hamper of wine, "of the same sort with that which is to be put to sale on Thursday next at Garraway's," and he sends for three friends, and they carouse together, drinking two bottles a man, until two o'clock in the morning."

But if it was bad in England it was worse in Scotland. There the ordinary drink was whisky, or claret, and the latter beverage must have seemed weak as water after the former. One of the Scotch judges, Lord Hermand, is said to have got drunk at Ayr while on circuit, and to have continued drunk until his work was finished at Jedburgh. In a house where Mackenzie, the author of the ' Man of Feeling,' was a visitor, a servant lad was kept, whose business was to " loose the neckcloths " of the guests who fell under the table, and at Castle Grant two Highlanders attended to carry the drunken company to bed. Dr. Carlyle (in 1751), describing in terms of praise Dr. Patrick Cumming, a clergyman, says that he "had both learning and sagacity and a very agreeable conversation, *with a constitution able to bear the conviviality of the times.*" Ladies were obliged to leave the dining-room that the *gentlemen* might get drunk, and had to receive afterwards those who could stand, staggering in the drawing-room.*

A natural accompaniment of hard drinking was hard swearing, and this was as common in fashionable as in vulgar life—in the dining-room and the drawing-room as in the kitchen or

* See for these facts Ramsay's ' Reminiscences of Scottish Life and Character.'

the stable. In most of the novels of the last century that we take up we find the pages studded with blanks and dashes, to denote the oaths of the speakers. I do not mean merely such characters as Squire Western or Commodore Trunnion, or Squire Tyrrel ; but it seems to have been considered the necessary stamp of a man of fashion to be in the habit of swearing. And the lady-novelists made no scruple in furnishing their pages with oaths, in order to give a life-like reality to the conversations of their *dramatis personæ*. This continued to the end of the century, and beyond it. In Miss Edgeworth's ' Belinda' Sir Philip Baddely and his friend Rochfort never speak without an oath, and in a single page I have counted nine. Even Miss Austen does not shrink from putting in the mouths of young men like John Thorpe a quantity of these expletives, which, of course, she would not have done if she had not thought it necessary in order to give *vraisemblance* to their characters.

The habit of swearing was so common that it hardly excited any attention ; and we find little notice taken of it by the essayists, who professed to attack every kind of folly and vice. In the ' Spectator,' indeed, swearing is described as a reproach to the nation. And there is a paper in the 'Tatler' upon this "blustering impertinence," as it is called, which " is already banished out of the society of well-bred men, and can be useful only to bullies and *ill* tragic writers, who would have sound and noise pass for courage and sense." But the number of well-bred men, if judged by this criterion, must have been extremely small. In the 'Microcosm' there is a paper by Canning, in 1786, which tries to make people ashamed of it by turning it into ridicule, and proposing to teach as a science "the noble art of swearing." We are there told, and beyond all doubt it was the truth, that "this practice pervades all stations and degrees of men, from the peer to the porter, from the minister to the mechanic . . . nay, even the female sex have, to their no small credit, caught the happy contagion ; and there is scarce a mercer's wife in the kingdom but has her innocent un-meaning imprecations, her little oaths 'softened into nonsense' and with squeaking treble, minc-ing blasphemy into *odsbodikins, slitterkins*, and such like, will 'swear you like a sucking dove, ay, an it were any nightingale.'" The writer then proposes that an advertisement should be issued in the following terms :—" Ladies and gentlemen instructed in the most fashionable and elegant oaths ; the most peculiarly adapted

to their several ages, manners and professions,
&c. He (the advertiser) has now ready for the
press a book entitled 'The Complete Oath
Register : or, Every Man his own SWEARER,'
containing oaths and imprecations for all times,
seasons, purposes and occasions. Also *Sentimental oaths* for ladies. Likewise *Execrations
for the year* 1786."

Gambling for high stakes was almost universal. In Lady Cowper's diary, under date
1715, she says, " My mistress (the Princess of
Wales) and the Duchess of Montague went
halves at hazard, and won £600. Mr. Archer
came in great form to offer me a place at the
table ; but I laughed, and said he did not know
me if he thought that I was capable of venturing
two hundred guineas at play—for none sit down
to the table with less."

On one occasion large sums of money were
lost and won on a race between two maggots
crawling across a table.* Horace Walpole,
writing to the Earl of Strafford in 1786, says :—
" If we turn to private life, what is there to
furnish pleasing topics ? Dissipation, without
object, pleasure, or genius, is the only colour of
the times. One hears every day of somebody

---

* ' Oxford Magazine,' October, 1770. ' Caricature History of
the Georges,' p. 319.

undone; but can we or they tell how, except
when it is by the most expeditious of all means,
gaming? And now even the loss of an hundred
thousand pounds is not rare enough to be surprising." *

At the end of the century three titled ladies,
Lady Buckinghamshire, Lady Archer, and Lady
Mount-Edgcumbe, were so notorious for their
passion for play that they were popularly known
as "Faro's daughters," and Gilray published, in
1796, a caricature representing two of them as
standing in the pillory, with a crier and his bell
in front. This was in consequence of what was
said by Chief Justice Kenyon in a case that
came before him in 1796, when he said, with
reference to the practice of gambling, "If any
prosecutions of this nature are fairly brought
before me, and the parties are justly convicted,
whatever be their rank or station in the country
—though they should be the first ladies in the
land—they shall certainly exhibit themselves in
the pillory."

In her novel of 'Belinda,' Miss Edgeworth
introduces a fashionable lady, Mrs. Luttridge,
as keeping an E. O. table at her house, where
heavy play goes on, and which is constructed
for the purpose of cheating. The consequence

* 'Walpole's Letters,' edited by Cunningham, vol. viii. p. 73.

is, that being detected, she is obliged, in order to prevent exposure, to give an acknowledgment that nothing is due for large sums won by her from one of her victims.

We know that Duelling, the offspring of the modern code of honour and involving the double crime of murder and suicide, flourished in full vigour during the whole of the last century and was continued down to our own day. In one of her letters Mrs. Delany calls it "that reigning curse." It was too common, and its existence too notorious to require even a passing illustration. Every gentleman who was challenged had to fight or forfeit his reputation; and we have a type of the character in Colonel Bath, one of the heroes in Fielding's 'Amelia,' who is described as "being indeed a perfect good Christian, except in the articles of fighting and swearing."* He is something like Captain Hector McTurk in 'St. Ronan's Well,' whose tears came into his eyes when he recounted the various quarrels which had become addled, not-

---

* With this we may compare Dr. Johnson's remark : "Campbell is a good man, a pious man. I am afraid he has not been in the inside of a church for many years : but he never passes a church without pulling off his hat : this shows he has good principles." On which passage Macaulay observes, in his review of Croker's edition of ' Boswell's Life of Johnson :' " Spain and Sicily must surely contain many pious robbers and well-principled assassins."

withstanding his best endeavours to hatch them
into an honourable meeting.   It was even
thought no violation of probability in a novel
to introduce clergymen as ready to give " satisfaction " with the pistol or the sword.   In Mrs.
Inchbald's ' Simple Story,' Dorriforth, a Roman
Catholic Priest, in a moment of irritation, strikes
Lord Frederick Lawnley, who, he thinks, is per-
secuting Miss Milner with his addresses, and then
accepts a challenge to fight a duel, in which he
comes off with a wounded arm.   And in ' Humphry
Clinker,' Mr. Prankley challenges at Bath the
Reverend Mr. Eastgate, after telling him that
unless he held his tongue he " would dust his
cassock for him "—and they go out together
armed with pistols—but the affair is amicably
settled on the ground.*   In Miss Edgeworth's
story of ' Belinda,' published in 1801, Lady
Delacour, a fashionable dame, narrates a " meeting " she had with Mrs. Luttridge, owing to a
quarrel that arose out of an election squib,
when each lady appeared on the ground in
male attire, with a pistol in her hand and attended by a female second.   The matter was

* The Rev. Henry Bate, who in 1781 took the name of
Dudley, fought two duels, and was afterwards made a Canon
and a Baronet.   See Croker's Edition of Boswell's ' Life of
Johnson.'

however arranged peaceably, and it was agreed that the combatants should fire their pistols into the air.

But what is not so generally known, is that the law steadily and consistently treated duelling as murder. Juries, indeed, might refuse to convict ; but that was not the fault of the law, but of a state of society which threw its shield over the transgressor. It would be easy to quote instances of the stern severity with which duelling was punished when judges had the opportunity of passing sentence. Thus, in 1708, one Mawgridge was executed at Tyburn for having killed William Cope, in a duel two years before.* He had in the meantime escaped to Flanders "washed and rubbed all over with green walnut shucks and walnut liquor to disguise him."

In 1729 Major Oneby was tried at the Old Bailey for killing Mr. Gower in a duel. The jury found a special verdict, stating the facts, and praying the advice of the Court " whether this be murder or manslaughter ? " Chief Justice Raymond delivered the opinion of all the Judges that the prisoner was guilty of murder, and he was sentenced to be hanged, but he escaped the gallows by destroying himself in

* Howell's 'State Trials,' vol. xvii. p. 57-71.

prison.* In 1753 John Barbot was tried in the Island of St. Kitts and found guilty of killing Mr. Mills in a duel after the President of the Court had told the jury that the offence was murder. He was afterwards executed.† But not only the law denounced duelling—the essayists and novelists emphatically condemned it.‡ And yet in Ireland in 1808 where two persons were tried for wilful murder, in a duel arising out of an election quarrel, and there were really no circumstances whatever in mitigation, the jury acquitted the prisoners, and Baron Smith, the Judge, "expressed his satisfaction at the

---

* Howell's 'State Trials,' vol. xvii. p. 30-55.

† Ibid. vol. xviii. 1316.

‡ Dr. Johnson, however, seriously defended duelling, on the ground that a man was justified in fighting, if he did so, not from passion against his antagonist, but in self-defence ; to avert the stigma of the world, and to prevent himself from being driven out of society. This he regretted as "a superfluity of refinement," but added, "while such notions prevail, no doubt a man may lawfully fight a duel." It is needless now-a-days to attempt to refute such a sophism as this, which makes the opinion of the world, however wrong it may be, the standard of what is right. On another occasion, Dr. Johnson said : " Sir, a man may shoot the man who invades his character, as he may shoot him who attempts to break into his house." But Boswell appends this note : " I think it necessary to caution my readers against concluding that in this or any other conversation of Dr. Johnson, they have his serious and deliberate opinion on the subject of duelling." He once confessed, "Nobody at times talks more laxly than I do." And in his 'Journal of a Tour to the Hebrides,' he owns that he could not explain the rationality of duelling.

verdict." * But this was in Ireland—where, according to a well-known story, a Judge who thought himself insulted by a Barrister told him that in a few minutes he would put off his official costume and be ready to meet him.

In her novel of ' Miss Betsy Thoughtless,' Mrs. Heywood says, " They then fell into some discourse on duelling; and Mr. Trueworth could not help joining with the ladies, in condemning the folly of that custom, which, contrary to the known laws of the land, and oftentimes contrary to his own reason too, obliges the gentleman either to obey the call of the person who challenges him to the field, or by refusing, submit himself not only to all the insults his adversary is pleased to treat him with, but also to be branded with the infamous character of a coward by all that know him." And in a conversation between Dr. Harrison and Colonel Bath in Fielding's ' Amelia,' the Doctor says of duelling, " In short it is a modern custom introduced by barbarous nations since the times of Christianity; though it is a direct and audacious defiance of the Christian law, and is consequently much more sinful in us than it would have been in the heathens."

Sir Charles Grandison declines to fight any

* 'Edinburgh Annual Register,' 1808, part ii. p. 55.

duel, and this on the high ground of religious principle. " I will not meet any man, Mr. Reeves," he said, "as a duellist. I am not so much a coward as to be afraid of being branded for one. I hope my spirit is in general too well known for anyone to insult me on such an imputation. Forgive the seeming vanity, Mr. Reeves ; but I live not to the world ; I live to myself ; to the monitor within me." And in his letter to Sir Hargrave Pollexfen, who had sent him a challenge to meet him at Kensington Gravel Pits, he replies, " My answer is this—I have ever refused (and the occasion has happened too often) to draw my sword upon a set and formal challenge .... Let any man insult me upon my refusal, and put me upon my defence, and he shall find that numbers to my single arm shall not intimidate me. Yet even in that case I would much rather choose to clear myself of them as a man of honour should wish to do, than either to kill or maim any one. My life is not my own ; much less is another man's mine. Him who thinks differently from me I can despise as heartily as he can despise me . . . . . In a word, if any man has aught against me, and will not apply for redress to the laws of his country, my goings out and comings in are always known; and I am any hour of the day to be found or met with, wherever I have a proper call. My sword is a sword of defence, not offence." It must be admitted that the tone of the last paragraph but one is not very conciliatory, nor likely to baulk an adversary of his wish to fight, and Richardson takes care to make his hero such a perfect master of his weapon and the trick of fence, that when attacked he is always able to overcome and disarm his opponent. Sir Charles, however, states the argument in a nutshell when he asks: " Of whose making, Mr. Bagenhall, are the laws of honour you mention? I own no laws but the laws of God and my country."

A lawyer in any shape is always supposed to be fair game, and hardly any character has been a more favourite butt of ridicule with the playwriters and novelists than that of a Justice of the Peace. I scarcely know an instance of his appearance in fiction, except to be quizzed; from Mr. Justice Shallow in Shakspeare to Mr. Justice Inglewood in Sir Walter Scott's 'Rob Roy,' who finds the legal knowledge of his clerk, Jobson, so inconveniently embarrassing. We have Mr. Thrasher in 'Amelia;' also Mr. Justice Buzzard in the same novel, whose ignorance of law is as great as his readiness to take a bribe; and Mr. Justice Frogmore in ' Humphry Clinker,' " sleek and corpulent, solemn and shallow, who had studied Burn with uncommon application, but he had studied nothing so much as the art of living (that is, eating) well." All who have read the book remember the laughable consequence that ensues to him from eating at supper a plate of broiled mushrooms. And there is the " Justass of Zumersettshire," who was going to commit Joseph Andrews and Fanny Goodwin for stealing a twig. When Lady Booby gets Joseph and Fanny taken before the justice they are charged with cutting and stealing one hazel-twig, on the deposition of Scout, an attorney.

" ' Jesu !' said the squire, ' would you commit two persons to Bridewell for a twig ?'—' Yes,' said the lawyer, ' and with great lenity too ; for if we had called it a young tree, they would both have been hanged.' " And Scout was not far wrong, for by the Act 9 Geo. I. c. 22, unlawfully and maliciously to cut down a tree growing in a plantation was a capital felony.

But the " great unpaid " may be laughed at and ridiculed with impunity ; for by the law of England it is not actionable to say of a justice of the peace " He is an ass, and a beetle-headed justice." " *Ratio est*, because a man cannot help his want of ability, as he may his want of honesty: otherwise where words impute dishonesty or corruption."* And an indictment for saying of Sir Rowland Gwyn, who was a justice of the peace, in a discourse concerning a warrant made by him, "Sir Rowland Gwyn is a fool, an ass, and a coxcomb, for making such a warrant, and he knows no more than a stickbill," was held naught on demurrer. Holt, C. J., there laid it down as law : "To say a justice is a fool, or an ass, or a coxcomb, or a blockhead, or a bufflehead, is not actionable."† So that Fielding was not guilty of *scandalum magnatum* in defining in his 'Modern Glossary' — "Judge, Justice ; an old woman."

We are apt to think that there is no position more fortunate, and no life likely to be happier, than that of a country gentleman. And certainly, at the present day, there is no class of men to whom the word "Gentlemen" more emphatically applies, or who are more generally distinguished for their culture and refinement. But the country squires of the last century were very different persons. According to almost unanimous testimony they were gene-

* *Howe* v. *Prinn*, 2 Salk. Reports, 695.
† *Reg.* v. *Wrightson*, Ibid. 698.

rally boorish and ignorant, mighty hunters, and hard drinkers, who swore loud oaths, and used in the drawing-room the language of the stable.

They are thus described in a paper in the 'Connoisseur' (1755): "They are mere vegetables which grow up and rot on the same spot of ground; except a few, perhaps, which are transplanted into the Parliament House. Their whole life is hurried away in scampering after foxes, leaping five-bar gates, trampling upon the farmer's corn, and swilling October." And, again: "The dull country squire, who with no taste for literary amusements, has nothing except his dogs and horses but his bumper to divert him; and the town squire sits soaking in a tavern for the same reason."

We may fairly consider Squire Western in 'Tom Jones' as an exaggerated caricature. Here is a specimen of his language, and, so far as I dare quote it, Fielding's description of the language of country gentlemen generally: "'I will have satisfaction o' thee,' answered the Squire; 'so doff thy clothes. At unt half a man, and I'll lick thee as well as wast ever licked in thy life.' He then bespattered the youth with abundance of that language which passes between country gentlemen who embrace opposite sides of the question, with frequent applications

to him to . . . . . ." And yet Squire Western
is hardly more boorish, and certainly he is far
less detestable, than Squire Tyrrel in Godwin's
novel of 'Caleb Williams,' published near the
end of the century. Tyrrel is a brute in every
sense of the word—a brute in language, in
heart and in conduct—without any of the
redeeming qualities which in Fielding's creation, to a certain extent, mitigate the sentiment
of disgust. But it is not safe to trust the fidelity
of any character drawn by such a democrat as
Godwin. There are of course exceptions to
the general description ; and we have Squire
Allworthy in 'Tom Jones,' and Sir William
Thornton in the 'Vicar of Wakefield,' who are
models of propriety.

And as a set-off to such a boorish brute as
Fielding has drawn, we have the delightful Sir
Roger de Coverley, the pattern of what a country gentleman should be, and the happiest creation of Addison. It is hardly worth while to
enter into a discussion whether the original
conception of the character is due to him or to
Steele. All the finer touches, and all the interest we feel in this worthy gentleman, are,
beyond doubt, due to Addison ; and we cannot
but be grateful to him for giving us so charming
a portrait. Alas ! for the caprice of woman,

that such a man was doomed to live and die a
bachelor.   That perverse widow for whom he
sighed in vain must indeed have been difficult
to please, and her rejection of his suit is almost
of itself sufficient proof that she was unworthy
of his hand.   It is strange that Dr. Johnson
should imagine that there are in the delineation
of his character "the flying vapours of incipient
madness, which from time to time cloud reason,
without eclipsing it ; " and he speaks of the irregularities of Sir Roger's conduct as the effects
of " habitual rusticity, and that negligence which
solitary grandeur naturally generates."   Never
were epithets more unfortunate.   Irregularities
and rusticity and solitary grandeur of Sir Roger !
His life is represented as one of blameless
virtue, full of good-humour, benevolence and
affection ; although it is admitted that when a
very young man, he so far yielded to the bad
custom of the age as once to fight a duel.   If
by " habitual rusticity " is meant anything more
than that he lived generally in the country, it is
entirely untrue, for a more polite and affable
gentleman could not have existed.   And as to
"solitary grandeur," the expression is ludicrously
false ; for sociability is his characteristic, and
he is distinguished for the gentleness and
considerate attention with which he treats his

neighbours and dependants. Dr. Johnson has mistaken humour of character for aberration of intellect; and as he had nothing of the former in his own composition, but was conscious of a dark stratum in his mind which made him often dread madness, he has fancied that the harmless eccentricities of the worthy baronet were due to the same cause. Surely we all know Sir Roger well, and fully agree with the 'Spectator' that "his singularities proceed from his good sense, and are contradictions to the manners of the world, only as he thinks the world is in the wrong." In early life he had been what was called a fine gentleman; had often supped with my Lord Rochester and Sir George Etherege, fought a duel upon his first coming to town, and kicked bully Dawson in a public coffee-house for calling him youngster. But then came the cruel widow, and she sobered him for life. He first saw her in an assize-court when he was serving the office of sheriff for the county, where, as he says himself, "at last with a murrain to her, she cast her bewitching eyes upon me." He no sooner met her glance than he bowed, "like a great surprised booby." He fell, in short, desperately in love with her; but met with little encouragement. This, however, was enough to make him resolve to offer her his

hand ; and, in the words of his own confession,
" I made new liveries, new paired my coach-
horses, sent them all to town to be bitted and
taught to throw their legs well and move all
together, before I pretended to cross the country
and wait upon her."   But she proved to be too
witty and learned for a plain country gentleman ; and Sir Roger was confounded with what
he calls her casuistry.   "Chance," he says, "has
since that time thrown me very often in her
way, and she has as often directed a discourse
to me which I do not understand.   This barbarity has left me ever at a distance from the
most beautiful object my eyes ever beheld.   It
is thus also she deals with all mankind, and you
must make love to her, as you would conquer
the Sphynx, by posing her. . . . You must know
I dined with her at a public table the day after
I saw her, and she helped me to some tansy
in the eye of all the gentlemen in the county.
She has certainly the finest hand of any woman
in the world."

We have a charming account of a visit paid by
the Spectator to Sir Roger's country seat, where,
to say nothing of the affection borne to him by
his servants, you might see "the goodness of the
master even in the old house-dog and in a gray
pad that is kept in the stable with great care

and tenderness, out of regard to his past ser-
vices, though he had been useless for several
years." There was a picture in his gallery of
two young men standing in a river, the one
naked and the other in livery. This was painted
in memory of an act of gallantry and devotion
by one of his servants, who jumped into the
water and saved his master from drowning.
His bounty was carried so far that the faithful
domestic was enabled to become the possessor
of a pretty residence, which the Spectator had
observed as he approached the house. "I remembered, indeed, Sir Roger said, that there
lived a very worthy gentleman to whom he was
highly obliged, without mentioning anything
farther." At a little distance from the house,
among the ruins of an old abbey, "there is a
long walk of aged elms, which are shot up so
very high that when one passes under them the
rooks and crows that rest upon the tops of
them seem to be cawing in another region."
"I am," continues the Spectator, "very much
delighted with this sort of noise, which I consider as a kind of natural prayer to that Being
who, in the beautiful language of the Psalms,
feedeth the young ravens that call upon him."
And Sir Roger at church! where he will not let
anybody take a quiet nap but himself, and

calls John Matthews to mind what he is about, and not disturb the congregation. For John Matthews was an idle fellow, who sometimes amused himself by kicking his heels during the sermon. The following passage has more than once formed the subject of a picture, and it would be difficult to find a more pleasing one of a country gentleman of the olden time. " As soon as the sermon is finished nobody presumes to stir till Sir Roger is gone out of church. The Knight walks down from his seat in the chancel between a double row of his tenants, that stand bowing to him on each side : and every now and then inquires how such a one's wife, or mother, or son, or father do, whom he does not see at church, which is understood as a secret reprimand to the person that is absent."

How touchingly is the death of the good old Knight related in the letter from his butler to the Spectator, written, of course, by Addison. " I am afraid," he says, " he caught his death the last county-sessions, where he would go to see justice done to a poor widow woman and her fatherless children, that had been wronged by a neighbouring gentleman ; for you know, sir, my good master was always the poor man's friend." And then he complained that he had lost " his roast-beef stomach," and grew worse and worse, although at one time he seemed to revive "upon a kind message that was sent him from the widow lady whom he had made love to the forty last years of his life." He bequeathed to her, "as a token of his love, a great pearl necklace and a couple of silver bracelets, set with pearls, which belonged to my good lady his mother. . . . It being a very cold day when he made his will, he left for mourning to every man in the parish a great frieze coat, and to every woman a black riding-hood." What a charming trait of considerate kindness is this! And then he took leave of his servants, most of whom had grown grey-headed in his service, bequeathing to them pensions and legacies. "The chaplain tells everybody that he made a very good end. . . . The coffin was borne by six of his tenants, and the pall held up by six of the quorum. The whole parish followed the corpse with heavy hearts and in their mourning suits; the men in frieze and the women in riding-hoods." As for the old house-dog, "it would have gone to your heart to have heard the moans the dumb creature made on the day of my master's death." *

* It has been said that Addison put Sir Roger to death to prevent liberties being taken with the character by Steele and others, in case he was supposed to remain alive.

In the 'Spectator' also we have the memoirs of a country gentleman, "an obscure man who lived up to the dignity of his nature and according to the rules of nature." Amongst other memoranda are the following :—

"*Mem.:* Prevailed upon M. T., Esq., not to take the law of the farmer's son for shooting a partridge, and to give him his gun again.

"Paid the apothecary for curing an old woman that confessed herself a witch.

"Gave away my favourite dog for biting a beggar.

"Laid up my chariot and sold my horses to relieve the poor in a scarcity of grain.

"In the same year remitted to my tenants a fifth part of their rents.

"*Mem.:* To charge my son in private to erect no monument for me; but put this in my last will."

Such a character we may hope was not merely ideal—and it may be fairly put into the scale against the Squire Westerns and Squire Tyrrels of the century.

CHAPTER IV.

THE PARSON OF THE LAST CENTURY.—FLEET MARRIAGES.

IN a famous chapter of his 'History of England,' Lord Macaulay has described the state of the Clergy in the seventeenth century in terms the truth of which has been much disputed. He refers to Eachard and Oldham as authorities for some of his most telling passages. Eachard was master of Catherine Hall at Cambridge, and published in 1670 a book called 'Causes of the Contempt of the Clergy and Religion.' Swift says of him— "I have known men happy enough at ridicule, who upon grave subjects were perfectly stupid ; of which Dr. Eachard of Cambridge, who writ 'The Contempt of the Clergy' was a great example." The book, which is very short, assigns as the chief reasons for the contempt of the clergy their ignorance and poverty. The remarks are, upon the whole, exceedingly sensible, and some of them well worthy of attention even now. A considerable part of the work is devoted to criticising the bad taste of the sermons of that period; and the author strongly complains also of the miserable stipends which a large portion of the clergy received, and which compelled them to eke out a support for their families by degrading employments. "What a becoming thing," he asks, "is it for him that serves at the altar to fill the dung-cart in dry weather, and to heat the oven and pull hemp in wet? . . . . Or to be planted on a pannier, with a pair of geese or turkeys bobbing out their heads from under his canonical coat, as you cannot but remember the man, Sir, that was thus accomplished?" In another passage he speaks of the chaplains in great houses as having "a little better wages than the cook or butler," and describes their degraded position in one respect, which continued to be literally true in the following century. He says he does not object to a young man becoming a chaplain, so that "he may not be sent from table picking his teeth, and sighing with his hat under his arm, whilst the knight and my lady eat up the tarts and chickens."

Oldham's poem is avowedly a satire, "addressed to a friend that is about to leave the university;" but the following lines express the exact truth :—

> Little the unexperienced wretch does know
> What slavery he oft must undergo ;
> Who, though in silken scarf and cassock drest,
> Wears but a gayer livery at best.
> When dinner calls the implement must wait
> With holy words to consecrate the meat,
> But hold it for a favour seldom known,
> If he be deigned the honour to sit down.
> Soon as the tarts appear ; " Sir Crape, withdraw,
> These dainties are not for a spiritual maw."

The same custom is thus alluded to by Gay in his 'Trivia :'

> Cheese, that the table's closing rites denies,
> And bids me with the unwilling chaplain rise.

For, strange as it may seem now, it was the usual custom for the domestic chaplain to retire from table at the second course. In the 'Tatler' there is a letter purporting to be written by a clergyman, in which he says,* " I am a chaplain to an honourable family, very regular at the house of devotion, and, I hope, of an unblameable life ; but for not offering to rise at the second course, I found my patron and his lady out of humour, though at first I did not know the reason of it. At length, when I hap-

* 'Tatler,' No. 255.

pened to help myself to a jelly, the lady of the
house, otherwise a devout woman, told me that
it did not become a man of my cloth to delight
in such frivolous food; but as I still continued
to sit out the last course, I was yesterday
informed by the butler, that his lordship had no
further occasion for my service."

And Steele, in his comment upon this letter,
observes, " The original of this barbarous custom I take to have been merely accidental.
The chaplain retires out of pure complaisance,
to make room for the removal of the dishes, or
possibly for the ranging of the dessert. This
by degrees grew into a duty, until at length, as
the fashion improved, the good man found himself cut off from the third part of the entertainment." In another letter a poor chaplain ac-
knowledges the benefit he has received from
the publication of the former one, and the
notice taken of it. He says that he was helped
by " my lord " to a slice of fat venison, and
pressed to eat a jelly or conserve at the second
course.

Lord Macaulay quotes also Swift's 'Advice to
Servants' to show that in the time of George II.
" in a great household the chaplain was the
resource of a lady's maid whose character had
been blown upon, and who was therefore forced

to give up hopes of catching the steward." But in a recent work this is denied, and the author calls it "an astounding blindness to the purposes of satire, and a still more extraordinary ignorance of the artistic devices by which it achieves its ends."* He says that throughout the early part of the eighteenth century the status of the wives of clergymen continued rapidly to improve. There can, however, be no doubt that during a great part of the century what in the Prayer Book are called "the inferior clergy," were in a very low and pitiable condition. They were looked down upon by the rich, and thought hardly fit to associate with the country squires. They drank ale and smoked tobacco in the kitchen with the servants, and frequently married the cast-off Abigails of the housekeeper's room.† It is impossible to doubt the testimony which the literature of the age bears to the truth of this.‡

* Jeaffreson's ' Book of the Clergy.'

† The menial thing, perhaps for a reward,
    Is to some slender benefice preferred,
    With this proviso bound, that he must wed
    My Lady's antiquated waiting-maid,
    In dressing only skilled and marmalade.
                      Oldham.
But these lines were written in the seventeenth century.

‡ In one of the letters of Lady Mary Wortley Montague, dated 1716, she says, that " Mrs. D—— is resolved to marry the old greasy curate. . . . . The curate indeed is very filthy—

Thus, when the young Squire in Richardson's 'Pamela' pretends that he will provide a husband for the servant-girl whose innocence he wishes to betray, and she asks him who the person is, he answers, " Why, young Mr. Williams, my chaplain, in Lincolnshire, who will make you very happy."

The coarse, fat, ignorant, and sensual Parson Trulliber, feeding his hogs and talking vulgar gibberish, is no doubt a caricature ; and if the story is true that he was intended to represent Fielding's own domestic tutor when he was a boy, he very likely wished to pay off old scores by making him as repulsive as possible. And although Richardson assures us that Parson Adams was drawn from the life, it is difficult to believe that a clergyman, however simple minded, could have been engaged in such scenes as are depicted in ' Joseph Andrews.' But the novels of the century furnish abundant and conclusive evidence of the low social position of the clergy, or at all events of the country clergy.*

such a red, spungy, warty nose ! . . . . I met the lover (*i. e.* the curate) yesterday, going to the ale-house, in his dirty night-gown, with a book under his arm to entertain the club."

  * " There is no doubt that in the low social estimation, as well as in the ignorance and coarseness of many of his clerical personages, Fielding has faithfully represented the degraded state

In 'Sir Charles Grandison,' the clergyman who is called in to perform the marriage which Sir Hargrave Pollexfen tries to force upon Harriet Byron is thus described by her, " A vast, tall, big-boned, splay-footed man. A shabby gown : as shabby a wig, a huge and pimply face ; and a nose that hid half of it when he looked on one side, and he seldom looked fore-right when I saw him. He had a dog-eared Common Prayer-book in his hand, which once had been gilt, opened, horrid sight ! at the page of matrimony. . . . . The man snuffled his answer through his nose. When he opened his pouched mouth, the tobacco hung about his great yellow teeth. He squinted upon me, and took my clasped hands which were buried in his huge hand." In 'Tom Jones,' Mrs. Honour, Sophia Western's maid, says, " I am a Christian as well as he, and nobody can say that I am base born : my grandfather was a clergyman, and would have been very angry, I believe, to have thought any of his family should have taken up with Molly Seagrim's dirty leavings." To this passage Fielding appends a note : " This is the second person of low condition whom we

of the rural clergy at the time when he wrote."—Shaw's ' History of English Literature,' p. 343.

have recorded in this history to have sprung from the clergy. It is to be hoped that such instances will, in future ages, when some provision is made for the families of the inferior clergy, appear stranger than they can be thought at present." A writer before the middle of the last century thus describes the conduct and occupation of a clergyman in a country house in Somersetshire. "There was indeed a clergyman in the house, who had quite laid aside his sacerdotal character, but acted in several capacities, as *valet de chambre*, butler, gamekeeper, pot-companion, butt, and buffoon, who never read prayers, or so much as said grace in the family while I was in it." *

In his preface to the 'Spiritual Quixote,' a novel written in the middle of the last century by a clergyman named Graves, he makes his imaginary landlord thus describe a jolly plump gentleman, who lodged "not far from the celebrated seat of the Muses called Grub Street," and left behind him the manuscript containing the story in the book. "By his dress, indeed, I should have taken him for a country clergyman, but that he never drank ale or smoked tobacco."

* 'The Contempt of the Clergy Considered,' 1739 ; quoted in Mr. Jeaffreson's 'Book of the Clergy,' vol. ii. 272.

A distinction was of course allowed to exist between the town and country parson, and the former might be a gentleman, while the latter was a boor. There is a paper in the 'Connoisseur' (1756), which was written to entertain "town readers, who can have no other idea of our clergy than what they have collected from the spruce and genteel figures which they have been used to contemplate here in doctors' scarfs, pudding-sleeves, starched bands, and feather-top grizzles." It purports to be a letter from Doncaster, and describes a Yorkshire parson, who is a jovial fox-hunter, and to whom Sunday is as dull and tedious "as to any fine lady in town." He takes his friend with him on horse-back on a Sunday, to serve a church twenty miles off, lamenting all the while that so fine and soft a morning should be thrown away upon a Sunday. "At length we arrived full gallop at the church, where we found the congregation waiting for us ; but as Jack had nothing to do but to alight, pull his band out of the sermon case, give his brown scratch bob a shake, and clap on the surplice, he was presently equipped for the service. In short, he behaved himself both in the desk and pulpit, to the entire satisfaction of all the parish, as well as the Squire of it."

K

This kind of clergyman was called a "buck-parson," and one of them, who was chaplain to Lord Delacour, in Miss Edgeworth's novel of 'Belinda,' is thus described by Lady Delacour: "It was the common practice of this man to leap from his horse at the church door after following a pack of hounds, huddle on his surplice, and gabble over the service with the most indecent mockery of religion. Do I speak with acrimony? I have reason; it was he who first taught my lord to drink. Then he was a *wit*—an insufferable wit! His conversation, after he had drank, was such as no woman but Harriet Freke could understand, and such as few *gentlemen* could hear. I have never, alas! been thought a prude, but in the heyday of my youth and gaiety, this man always disgusted me. In one word, he was a buck parson." *

It is difficult to decide whether the contempt in which the clergy were held ought to be considered as the cause or the effect of such habits,

---

* The term "parson" is generally used in a contemptuous sense. But not so originally. He is the clergyman, *qui* PER-SONAM *gerit ecclesiæ*, and 'Blackstone' says, book i. c. 2:—"The appellation of *parson* (however it may be depreciated by familiar, clownish, and indiscriminate use) is the most legal, most beneficial, and most honourable title that a parish-priest can enjoy; because such a one (Sir Edward Coke observes) is said *vicem seu personam ecclesiæ gerere.*"

but most certainly contempt is the word which best expresses the estimation in which their calling was very generally regarded.

Dr. Wolcott, the well known Peter Pindar, was for many years a physician, and in that capacity, in 1767, accompanied Sir William Trelawny to Jamaica, of which that officer was appointed Governor. But Trelawny thought that he could promote his interests better in the church, and recommended him to take orders, saying, " Away then for England. *Get yourself japanned*, but remember not to return with the hypocritical solemnity of a priest. I have just bestowed a good living on a parson who believes not all he preaches, and what he really believes he dares not preach. You may very conscientiously declare that you have an internal call, as the same expression will equally suit a hungry stomach and the soul."

Although all the parsons in the novels of the century are not low, vulgar, or simple-minded fools, it is undeniable that those to whom such epithets are applicable leave by far the strongest impression on the mind of the reader. Dr. Bartlett, the family chaplain in 'Sir Charles Grandison,' is a respectable colourless person, quite unexceptionable as regards language and conduct, as every one who lived in Sir Charles's house must of course be.   He is never tired of singing the praises of his patron, and rather wearies us with his trite and sententious morality.   In 'Clarissa Harlowe' we have the worthy Dr. Lewen, and the pedantic Elias Brand, but none of them are types of a class; and, like Dr. Harrison in 'Amelia,' they soon fade away from the memory.   Dr. Primrose is, of course, an exception, but we must remember that he is the hero of the story, the pivot on which all the family history turns.   And it is indeed refreshing to make the acquaintance of such a delightful character.   But as a set-off against the typical parson of the novels, we may cite the example of Sir Roger de Coverley's chaplain in the 'Spectator,' "a person of good sense and some learning, of a very regular life and obliging conversation," who understood backgammon, and lived in the family rather as a relation than a dependent, and who showed his good sense by preaching in regular succession the sermons of Tillotson, Saunderson, Barrow, Calamy, and South, "instead of wasting his spirits in laborious compositions of his own."   He heartily loved Sir Roger, and stood high in the old knight's esteem, having lived with him thirty years, during which time there had not been a law-suit in the parish.

It was the custom for a clergyman always to go abroad in his cassock, and if we might trust Mr. Disraeli's ' Lothair,' we should believe it to be the custom now, for he represents curates at Muriel Towers playing at croquet in this dress: Parson Adams, in ' Joseph Andrews,' sits smoking his pipe with a night-cap drawn over his wig, and "a short great-coat which half covered his cassock." " Is the gentleman a clergyman then ? says Barnabas, for his cas-sock had been tied up when he first arrived." When Adams visits Trulliber,—" After a short pause Adams said, ' I fancy, sir, you already perceive me to be a clergyman.' ' Ay, ay,' cries Trulliber, grinning, ' I perceive you have some cassock, I will not venture to call it a whole one.' Adams answered, ' It was indeed none of the best, but he had the misfortune to tear it about ten years ago in passing over a stile.' " And when he is attacked by the hounds, they mistake the skirts of his cassock for a hare's skin, and he escapes by leaving a third part of it as *exuviæ* or spoil to the enemy. In going about thus clothed, the clergy, how-ever, obeyed one of the canons of the church; for by the 74th it is enjoined that they " shall usually wear in their journeys cloaks with sleeves, commonly called priests' cloaks, without guards, welts, long buttons, or cuts. And no ecclesiastical person shall wear any coif or wrought night-cap, but only plain night-caps of black silk, satin, or velvet . . . . and that in public they go not in their doublet and hose, without coats or cassocks ; and that they wear not any light-coloured stockings."*

One of the most curious things, as throwing light upon the position of many of the clergy, is the history of Fleet marriages, on which I will say a few words.

While the hero in ' Peregrine Pickle' is in the Fleet Prison, he makes the acquaintance of a clergyman "who found means to enjoy a pretty considerable income by certain irregular practices in the way of his function." That this was quite possible, we know from the entries that still exist in those very curious books called Fleet Registers. On the cover of one of them there is the following memorandum—

---

* In 1729, the Rev. Thomas Kinnersley was convicted of forging a promissory note, and being sentenced to stand twice in the pillory, he appeared both times, first at the Royal Exchange, and next at Fetter-lane end in Fleet Street, " in his canonical habit, thinking to draw compassion and respect from the populace, but it had the contrary effect."—Howell's ' State Trials,' vol. xvii. p. 296.

"Mr. Wyatt, Minister of the Fleet, is removed from the Two Sawyers, the corner of Fleet Lane (with all the Register Books) to the Hand and Pen, near Holborn Bridge, where marriages are solemnised without imposition."

And it appears that he received for weddings in the month of October, 1748, no less a sum than 57*l.* 12*s.* 9*d.*

These parsons used to advertise their trade in handbills of which I will give a specimen.

G. R.
At the true Chapel
at the old red Hand and Mitre, three doors from Fleet Lane,
and next Door to the White Swan ;
Marriages are performed by authority by the Reverend Mr.
Symson, educated at the University of Cambridge, and late
Chaplain to the Earl of Rothes.
N.B. Without Imposition.

How the practice began is not altogether clear. The earliest Register is dated 1674, but it must have commenced much earlier, for in a letter from Alderman Lowe to Lady Hickes, in 1613, he says, " Now I am to inform you that an ancyent acquayntance of y^{rs} and myne is yesterday married in the Fleete, one Mr. George Lester, and hath maryed M^{ris} Babbington, Mr. Thomas Fanshawe's mother-in-lawe. It is sayed she is a woman of good wealthe, so as nowe the man wylle be able to lyve and mayntayn hymself in prison, for hether unto he hath byne in poor estate."

The entries in these Registers and the pocket books of the parsons, reveal a shocking state of profligacy and vice. In one of the latter, belonging to the same Mr. Wyatt, who carried on so lucrative a trade, under the date of 1736, he says :*—

" Give to every man his due, and learn ye way of Truth.

" This advice cannot be taken by those that are concerned in ye Fleet marriages ; not so much as ye priest can do ye thing y^t is just and right there, unless he designs to starve. For by lying, bullying, and swearing, to extort money from the silly and unwary people, you advance your business, and gets ye pelf which always wastes like snow in sun shiney day.

" The fear of the Lord is the beginning of wisdom. The marrying in the Fleet is the beginning of eternal woe.

" If a clark or plyer tells a lye, you must vouch it to be as true as ye gospel, and if disputed you must affirm with an oath to ye truth

---

* Lansdowne MSS. 93-17, quoted in Burn's ' History of Fleet Marriages,' to which I am indebted for many of these curious particulars.

of a downright damnable falsehood. *Virtus laudatur et alget.*

"May God forgive me what is past, and give me grace to forsake such a wicked place, where truth and virtue can't take place unless you are resolved to starve."

Tavern keepers within the Rules of the Fleet used to keep clergymen in their pay at a salary of a pound a week—and touters or "plyers," as they were called, were always on the look out for customers. From an anonymous letter in the Bishop of London's Registry, written between 1702 and 1714, we learn something of the character of these parsons. "There is also one Mr. Nehemiah Rogers; he is a prisoner, but goes at large to his Living in Essex, and all places else; he is a very wicked man as lives for drinking . . . . and swearing; he has struck and boxed the bridegroom in the chapple, and damned like any com'on souldier; he marries both within and without the chapple like his brother Colton." And in the 'Weekly Journal' of February 1717, there is an account of a trial of one John Mottram, clerk, for solemnizing clandestine and unlawful marriages in the Fleet Prison, and keeping fraudulent registers, in which it was proved that he kept nine separate registers at different houses which contained many scandalous frauds. "It rather appeared from evidence that these sham marriages were solemnized in a room in the Fleet they call the Lord Mayor's Chappel, which was furnished with chairs, cushions, and proper conveniencies, and that a coal-heaver was generally set to ply at the door to recommend all couples that had a mind to be married, to the prisoner, who would do it cheaper than anybody. It further appeared, that one of the registers only, contained above 2200 entrys which had been made within the last year." The reverend gentleman was tried at Guildhall, before Chief Justice Parker, found guilty, and fined £200.

In the 'Grub Street Journal' of Jan. 15, 1734, there is a letter signed "Virtuous," which gives a graphic account of the scandalous way in which such marriages took place.

"These ministers of wickedness ply about Ludgate Hill, pulling and forcing people to some pedling ale-house, or a brandy shop, to be married; even on a Sunday, stopping them as they go to Church, and almost tearing their clothes off their backs. To confirm the truth of these facts, I will give you a case or two which lately happened. Since Midsummer last, a young lady of fortune was deluded and forced

from her friends, and by the assistance of a
wry-necked swearing parson, married to an
atheistical wretch, whose life is a continued
practice of all manner of vice and debauchery.
And since the ruin of my relation, another lady
of my acquaintance had like to have been tre-
panned in the following manner :—This lady had
appointed to meet a gentlewoman at the Old
Playhouse in Drury Lane; but extraordinary
business prevented her coming. Being alone
when the play was done, she bade a boy call a
coach for the City. One dressed like a gentleman helps her into it, and jumps in after her.
' Madame,' says he, "this coach was called for
me, and since the weather is so bad and there
is no other, I beg leave to bear you company :
I am going into the City, and will set you down
wherever you please.' The lady begged to be
excused, but he bade the coachman drive on.
Being come to Ludgate Hill, he told her his
sister, who waited his coming, but five doors up
the Court, would go with her in two minutes.
He went and returned with his pretended
sister, who asked her to step in one minute,
and she would wait upon her in the coach.
Deluded with the assurance of having his
sister's company, the poor lady foolishly followed her into the house, when instantly the

sister vanished; and a tawny fellow in a black
coat and a black wig appeared. 'Madam, you
are come in good time, the Doctor was just a
going.' 'The Doctor!' says she, horribly
frighted, fearing it was a mad house. 'What
has the Doctor to do with me?' 'To marry
you to that gentleman; the Doctor has waited
for you these three hours, and will be paid by
you or by that gentleman before you go!'
'That gentleman!' says she, recovering herself, 'is worthy a better fortune than mine;'
and begged hard to be gone. But Doctor
Wryneck swore she should be married, or if she
would not, he would still have his fee, and
register the marriage from that night. The
lady finding she could not escape without
money or a pledge, told them she liked the
gentleman so well, she would certainly meet
him to-morrow night, and gave them a ring as
a pledge, which, says she, 'was my mother's
gift on her death bed, enjoining that if ever I
married, it should be my wedding ring.' By
which cunning contrivance she was delivered
from the black Doctor and his tawny crew.
Sometime after this, I went with this lady and
her brother in a coach to Ludgate Hill, in the
day time, to see the manner of their picking up
people to be married. As soon as our coach

stopped near Fleet Bridge, up comes one of the myrmidons. 'Madam!' says he, 'you want a parson?' 'Who are you?' says I. 'I am the Clerk and Register of the Fleet.' 'Show me the Chapel.' At which comes a second, desiring me to go along with him. Says he, 'that fellow will carry you to a pedling ale-house.' Says a third, 'go with me, he will carry you to a brandy-shop.' In the interim comes the Doctor. 'Madam,' says he, 'I'll do your job for you presently.' 'Well, gentlemen,' says I, 'since you can't agree, and I can't be married quietly, I'll put it off till another time,' so drove away."

Nor were these marriages confined to the lower classes. In 1724, Lord Abergavenny was married at the Fleet to Miss Tatton; and in 1744 Mr. Henry Fox, afterwards created Baron Holland, was married there to Lady Georgiana Gordon, the eldest daughter of the Duke of Richmond.

One of the most notorious of the Fleet parsons was Doctor Gaynham or Garnham, popularly known as the Bishop of Hell, "a very lusty, jolly man," who being asked at a trial, where he gave evidence, whether he was not ashamed to come and own a clandestine marriage in the face of a Court of Justice, replied, bowing to the Judge, "*video meliora, deteriora sequor.*"   On another occasion, when questioned as to his recollection of the prisoner, he said, "Can I remember persons? I have married 2000 since that time."   The entry of a marriage by the Rev. John Evans has the following memorandum attached to it :—

" Pd. one shilling only ; the Bridegroom a boy about eighteen years of age, and the Bride about sixty-five.   They were brought in a coach and attended by four θυμπιvg whopηs (*sic*) out of Drury Lane as guests."

Another of these worthies was the Rev. John Flint, who died in 1729.   He dispensed with marriage in his own case and kept a mistress, called Mrs. Blood.   One of his entries is, " Paid three shillings and sixpence, certificate one and sixpence ; it being pretty late, they lay here, and paid me one shilling for bed (a kind girl). "   Another is, " The man had five shillings for marrying her, of which I had one and sixpence.   N.B. The above said person marries in common."   In several cases it is noticed that the bridegroom had something paid to him " for his trouble," the object of the lady being to be able to plead coverture in case of her arrest for debt.   Other memoranda in these books are, " I gave a certificate, for which I had only quartern of brandy." "Two most notorious Thieves." "This marriage upon honour." "Brought by a Counsellor." "Married upon Tick." "N. B. married for nothing to oblige Mr. Golden, Attorney-att-Law." "Stole my clothes brush." "Her eyes very black, and he beat about yᵉ face very much."

"Having a mistrust of some Irish roguery, I took upon me to ask what yᵉ gentleman's name was, his age, &c., and likewise the lady's name and age. Answer made me—What was that to me. G— dam me, if I did not immediately marry them he would use me ill; in short, apprehending it to be a conspiracy, I found myself obliged to marry them in *terrorem.* N.B. Some material part was omitted."

"The woman ran across Ludgate Hill in her shift." *

"He dressed in a gold waistcoat like an officer; she a beautiful young lady with two fine diamond rings and a Black high crown Hat, and very well dressed—at Boyce's."

These extracts are sufficient to prove the prevalence of such disreputable practices, and to justify what Smollett says in his novel called

---

* This was owing to a vulgar opinion that a husband was not liable for his wife's debts if he took her in no other dress but her shift. For an instance of the custom, see 'Ann. Reg.' 1766, Chron. p. 106.

'The Adventures of Count Fathom': "This would have been a difficulty soon removed had the scene of the transaction been laid in the metropolis of England, where passengers are plied in the streets by clergymen, who prostitute their characters and consciences for hire, in defiance of all decency and law."

Notwithstanding the infamous character of such marriages, those that took place before the Marriage Act 26 Geo. II. c. 33 (1753), came into operation on the 25th of March, 1754, were unquestionably valid. It was at one time doubted whether the Fleet Registers were or were not admissible in evidence to prove a marriage. They seem to have been admitted by Mr. Justice Willes on a trial at York in 1780; by Mr. Justice Heath in 1794; and in the same year, with considerable doubt, by Lord Chief Justice Kenyon.* But soon afterwards he refused to admit them, and said that in a

---

* A Fleet Register was admitted as evidence by Mr. Justice Powel, on the trial of Beau Fielding, in 1706, for bigamy, in intermarrying with the Duchess of Cleveland, in order to prove that his first wife, Mary Wadsworth, had been previously married to, and was then, the wife of one Bradley. But even according to the loose notions of evidence which then prevailed, the entry for other reasons, which it would be too technical to discuss here, ought to have been peremptorily rejected. Beau Fielding was found guilty, but escaped punishment by having the benefit of clergy. See 'State Trials,' vol. xiv. 1327.

case before Lord Hardwicke, where one of the
Register books was offered in evidence, he tore
the book and declared that such evidence could
never be admitted in a court of justice. It is
now settled law that the Registers are not admissible as evidence to prove a *marriage;* but
they may, when signed by the parties, be received in *pedigree* cases as declarations of deceased members of the family.

A great destruction of papers and documents
at the Fleet took place at the time of the Lord
George Gordon riots, in 1780; but a large number of the Registers and pocket-books, which
were in the possession of the proprietors of the
taverns and houses where marriages were celebrated after passing through parsons' hands,
were purchased by Government, and deposited
in the Registry of the Consistory Court of London. There are two or three hundred large
Registers, and upwards of a thousand dirty little
pocket-books, in which entries of the marriages
were made. Besides these, there are registers
of marriage performed in the King's Bench
Prison, the Mint, and May Fair, where the
same practice existed. The May Fair Chapel
was built in 1730, and was a sort of opposition
house to the Fleet for the purpose of matrimony. It seems, however, to have been sup-

pressed, and in the 'Daily Post' of July, 1744, the following advertisement appears :—

"To prevent mistakes, the little new chapel in May Fair, near Hyde Park Corner, is in the corner house opposite to the city side of the great chapel, and within ten yards of it, and the minister and clerk live in the same corner house, where the little chapel is, and the license on a crown stamp, and the minister and clerk's fees, together with the certificate, amount to one guinea as heretofore, at any hour till four in the afternoon. And that it may be the better known, there is a porch at the door like a country church porch." In 1752 the marriage of the Duke of Hamilton and Miss Gunning took place in a May Fair chapel. One of these chapels belonged to the Rev. Mr. Keith, who is said to have married in one day 173 couples. He thus advertises his place of business in the 'Daily Advertiser' in 1753 :—

"Mr. Keith's chapel, in May Fair, Park Corner, where the marriages are performed, by virtue of a license on a crown stamp, and certificate for a guinea, is opposite to the great chapel, and within ten yards of it. The way is through Piccadilly, by the end of St. James's Street, down Clarges Street and turn on the left hand."

On many houses signs were hung out, and over the door were written the words " Marriages done here ; " while touters accosted passengers with the cry " Do you want a parson ? " " Will you be married ? " Sion Chapel, at Hampstead, which seems to have belonged to the keeper of an adjoining tavern, was a favourite place of resort, and was thus advertised in the ' Weekly Journal ' of Sept. 8, 1718 :—

" Sion Chapel, at Hampstead, being a private and pleasant place, many persons of the best fashion have lately been married there. Now, as a minister is obliged constantly to attend, this is to give notice, that all persons upon bringing a license, and who shall have their wedding dinner in the gardens, may be married in the said chapel without giving any fee or reward whatsoever ; and such as do not keep their wedding dinner in the gardens, only five shillings will be demanded of them for all fees." Like most abuses, the facility of celebrating clandestine marriages was clung to as a great social privilege ; and the Marriage Act, 26 Geo. II. c. 33, which put an end to them, was strongly opposed. Horace Walpole says, in one of his letters, that the Act was so drawn by the judges "as to clog all matrimony in general." *

* When Dr. King, the public orator at Oxford, presented can-

It was for some time evaded by persons going
to the Channel Islands, which were not within its
operation ; and in the 'Gentleman's Magazine'
of 1760 we read that there were "at South-
ampton vessels always ready to carry on the
trade of smuggling weddings, which for the price
of five guineas transport contraband goods into
the land of matrimony."

didates for the degree of Doctor of Law at the Installation in
1754, he fiercely denounced the new law.   "The times," he said,
"were so horribly corrupt that we had agreed to sell our daughters by the late Marriage Act.   Sweet creatures ! it was ten
thousand pities that such fine girls as then filled the theatre
should be sold by their unnatural parents, and perhaps (dreadful
thought !) even to Whig husbands.   But he was sure that such
beautiful and elegant ladies as were there assembled were on the
right side, and he advised them to wear upon their rings, and
embroider upon their garments, the maxim : '*The man who sells
his country will sell his wife or his daughter,*'—upon which there
was loud applause."— 'Correspondence of Richardson,' vol. ii.
p. 190.

CHAPTER V.

THE OLD ROMANCES—'THE FEMALE QUIXOTE.'—NOVELS OF
THE LAST CENTURY.—THEIR COARSENESS AND ITS APOLO-
GISTS.—'CHRYSAL, OR THE ADVENTURES OF A GUINEA.'
—'POMPEY.'—'THE FOOL OF QUALITY.'—TWO CLASSES
OF NOVELS.—'SIMPLE STORY.'—THE COMIC NOVELS.

 COME now to speak more particularly of the novels. It would be
easy for an author to make a parade
of learning, if an acquaintance with novels and
romances can be called learning, by quoting
the names of old authors and their works,
and leaving the reader to suppose that he
was familiar with their contents. I might go
back to remote antiquity and speak of the
'Books of Love' of Clearchus the Cilician
—of Jamblichus, who wrote the 'Adventures
of Rhodanes,'—of Heliodorus of Emesus, the
author of 'Theogenes and Chariclea'—of
Achilles Tatius, who wrote the 'Amours of
Clitophon and Leucippe'—of Damascius, who
composed four books of fiction — of the
three Xenophons mentioned by Suidas—of
the parables of the Indian Sandabar and the

fables of Pilpay—of the lying legends of the
Talmud—of the famous Milesian tales, and
Aristides the most famous of the authors—of
Dionysius the Milesian who wrote fabulous
histories—of the romance of 'Dinias and Der-
cyllis,' of which Antonius Diogenes was the
author, or the still older romances of Anti-
phanes—of Parthenius of Nice—of the 'True
and Perfect Love' of Athenagoras—of the
'Golden Ass' of Apuleius — of the 'Amours
of Diocles and Rhodanthe,' by Theodorus
Prodromus, and those of 'Ismenias and Ismene'
by Gustathius, Bishop of Thessalonica; and,
coming lower down into the Middle Ages, of
the novels of Boccaccio and the Romances
of Garin de Loheran, 'Tristan,' 'Lancelot du
Lac,' 'St. Greal,' 'Merlin,' 'Arthur,' 'Perceval,'
'Perceforêt,' 'Amadis de Gaul,' 'Palmerin of
England,' and 'Don Beliaris of Greece;' and in
more modern times, of the 'Astræa' of Monsieur
d'Urfé, and the 'Illustrious Bassa,'—the 'Grand
Cyrus' and 'Clelia' of Mademoiselle de Scuderi,
who is called by Monsieur Huet, the Bishop
of Avranches, in his letters to Monsieur de
Legrais 'On the Original of Romances' a grave
and virtuous virgin—the 'Roman Comique'
of Scarron, and the 'Zaide' and 'Princesse de
Cleves' of Madame de la Fayette—the 'Phara-

mond,' 'Cassandra,' and 'Cleopatra' of M. de la Calprenede; and, to come to our own country, of 'Euphues' by John Lylie who was born in 1553—of 'the famous delectable and pleasant Hystorie, of the renowned Parrissius, Prince of Bohemia' and the 'Ornatus and Artesia' of Ford, who lived in the reign of Elizabeth— of Greene's 'Philomela' "penned to approve women's chastity," and his 'Pandosto the Triumph of Time,' from which Shakspeare borrowed the plot of his 'Winter's Tale,'—of Barclay's 'Argenis,'—of 'Eliana,' published in 1661 —and of the 'Parthenissa' of Roger Boyle, Earl of Orrery—I might, I say, pretend to be familiar with these works, but for two reasons, first, that many of them have long ceased to exist, and, secondly, that no appetite for books could be supposed to induce a man now to face the appalling dulness and interminable length of most of these old romances. As Sydney Smith says, "human life has been distressingly abridged since the flood," and considering the multiplicity of demands upon one's time now, it is really too short to wade through the ponderous romances of the seventeenth century, which Sir Walter Scott aptly described when he called them "huge folios of inanity over which our ancestors yawned themselves to sleep."

In Leonora's Library, which the 'Spectator' visited in order to deliver to her a letter from Sir Roger de Coverley, he found 'Astrea,' 'The Grand Cyrus,' "with a pin stuck in one of the middle leaves," 'Clelia,' which opened of itself in the place that describes two lovers in a bower, the 'New Atalantis' "with a key to it," and all the classic authors " in wood."

It was to ridicule the taste for such romances as these that Mrs. Lennox published her 'Female Quixote,' in 1752,* in which the heroine Arabella, the only child of a widowed and misanthropic marquis, is supposed to be brought up in seclusion in the country, where she has access to a library full of old romances, by which her head is almost as much turned as that of the Knight of La Mancha was by the same kind of study. She takes a young gardener in her father's service for a nobleman in disguise, and is with difficulty undeceived when he gets a thrashing for stealing carp from a pond. The book is cleverly written, and is useful as enabling us to get at second hand a knowledge of the romances which were Lady Arabella's favourite reading. She has a cousin

---

* Richardson says of the authoress : " The writer has genius. She is hardly twenty-four, and has been unhappy."—'Correspondence,' vol. vi. p. 243.

named Glanville, who is in love with her for her beauty, but is sorely puzzled by her conduct, and wholly ignorant of the books on which she has modelled it. In order to instruct him, she bids one of her women to bring from her library 'Cleopatra,' 'Cassandra,' 'Clelia,' and 'the Grand Cyrus,' and leaves him to peruse them. But he is bewildered by their length and turns over the pages in despair. She then examines him as to his proficiency, and convicts him of his deception in pretending to have read them, when he talks of Orontes and Oroontades as two lovers of Statira, whereas " if he had read a single page, he would have known that Orontes and Oroontades was the same person, the name of Orontes being assumed by Oroontades to conceal his real name and quality."

But although the Lady Arabella talks in the strain of Cathos and Madelon in '*Les Précieuses Ridicules*' of Molière, the novel wants the wit of that admirable comedy, and as a satire it has lost its point, for nobody—certainly no young lady—at the present day knows or cares anything of the ' Loves of Artemisa and Candace,' of the ' Great Sisygambis,' or the renowned ' Artaban '—and I fear that such illustrations of love as are quoted by Arabella, would now be the utterance of an unknown tongue. For instance—" Love is ingenious in artifices ; who would have thought that under the name of Alcippus, a simple attendant of the fair Artemisa, princess of Armenia, the gallant Alexander, son of the great and unfortunate Antony, by Queen Cleopatra, was concealed, who took upon himself that mean condition for the sake of seeing his adored princess ? "

The time has gone by when, as the Bishop of Avranches tells us, he and his sisters were often obliged to lay down the 'Astræa' of M. d'Urfé while reading it, in order that they might indulge freely in their tears; and it would be difficult for Boileau, if he were alive, to find now, in either town or country,

> Deux nobles campagnards, grands lecteurs de romans,
> Qui m'ont dit tout Cyrus dans leurs longs complimens.*

---

* In '*Les Précieuses Ridicules*,' Marotte, the lady's maid, says : " Dame ! je n'entends point le latin, et je n'ai pas appris, comme vous, la filophie dans le grand Cyre." Boswell tells us, on the authority of Bishop Percy, that when Dr. Johnson spent part of a summer at his parsonage in the country, he chose for his regular reading the old Spanish romance of 'Felixmarte of Hyrcania,' in folio, which he read quite through. This was the book which the curate in 'Don Quixote' condemned to the flames. These romances are satirised by the youthful Canning in the 'Microcosm,' where he describes the hero sighing respectfully at the feet of his mistress during a ten years' courtship in a wilderness ; and quotes the adventures of St. George, " who mounts his horse one morning at Cappadocia, takes his way through Mesopotamia, then turns to the right into Illyria, and

Old Thomas Gent, " Printer of York," when describing his intercourse with his dear niece, Anne Standish, " a perfect beauty," says in his autobiography, " Often did we walk till late hours in the garden ; she could tell me almost every passage in ' Cassandra,' a celebrated romance that I had bought for her at London." And to come to a later period, the close of the century, we have a list of the novels, which Miss Thorpe tells Catherine Morland, the heroine in Jane Austen's story of ' Northanger Abbey,' she has written down in her pocket-book ; ' Castle of Wolfenbach,' ' Clermont,' ' Mysterious Warnings,' ' Necromancer of the Black Forest,' ' Midnight Bell,' ' Orphan of the Rhine,' and the ' Horrid Mysteries.' Possibly these novels are merely imaginary, but if they are real books, where are any of them to be found now ? and where could readers be found for them if they existed ? Few have the courage to wade through the twenty-one volumes of Richardson,—for in no less a number are contained his ' Pamela,' ' Clarissa Harlowe,' and ' Sir Charles Grandison,' and the man who has performed the feat in these degenerate days may plume himself upon the achievement.

so by way of Grecia and Thracia, arrives in the afternoon in England."

For a long list of the novels in vogue in the
middle of the last century we may refer to the
preface to George Colman's comedy of 'Polly
Honeycomb,' first acted in 1760, and intended
to expose the mischiefs of novel reading, although it really does nothing of the kind.*
The names of nearly two hundred are given,
of which very few, exclusive of the fictions of
Richardson, Fielding and Smollett, are now
known even by name, or could be procured
without a good deal of hunting at second-hand
bookstalls. But the same will be true a century
hence of most of the novels of this generation.
As Fielding says in 'Tom Jones,' "The great
happiness of being known to posterity is the
portion of few." Amongst those works that are
practically lost there are some whose names, like
that of the 'Fair Adulteress,' sufficiently indicate their contents. Some for a long time
lingered in circulating libraries, and, perhaps,
may still be found there, although they are
seldom or never asked for by readers whose
taste has been reformed and purified by the
writings of such authors as Scott, Thackeray,
Dickens and Trollope. Of very few of these

* 'Polly Honeycomb' ends thus :—"Zounds . . . a man
might as well turn his daughter loose in Covent Garden, as trust
the cultivation of her mind to a circulating library."

old novels can be predicated what Dr. Johnson said of Prior's poems, " No, sir, Prior is a lady's book. No lady is ashamed to have it standing in her library." Their character may be described by two lines from the prologue to ' Polly Honeycomb '—

> Plot and elopement, passion, rape and rapture,
> The total sum of every dear—dear—chapter.

or by the following verses of Cowper :—

> Ye novelists who mar what ye would mend,
> Snivelling and drivelling, folly without end ;
> Where corresponding misses fill the ream
> With sentimental frippery and dream,
> Caught in a delicate soft silken net
> By some lewd earl or rake-hell baronet.*

The subject of most of them is, in fact, what Charles Lamb calls " the undivided pursuit of lawless gallantry." In his essay on the artificial comedy of the last century he attempts a defence of this where he says, " The Fainealls and the Mirabels, the Doricourts and Lady Touchwoods, in their own sphere, do not offend any moral sense ; in fact, they do not appeal to it at all. They seem engaged in their proper element. They break through no laws or conscientious restraints. They know of none. They have got out of Christendom into the land—what shall I call it ?—of cuckoldy—the

* ' Progress of Error.'

Utopia of gallantry, where pleasure is duty, and the manners perfect freedom."

I think this is a bad and false apology even for the stage. But whatever may be the case with the plays such a defence is not available for the novels. The object in writing them was not merely to amuse but to instruct, as the authors assure us over and over again in their prefaces and dedications, and they certainly did not intend their heroes and heroines to be mere shadowy abstractions, but representations of real flesh and blood. And our forefathers so regarded them, looking to them for lessons in morality and conduct. It is in this light that Dr. Young, in one of his letters, calls Richardson " an instrument of Providence." A writer in the ' Olla Podrida ' (A.D. 1787), says, that " if we wish for delicate and refined sentiments we can recur to ' Grandison ' and ' Clarissa ;' if we would see the world more, perhaps, as it is than it should be, we have ' Joseph Andrews ' and ' Tom Jones;' or can we find the happy mixture of satire and moral tendency in the ' Spiritual Quixote ' and ' Cecilia.' " And the Rev. Mr. Graves in his preface or apology, as he calls it, for his ' Spiritual Quixote,' says, " Nay, I am convinced that ' Don Quixote ' or ' Gil Blas,' ' Clarissa ' or ' Sir Charles Grandison,' will

furnish more hints for correcting the follies and
regulating the morals of young persons, and im-
press them more forcibly on their minds, than
volumes of severe precepts seriously delivered
and dogmatically enforced." Now, what is the
character of most of these books which were to
correct follies and regulate morality? Of a
great many of them, and especially those of
Fielding and Smollett, the prevailing features
are grossness and licentiousness. Love degenerates into mere animal passion, and almost
every woman has to guard her chastity—if,
indeed, she cares to guard it at all—against the
approaches of man as the sworn enemy of her
virtue. The language of the characters abounds
in oaths and gross expressions, and to swear
loudly and to drink deeply are the common
attributes of fashionable as well as vulgar life.
The heroines allow themselves to take part in
conversations which no modest woman could
have heard without a blush.

And yet these novels were the delight of a
bygone generation and were greedily devoured
by women as well as men. Are we, therefore,
to conclude that our great-great-grandmothers,
—those stately dames, whose pictures by Gainsborough and Reynolds look down upon us in
our dining rooms,—were less chaste and moral

than their female posterity? I answer, certainly not; but we must infer that they were inferior to them in delicacy and refinement. They were accustomed to hear a spade called a spade, and words which would shock the more fastidious ear in the reign of Queen Victoria were then in common and daily use. We see this in the diaries and journals of the time, but it would not be pleasant to quote passages in proof of the statement; and, perhaps, the women of that day would defend themselves in some such way as Charlotte Grandison does in Richardson's novel, " Let me tell you that there is more indelicacy in delicacy than you *very* delicate people are aware of."

There is in ' Richardson's Correspondence ' a long extract from a letter written by a young lady in London to another lady, her friend, in the country, in which she laments the hard necessity she supposed she was under of having been obliged to read ' Tristram Shandy.' " Happy are you in your retirement, where you read what books you choose, either for instruction or entertainment; but in this foolish town we are obliged to read every foolish book that fashion renders prevalent in conversation; and I am horribly out of humour with the present

taste which makes people ashamed to own they
have not read, what, if fashion did not authorise,
they would with more reason blush to say they
had read. Perhaps some polite person from
London may have forced this piece into your
hands ; but give it not a place in your library ;
let not 'Tristram Shandy' be ranked among the
well-chosen authors there.. It is indeed a little
book, and little is its merit, though great has
been the writer's reward. Unaccountable wildness, whimsical digressions, comical incoheren-
cies,, uncommon indecencies, all with an air of
novelty has catched the reader's attention, and
applause has flown from one to another, till it is
almost singular to disapprove. . . . Yet I will
do him justice ; and if, forced by friends, or led
by curiosity, you have read and laughed and
almost cried at Tristram, I will agree with you
that there is subject for mirth and some affecting
strokes. . . . But mark my prophecy, that by
another season this performance will be as much
decryed as it is now extolled ; for it has not
sufficient merit to prevent its sinking when no
longer upheld by the short-lived breath of
fashion : and yet another prophecy I utter, that
this ridiculous compound will be the cause of
many more productions, witless and humourless,
perhaps, but indecent and absurd, till the town

M

will be punished for undue encouragement by being poisoned with disgustful nonsense."*

In his 'Essay on Conversation,' which contains some admirable precepts, Fielding strongly insists against indecency, and proscribes "all *double-entendres* and obscene jests" as carefully to be avoided before ladies. And yet in that very essay he offends against decency, according to modern notions, by using words with which no writer of reputation would now sully his pen. This is curious, and proves what I contend for, namely, that in the last century men and women were so accustomed to coarse language that they hardly knew what was a sin against decorum. Necessarily I cannot give quotations to show this, for in doing so I should myself offend; but I may state, without fear of contradiction, that there is hardly a novel of the eighteenth century which does not contain expressions and allusions which would at the present day be thought not only vulgar but indecorous.

And this is true not only of the beginning and middle, but the end of the period, not only of Defoe, Swift, Richardson, Fielding and Smollett, but of Mrs. Inchbald, Miss Burney and Miss Edgeworth. Nobody can think higher of the

* 'Correspondence of Richardson,' vol. v. p. 147.

last-named authoress than myself, and I attribute whatever faults of this kind she has committed to the manners of the age. She could never have put into the mouth of a fashionable lady such language as Mrs. Freke in ' Belinda' uses, unless she had thought it at least possible that a fashionable lady could so talk.

I will give one or two specimens of it, addressed, be it observed, to a young lady :—

" The devil! they seem to have put you on a course of the bitters—a course of the woods might do your business better. Do you ever hunt? Let me take you out with me some morning. You'd be quite an angel on horseback, or let me drive you out some day in my unicorn."

" I only wish, I only wish his wife had been by. Why the devil did not she make her appearance? I suppose the prude was afraid of my demolishing and unrigging her."

" ' Drapery, if you ask my opinion,' cried Mrs. Freke, ' drapery, whether wet or dry, is the most confoundedly indecent thing in the world.' "

I know that there are writers who assert that we have not gained by the difference; but I think they are wholly wrong. The gain is immense, when we remember all that such want

of refinement implies.   Coarseness of language
is a proof of coarseness of thought, and too
often leads to coarseness of conduct.   And the
same is equally true of profanity and vice.
Studia abeunt in mores.   A profane talker is a
profane liver, and the man who revels in licentious conversation is not likely to be a Joseph
in morals.

Two of the most popular novels mentioned
in the preface to 'Polly Honeycombe,' next to
those of Richardson, Fielding and Smollett, are
'Chrysal, or the Adventures of a Guinea,' and
'The Fool of Quality.'

I have looked through the four volumes of
'Chrysal'—it is impossible for human patience
now to peruse them—to see if there was anything which could interest a reader at the present day ; but the attempt was vain.   The book
in both style and matter is execrably bad.   And
yet it was once very popular.*   But see the
uncertainty of fame !   I had the greatest difficulty in procuring a copy, although I inquired

---

* The author of 'The Adventures of a Guinea' was Charles
Johnson, a barrister, whose deafness prevented him from following his profession.   The bookseller to whom it was offered for
publication, sent the first volume to Dr. Johnson, in manuscript,
to have his opinion whether it should be printed, and he thought
it should.   We can only wonder that such a stupid book met
with Johnson's approval.

of many booksellers and hunted many book-stalls. It has sunk into total oblivion, and I am bound to say that it deserves its fate.

The 'Guinea' passes from hand to hand, and this gives the author the opportunity of describing all kinds of characters and all kinds of scenes. I need not say that many of them are licentious and impure; but the vice is not redeemed by wit or grace of style, and the book is simply unreadable. The same idea is produced in the novel of 'Pompey, or the Adventures of a Lap-dog,' by Coventry, where the dog becomes the property of a variety of persons, of whom it is sufficient to say that all the women are rakes and the men libertines and scamps. Many of the scenes can only be described by one word, and that is—filthy—and there is nothing in Swift which is more gross or more offensive. I cannot understand how it obtained the honour of being allowed a place in the edition of the British Novelists.

'The Fool of Quality' was written by Henry Brooke, and published by him in 1766. It was republished by the Rev. Charles Kingsley, with a preface and life of the author, in 1859; and he speaks with enthusiasm of the causes which have made the book to be forgotten for a while, and which, he says, are to be found " in its deep and grand ethics, in its broad and genial humanity, in the divine value which it attaches to the relations of husband and wife, father and child, and to the utter absence both of that sentimentalism and that superstition which have been alternately debauching of late years the minds of the young." He calls it a "brave book." I am bound to say that I wholly disagree with him. A more horribly dull and tedious book it was never my misfortune to read ; and as a fiction, or a story, or a work of art, it is beneath criticism. Mr. Kingsley admits that "an average reader" would say that "the plot is extravagant, as well as ill woven, and broken besides by episodes as extravagant as itself. The morality is Quixotic and practically impossible. The sermonizing, whether theological or social, is equally clumsy and obtrusive. Without artistic method, without knowledge of human nature and the real world, the book can never have touched many hearts, and can touch none now."

I willingly rank myself amongst the average readers as regards my estimate of the book, and can only wonder at Mr. Kingsley having taken the trouble to republish it, and still more at the praise which he lavishes upon it. It is made up of dull sermons and dull disquisitions

on morality and the British Constitution, with
an absurd attempt at a story, in which it is
impossible to take interest, running through it.
Harry Clinton, afterwards Earl of Moreland,
the hero, is carried off by a benevolent old
gentleman, who turns out to be his uncle in
disguise, and supplies him while a boy with
almost unlimited sums of money to scatter
broadcast in prisons, hospitals, and the abodes
of poverty. To slip a hundred guineas into a
poor man's pocket is with him quite an ordinary
occurrence; and his uncle kisses him and exclaims, "Oh, my noble, my generous, my incomparable boy!" Another gentleman is so
enraptured by the generous manner in which
the hero spends his uncle's money that he
exclaims in ecstasy, "Let me go, let me go
from this place. This boy will absolutely kill
me if I stay any longer. He overpowers, he
suffocates me with the weight of his sentiments." The author certainly overpowers the
reader with the weight of his dulness. The
dress of a lady is thus described :—"A scarf of
cerulean tint flew between her right shoulder
and her left hip, being buttoned at each end by
a row of rubies . . . . A coronet of diamonds,
through which there passed a white branch of
the feathers of the ostrich, was inserted on the

left decline of her lovely head, and a stomacher
of inestimable brilliance rose beneath her daz-
zling bosom, and by a fluctuating blaze of un-
remitted light, checked and turned the eye
away from too presumptuous a gaze"! When
the hero goes to Court, Queen Mary sends the
Lord Chamberlain to tell him to come to her,
and after a few words of conversation cries out,
"You are the loveliest and sweetest fellow I
ever knew. My eye followed you all along,
and marked you for my own, and I must either
beg or steal you from our good friend your
father." Her Majesty then gives him her
picture! There is a caricature of a trial at
the Old Bailey, where a woman is tried for
killing a nobleman in defence of her chastity,
and where the judge is represented as summing
up for a conviction in a way which would have
shocked a Jeffreys or a Scroggs. The foreman
of the jury prefaces their verdict of Not Guilty
with a sentimental speech, calling the prisoner
"an honour to human nature and the first grace
and ornament of her own sex." But *Ohe jam
satis.* Considering the nature of the book, it
is not surprising that John Wesley "bowd-
lerized" the 'Fool of Quality,' striking out
such passages as he did not like, and then
published it during the author's lifetime as the

' History of Harry, Earl of Moreland,' which was long believed by the Wesleyans to be the work of the great John himself.

The novels of the last century may be divided into different classes. In the first we have the domestic life of our ancestors pourtrayed under the guise of fiction, of which the staple generally is the story of a young lady who has great difficulty in preserving her honour intact from the pursuit of libertine admirers. Thus in ' Clarissa Harlowe,' the heroine falls a victim to her seducer, while in ' Pamela ' she triumphs over his arts, and the result is a happy marriage. In ' Sir Charles Grandison,' the lady is forcibly carried off by Sir Hargrave Pollexfen, whose object is to compel her to marry him, but she is rescued by Sir Charles, and after an intolerably tedious courtship becomes his wife. It is the same idea in a more disguised form which forms the subject of the story in Miss Burney's ' Evelina,' or the ' History of a Young Lady's Introduction to the World.' There Miss Anville comes up to town from the country on a visit to Mr. and Mrs. Mirvan in Queen Anne Street, and she is immediately beset by admirers, one of whom, Lord Orville, is a gentleman not only by birth but in character and conduct; while another, Sir Clement Wil-

loughby, pursues her with no other object than
that of " lawless gallantry."   She has a narrow
escape when she trusts herself with him in his
carriage to take her home from the theatre.
She is insulted at Ranelagh, and " Marybone,"
and the Hotwells by libertine addresses.

In Mrs. Inchbald's 'Simple Story' we have
the tale of a young lady, Miss Milner, left to
the care of a Roman Catholic priest, Dorriforth,
with whom she falls in love ; and as he becomes
the Earl of Elmwood, and is released from his
ordination vows, she marries him ; but afterwards
becomes unfaithful and dies in great misery.
The latter part of the novel is occupied with
the story of her daughter, an only child, whom
the father allows to live at one of his country
residences ; but, in bitter resentment at her
mother's misconduct, obstinately refuses to see
or allow her name to be mentioned in his presence, until he hears that she has been carried
off by a libertine nobleman, when he rushes to
her rescue, and then opens his heart to her with
parental fondness, and sanctions her marriage
with his nephew, who has long been her secret
adorer.

A favourite form in which many of these
novels are written is a series of letters, which
seems to me the most uninteresting mode in

which a story can be told. It is difficult not to compassionate the persons who sit down day after day and night after night to pen their long-winded epistles, and fill them with the most trivial and egotistical details. Perhaps in these days of the penny-post one is more impatient of the length of a letter; but no mortal men nor women could have spun out in real life such a correspondence as is carried on in 'Clarissa Harlowe,' 'Sir Charles Grandison,' and 'Evelina.'*

Another class of novels consists of comic stories of low life, in which the hero or heroine is engaged in ludicrous adventures, where the scenes are often laid in a country inn, and the interior of a prison, and where such events as are likely to happen there are described with all the fidelity and, I will add, all the coarseness of a Dutch picture. Such are 'Roderick Random' and 'Peregrine Pickle,' 'Tom Jones' and 'Joseph Andrews.' The men riot in every kind of dissipation and the women indulge in every species of intrigue. But there is always some virtuous figure who is generally the heroine—like Sophia Western, or Fanny Goodwin,

* These letters were supposed to be sent by private hands, not the post. " Letters from Northamptonshire, by Farmer Jenkins ; I kiss the seals." 'Sir Charles Grandison :' Letter XIV.

or Emilia—who resists all libertine advances, and whose constancy is at last rewarded by marriage. It is with reference to this class of novels that an accomplished French critic, M. Taine, speaking of 'Tom Jones,' says,* "One becomes tired of your fisty-cuffs and your alehouse adventures. You dirty your feet too much in the stables amongst the ecclesiastical pigs of Trulliber. One would like to see more regard for the modesty of your heroines; the roadside accidents disturb their dresses too often, and it is in vain that Fanny, Sophy, and Mistress Heartfree preserve their purity; one can't help remembering the assaults which have lifted their petticoats. You are so rude yourself that you are insensible to what is atrocious. . . . . Man, such as you conceive him, is a good buffalo, and perhaps he is the kind of hero required by a people which is itself called John Bull." It is curious to contrast with this the opinion of Coleridge. "How charming, how wholesome, Fielding always is! To take him up after Richardson is like emerging from a sick room heated by stoves, into an open lawn on a breezy day in May." † In so far as Fielding is opposed to Richardson, we

---

* 'Histoire de la Littérature Anglaise,' vol. iii. pp. 317-18.
† 'Table Talk,' p. 332.

should all agree in this; but I cannot think that the pure breeze of a May morning is a proper metaphor to describe such scenes as occur in ' Tom Jones ' and ' Joseph Andrews.'

CHAPTER VI.

MRS. BEHN AND HER NOVELS.—'OROONOKO.'—'THE WAN-
DERING BEAUTY.'—'THE UNFORTUNATE HAPPY LADY.'
—MRS. MANLEY AND 'THE NEW ATALANTIS.'—'THE
POWER OF LOVE IN SEVEN NOVELS.'—'THE FAIR HYPO-
CRITE.'—MRS. HEYWOOD.—HER NOVEL, 'MISS BETSY
THOUGHTLESS.'

IT is remarkable that some of the most immoral novels in the English language should have been written by women. This bad distinction belongs to Mrs. Behn, Mrs. Manley, and Mrs. Heywood;— *Corruptio optimi est pessima*, and that such corrupt stories as they gave to the world were the offspring of female pens is an unmistakable proof of the loose manners of the age. Mrs. Behn, indeed, belongs to an earlier period. She wrote in the reign of Charles II., when vice was triumphant, and modesty, like 'Astræa,' had left her last footsteps upon earth.* Strictly, therefore, she does

---

* Mrs. Behn called herself 'Astræa,' and as such is alluded to by Pope in the lines—

not come within the scope of the present work; but as some of her stories were the first that at all approached in idea the modern novel, and in that respect she may be considered as the literary progenitor of a most numerous race, I may be excused for saying something about her, and so far as I dare, giving some specimens of her works.

Her maiden name was Aphra Johnson; her father was made Governor of Surinam, whither she accompanied him, and then she became acquainted with the negro slave Oroonoko and his wife Imoinda, whose adventures she has made the subject of the best known one of the least objectionable of her novels, called 'Oroonoko.' She afterwards married a Dutch merchant named Behn, and went to Antwerp, where she was employed by Charles II. in some political intrigues during the war with Holland. After various vicissitudes of fortune she settled in England and devoted herself to literature, chiefly novels and comedies, the titles of some of which sufficiently indicate their contents. In her preface to 'The Lucky Chance' she attempts to defend herself against the charge of indecency and indelicacy; but it is by what

The stage how loosely does Astræa tread,
Who fairly puts all characters to bed!

lawyers call a plea in confession and avoidance
—retorting the charge of prudery on her ac-
cusers. She died in 1689, and was buried in
Westminster Abbey. In a curious memoir of
her prefixed to a volume of her novels which
was published in 1705, and written "by one of
the Fair Sex," she is described as an honour
and glory to women, and possessed of uncommon charms of person. The lady takes pains
to deny the truth of an ill-natured rumour
which it seems was current as to some love
affair between Mrs. Behn, or Astræa, as she is
called, and Oroonoko, whose heart she said was
too devoted to Imoinda to be shaken in its
constancy by the charms of a white beauty,
"and Astræa's relations who were there present
had too watchful an eye over her to permit the
frailty of her youth, if that had been powerful
enough." While she was at Antwerp more
than one lover paid his addresses to her, but
she merely used them as tools to worm out
political secrets, and, in the words of the lady
who wrote her life, "she contrived to preserve
her honour without injuring her gratitude."
She adds, "They are mistaken who imagine
that a Dutchman can't love; for, though they
are generally more phlegmatic than other men,
yet it sometimes happens that love does pene-

trate their lumps and dispense an enlivening fire, that destroys its graver and cooler considerations." One of her lovers met with a rather unlucky adventure in pursuit of his object. He bribed an old lady who slept with Mrs. Behn to put him, dressed in her nightclothes, in their bed, while Mrs. Behn was absent at an evening party, in Antwerp; when she came home, attended by some friends, one of them "a brisk, lively, frolicsome young fellow," proposed as a practical joke to go to the old lady's bed, "whilst they should all come in with candles and complete the merry scene." This he did, but was not a little confounded when he encountered, not an old woman, as he expected, but Mrs. Behn's Dutch lover, who was occupying the bed. The rest of the company came in, and it is needless to say that her admirer, thus caught in his own trap, was ignominiously dismissed. Her female biographer praises her for her virtue and self-command, but she prints some " Love Letters to a Gentleman by Mrs. A. Behn " which she declares are genuine, and if so they leave little doubt that her conduct was as loose as her writings, notwithstanding the assertion, " I knew her intimately and never saw ought unbecoming the just modesty of our sex, though more gay and free than the folly of the precise will allow. She was, I am satisfied, a greater honour to our sex than all the canting tribes of dissemblers that die with the false reputation of saints."

She was a learned lady, and amongst other things wrote a treatise on the 'History of Oracles,' which is in part a translation of the Latin work of Van Dale, ' De Oraculis Ethnicorum,' on the same subject. Mrs. Behn tells us in her preface, that she had taken great liberties with Van Dale, and had changed the whole disposition of the book, retrenching and adding as she thought fit, and sometimes arguing in direct opposition to him. " In fine," she says, " I have new cast and modelled the whole work, and have put it into the same order as I should have done at first to have pleased my particular view, had I had so much knowledge as Mr. Van Dale, but since I am far from it, I have borrowed his learning, and ventured to make use of my own wit and fancy (such as it is) to adorn it." The object of Van Dale's work was to refute the opinion that the ancient oracles were delivered by Dæmons, and that they ceased wholly at the coming of Jesus Christ. Mrs. Behn also translated Fontenelle's work on the ' Plurality of Worlds,' but her version was first published after her death. In

the dedication to the Earl of Kingston, by
Briscoe, who seems to have brought it out, he
calls her "the Sappho of our nation, the incomparable Mrs. Behn," and describes himself as
one who has been "only a necessary appendix
to the traders in Parnassus." Although utterly
forgotten now, Mrs. Behn's name once occupied a prominent place in the world of letters.
In 'Tom Jones' occurs the following passage—
"This young fellow lay in bed, reading one of
Mrs. Behn's novels, for he had been instructed
by a friend that he could not find a more
effectual method of recommending himself to
the ladies, than by improving his understanding, and filling his mind with good literature."
This of course is Fielding's sarcasm.

I have said that 'Oroonoko' is the best known
of Mrs. Behn's novels, but I doubt whether more
than a very few of the present generation have
read or even seen it, and I had some difficulty
in procuring a copy. The story is founded on
fact, and became known to the authoress while
she was residing at Surinam, of which her
father was Governor. The real history of
Oroonoko and Imoinda seems to be this. He
was a young negro chief, whose grandfather
was ruler of a country in Africa, not **far** from
the coast. He had just married a negress

named Imoinda, when the old king, having seen her, and being struck with her beauty, ordered that she should be brought to him to live as his concubine. Notwithstanding her opposition and despair, the royal will was law, and she took up her residence with the king. Oroonoko, however, contrived to get access to her apartment, and being discovered, she was sold as a slave, while he managed to make his escape. He got down to the coast, and was there basely inveigled on board a slave ship, and carried off to Surinam. Here he was sold as a slave, and became the property of a kind-hearted master named Trefry. It happened that Imoinda was working as a slave on the same plantation, and the unfortunate husband and wife thus unexpectedly met. They told their story to their master, who showed sympathy with their sorrows, and they were allowed to live together as man and wife, in a cottage on the estate, where, Mrs. Behn says, she frequently visited them. Oroonoko was known by the name of Cæsar, and Imoinda by that of Clemene. He tried in vain to purchase his liberty, and at last excited his fellow-slaves to a revolt, which was quickly suppressed. He and Imoinda had escaped into the woods, but they were taken, and he was barbarously flogged.

Enraged at this, he brooded over a scheme of
signal vengeance on the whites, but fearing
that his wife would become a prey to their
lawless caprice, and that the child she then
bore in her bosom was doomed to slavery, he
determined to kill her. Taking her into the
woods, he cut her throat, and remained for
some days beside her dead body, until he was
found by those who went in search of the run-
aways. He was brought back, tied to a post,
and literally cut to pieces. I may give the
death scene in Mrs. Behn's own words—" He
had learned to take tobacco; and when he was
assured he should die, he desired they would
give him a pipe in his mouth, ready lighted,
which they did : and the executioner came
. . . . . . and threw them into the
fire; after that, with an ill-favoured knife, they
cut off his ears and nose, and burned them;
he still smoked on as if nothing had touched
him; then they hacked off one of his arms, and
still he bore up, and held his pipe; but at the
cutting off the other arm, his head sank, and
his pipe dropped, and he gave up the ghost
without a groan or a reproach.—My mother
and sister," she adds, "were by him all the
while, but not suffered to save him."

Such, I believe, to be the true facts of this

tragic tale, which Mrs. Behn took as the basis
of her story, and which she has of course
amplified and altered as suited her purpose.
She has made Oroonoko a most accomplished
prince, well acquainted with English, French,
and mathematics, and says, " I have often seen
and conversed with this great man, and have
been a witness to many of his mighty actions,
and do assure my reader that the most illustrious courts could not have produced a braver
man, both for greatness of courage and mind,
a judgment more solid, a wit more quick, and
a conversation more sweet and diverting.   He
knew almost as much as if he had read much ;
he had heard of the late civil wars in England,
and the deplorable death of our great monarch ;
and would discourse of it with all the sense and
abhorrence of the injustice imaginable.   He
had an extreme good and graceful mien, and all
the civility of a well-bred great man.   He had
nothing of barbarity in his nature, but in all
points addressed himself as if his education had
been in some European court." This shows
the key in which the tone of the novel is
pitched, and the person of the sable hero is
described in corresponding style.   " He was
pretty tall, but of a shape the most exact that
can be fancied.   The most famous statuary

could not form the figure of a man more admirably turned from head to foot. His face
was not of that brown rusty black which most
of that nation are, but a perfect ebony or
polished jet. His eyes were the most awful
that could be seen, and very piercing, the white
of them being like snow, as were his teeth.
His nose was rising and Roman, instead of
African and flat. His mouth the finest shaped
that could be seen, far from those great turned
lips which are so natural to the rest of the
negroes. . . . . His hair came down to his
shoulders by the aids of art, which was by
pulling it out with a quill, and keeping it
combed, of which he took particular care." As
to Imoinda, "one need say only that she was
female to the noble male; the beautiful black
Venus to our young Mars, as charming in her
person as he, and of delicate virtues. I have
seen an hundred white men sighing after her,
and making a thousand vows at her feet, all
vain and unsuccessful." After thus turning a
woolly-headed negro into an Adonis, with a
Roman nose and flowing hair, it is not surprising that Mrs. Behn should metamorphose
the hut of an African chief into a palace where
the king is surrounded by oriental luxury, and
where the usages are borrowed from such tales

as the 'Arabian Nights.' When Oroonoko
was about to be treacherously carried off by the
slaver, "the captain in his boat richly adorned
with carpets and velvet cushions went to the
shore to receive the prince, with another long-
boat where was placed all his music and
trumpets." When he got on board, his High-
ness drank too much wine and punch, and so
fell an easy prey to the cupidity of the captain,
who seized on him and put him in irons, and
then "made from the shore with this innocent
and glorious prize, who thought of nothing less
than such an entertainment." I will only add
that the novel contains a rather interesting
account of the country around Surinam, and
the mode of life there. On one occasion when
Mrs. Behn, with some women, Cæsar, and "an
English gentleman, brother to Harry Marten,
the great Oliverian,"—that is Marten, the re-
gicide, on whom Southey wrote the sonnet
parodied by Canning in the 'Antijacobin'—
were out "surprising, and in search of young
tigers in their dens," they were themselves
surprised by the appearance of an enormous
tigress, and would have been torn to pieces if
the monster had not been killed by the valiant
Cæsar—that is Oroonoko.

Two others at least of Mrs. Behn's stories—

they are almost too short to be called novels— may be still read without offence, and if better handled might be made interesting even now. One is 'The Wandering Beauty,' and the other 'The Unfortunate Happy Lady,' and it may be worth while to sketch the plots, and give a few specimens of the style,

In the first Arabella Fairname, the youthful daughter of a gentleman of large fortune in the west of England, in order to avoid being forced by her parents into a marriage with a neighbouring squire old enough to be her father, runs away from home, and disguising her skin with walnut-juice, changes clothes with a labourer's daughter, and wanders on foot as far as Lancashire. There she reaches the house of Sir Christian Kindly, and offering herself as a servant under the name of Peregrina Goodhouse, becomes the attendant of his daughter, who is almost the same age as herself.

" In this state of easy servitude she lived there for near three years, very well contented at all times but when she bethought herself of her father, mother, and sisters ; courted by all the principal men-servants, whom she refused in so obliging a manner, and with such sweet, obliging words, that they could not think themselves injured, though they found

their addresses were in vain. Mr. Prayfast, the
chaplain, could not hold out against her charms.
For her skin had long since recovered its native
whiteness; nor did she need ornaments of
clothes to set her beauty off, if anything could
adorn her, since she was dressed altogether
as costly, though not so richly (perhaps) as
Eleanora. Prayfast, therefore, found that the
spirit was too weak for the flesh, and gave
her very broad signs of his kindness in sonnets,
anagrams, and acrostics, which she received
very obligingly of him, taking a more convenient
time to laugh at 'em with her young lady."

The Rev. Mr. Prayfast, however, was informed that Peregrina's father was a "husband-
man," or something inferior to that, and had,
when she first appeared at Sir Christian Kindly's
house, begged "one night's entertainment in the
barn." "'Alas! sir, then" (returned the proud,
canonical sort of a farmer, *sic*) "she is no wife for
me; I shall dishonour my family by marrying so
basely.'" The chaplain, therefore, declined to
pursue his addresses, and a young knight, Sir
Lucius Lovewell, coming to the mansion to pay
court to Eleanora, Sir Christian's daughter, fell in
love with Peregrina instead, and soon afterwards
married her. She did not reveal to her husband the secret of her birth; but as she longed

to see her parents again, whom he believed to
be poor labourers, they both set out for the
west of England, "and in five or six days
more, by the help of a coach and six, they got
to Cornwall," and put up at a little inn near the
residence of Sir Francis and Lady Fairname.
Sir Lucius is persuaded by his wife to go and
see the house, where he is courteously received
by Sir Francis, and invited to dinner.   He is
much struck by a picture in the room, which is
the likeness of his own wife, and also by the
appearance of her two sisters, who greatly re-
sembled her.   He mentions the circumstance
to his host, who begs him to fetch his wife, that
they may see one who bears a likeness to their
lost Arabella.   He returns to the inn and
brings her back with him.   "The boot of the
coach (for that was the fashion in those days)
was presently let down, and Sir Lucius led his
lady forwards to them, who, coming within three
or four paces of the good old Knight, his lady
fell on her knees and begged their pardon and
blessing. . . . She then gave her father, mother,
and sisters a relation of all that had happened
to her since her absence from her dear parents,
who were extremely pleased with the account
of Sir Christian and his lady's hospitality and
kindness to her; and in less than a fortnight

after, they took a journey to Sir Lucius's, carrying the two other young ladies along with 'em ; and by the way they called at Sir Christian's, where they arrived in time enough to be present the next day at Sir Christian's daughter's wedding, which they kept there for a whole fortnight."

In 'The Unfortunate Happy Lady,' which Mrs. Behn calls "a true history," we have the story "of the uncommon villany of a gentleman of good family in England, practised upon his sister, which was attested to me by one who lived in the family, and from whom I had the whole truth of the story." Whether or not this is only a device to attract the interest of the reader, I cannot say ; but, in either case, it affords a curious picture of what was possible in those days, which we must, however, remember were the days of the *seventeenth* century. The brother is introduced under the name of Sir William Wilding, who has a sister called Philadelphia. He gets heavily into debt, " contracted in his profuse treats, gaming and women," and is obliged to mortgage part of his estate. His sister begs him to pay her her portion ; and he promises to do this if she will accompany him to town, where, he tells her, he will place her with an ancient lady " of incomparable morals and of a matchless life and conversation." When they reach London, Sir William goes to Lady Beldam and tells her that his sister was a cast-off mistress of his, asking her to give her "a wholesome lesson or two before night" for a pecuniary reward, and giving the old harridan three guineas. Poor Philadelphia falls into the trap, and takes up her abode with Lady Beldam. In answer to her Ladyship's inquiry, she assures her that she is Sir William's sister, and tells her that she is assured he intends to deprive her of her portion. "I will show you," said the other, "the means of living happy and great without your portion, or your brother's help; so much I am charmed with your beauty and innocence." The means may be easily conjectured. In the afternoon three or four young women visit Lady Beldam, and are introduced by her to Philadelphia as her nieces. They adjourn after dinner into the garden, where there was "a very fine dessert of sweetmeats and fruits brought into one of the arbours. Sherbets, Ros Solis, rich and small wines, with tea, chocolate, &c., completed the old lady's treat, the pleasure of which was much heightened by the voices of two of her Ladyship's sham nieces, who sang very charmingly." Next day a servant came to say that Sir William would come at one o'clock, and desired that

he might dine in the young lady's apartment,
adding that he had invited a gentleman, his
particular friend, to join them at dinner. The
gentleman comes—a Mr. Gracelove—but not
Sir William ; and the poor girl is in the most
imminent peril. She, however, undeceives
Gracelove as to her real position and character,
and he behaves very well, offering to rescue her
and get her out of the house. Under pretence
of taking her to the play, he is allowed by Lady
Beldam to call a coach, and they go at once "to
Counsellor Fairlaw's house, in Great Lincoln's
Inn Fields, whom they found accidentally at
home ; but his lady and daughter were just
gone to chapel, being then turned of five." The
old counsellor was a relation of Gracelove, and
when he heard her story, promised to take every
care of her. He introduced her to his family,
and " the mother and daughter both kindly and
tenderly embraced her, promising her all the
assistance within their power, and bid her a
thousand welcomes." Gracelove afterwards
went with a constable to Lady Beldam's house
and demanded Miss Wilding's trunk, "which
at first her reverence denied to return, till
Mr. Constable produced the emblem of his authority, upon which it was delivered." He then
found out Sir William and reproached him with

his villany, threatening him with the conse-
quences. Sir William, upon this, "retreated
into a place of sanctuary called the Savoy,
whither his whole equipage was removed as
soon as possible," and he assumed a false name.
Gracelove then avowed his passion to Philadelphia; but the marriage could not immediately take place, as he was obliged to go to
Turkey on business. News afterwards arrived
that the ship in which he sailed was lost, and
he was supposed to be drowned. Two years
passed away, at the end of which old Lady
Fairlaw died, "and dying told her husband
that she had observed he had a particular esteem or kindness for Philadelphia, which was
now a great satisfaction to her; since she was
assured that if he married she would prove an
excellent nurse to him, and prolong his life by
some years." And so, at the expiration of a
decent time from the funeral, they were married, and "kept the wedding very nobly for a
month at their own house, in Great Lincoln's
Inn Fields." But at the end of four months
the old gentleman fell sick and died. "Whether
it was the change of an old home for a new (for
they had removed to Covent-Garden), or an old
wife for a young, is yet uncertain, though his
physicians said, and are still of opinion, that

doubtless it was the last." The young and
beautiful widow, who was left in affluence, was
now addressed "by as many lovers, or pretended lovers, as our dear King Charles, whom
God grant long to reign, was lately by the
Presbyterians, Independents, Anabaptists, and
all those canting whiggish brethren;" but she
yielded her hand to none of them. In the
meantime her worthless brother was arrested
for debt, and thrown into gaol in the King's
Bench, where the Marshal "turned him to the
common side, where he learned the art of peg-
making." Philadelphia used to send money and
provisions to relieve the poor prisoners, and she
thus became acquainted with her brother's for-
lorn position, and took measures unknown to him
to extricate his property from its load of debt.
One day, "looking out of her coach on the road
near Dartford, she saw a traveller on foot, who
seemed to be tired with his journey, whose face
she thought she had formerly known." This,
of course, was Gracelove, "now very pale and
thin, his complexion swarthy, and his clothes
(perhaps) as rotten as if he had been buried in
them." Philadelphia did not make herself
known to him; but took care to find out where
he lodged, and sent her steward, who told him
that he came from the young widow of Coun-

sellor Fairlaw, and ordered that he should "be taken measure of by the best tailor in Covent-Garden ; that he should have three of the most modish rich suits made that might become a private gentleman of a thousand pounds a year, and hats, perukes, linen, swords, and all things suitable to them."   She then invited her brother and Gracelove and three of her admirers to dine with her.   "After dinner the cloth was taken away.   She thus began to her lovers: —' My Lord, Sir Thomas and Mr. Fat-acres! I doubt but that it will be some satisfaction to you to know that I have made choice for my real husband, which now I am resolved no longer to defer.'"   She then took a diamond ring from her finger, and, putting it into a wine-glass, said, "My dear Gracelove! I drink to thee ; and send thee back thy own ring with Philadelphia's heart."   The rest may be easily imagined, and she invited the party to her wedding on the morrow.   The graceless Sir William is by this time supposed to be re-formed, and he is off-hand accepted as a husband by the step-daughter Eugenia.   "The whole company in general went away very well that night, who returned the next morning and saw the two happy pair firmly united."

Some of this lady's descriptions it would be impossible to quote ; but an idea of their *warmth* may be gathered from the following passage in 'The Unfortunate Bride,' where the mutual passion of Frankwit and Belvira is thus related :—" Their flames, now joined, grew more and more, glowed in their cheeks and lightened in their glances. Eager they looked, as if there were pulses beating in their eyes ; and all endearing at last, she vowed that Frankwit living 'she would ne'er be any other man's.' Thus they past on some time, while every day rolled over fair ; Heaven showed an aspect all serene, and the sun seemed to smile at what was done. He still caressed his charmer with an innocence becoming his sincerity ; he lived upon her tender breath, and basked in the bright lustre of her eyes, with pride and secret joy."

In the 'Unhappy Mistake' a lover, who is about to fight a duel, goes early in the morning to his sister's bedroom, with whom Lucretia, the mistress of his affections, is sleeping. " They both happened to be awake, and talking as he came to the door, which his sister permitted him to unlock, and asked him the reason of his so early rising ? who replied, that since he could not sleep he would take the air a little. 'But first, sister (continued he), I will refresh myself at your lips. And now, madam (added he to Lucretia), I would beg a cordial from you.' 'For that (said his sister) you shall be obliged to me for this once.' Saying so, she gently turned Lucretia's face towards him, and he had his wish. Ten to one but he had rather have continued with Lucretia than have gone to her brother, had he known him, for he loved her truly and passionately. But being a man of true courage and honour, he took his leave of them, presently dressed, and tripped away with the messenger, who made more than ordinary haste."

Mrs., or rather Miss Manley, for she was never married, is best known as the authoress of the 'New Atalantis,' a scandalous work, which she published at the end of the seventeenth or the beginning of the eighteenth century. Her life was a sad career of dissipation, and as licentious as her books. But she was much to be pitied. Her father, Sir Roger Manley, was Governor of Guernsey, and after his death she was seduced under a promise of marriage and abandoned by a cousin, who was, unknown to her, a married man. Her 'New Atalantis,' which was published anonymously, was such a satire upon many of the eminent men of the time that both the printer and publisher were imprisoned under a warrant of the Secretary of State, when she came forward and avowed herself the authoress. She was arrested, but sued out a writ of *habeas corpus*, and was admitted to bail. After her final discharge she plunged afresh into vice, and died in 1724, the mistress of a printer named Barber. The 'New Atalantis, or Secret Memoirs and Manners of Persons of Quality,' is one of the worst books I know—the worst in style and worst in morals, and fully deserves the oblivion into which it has fallen. It is impossible to read it through ; and that it should ever have been popular—the edition I have before me is the seventh — notwithstanding Pope's line,

As long as Atalantis shall be read,

is almost incredible, and denotes a taste utterly depraved. To a certain extent, however, this may be accounted for by the fact that it is a scandalous chronicle of persons in high life under thinly disguised names, and reveals or invents their amours and intrigues.

Besides this 'New Atalantis' Mrs. Manley wrote 'The Power of Love, in seven Novels,' under the following names : — ' The Fair Hypocrite,' ' The Physician's Stratagem,' ' The Wife's Resentment,' ' The Husband's Resentment in two Examples,' 'The Happy Fugitive,' and 'The Perjured Beauty;' and in her dedication to Lady Lansdowne she says that they have truth for their foundation, and several of the facts are to be found in ancient histories.

In 'The Fair Hypocrite' Reginia, the young and beautiful daughter of Charles the German Emperor, is, for reasons of state, married to the Duke of Savoy, an old man past seventy, who "to please her fond girlish fancy," entertains her with "collations, pretty sports, fine clothes, rich jewels, coaches and equipage;" and she in return for his complaisance, "hugged the fond Duke in her arms, with this fond, this passionate expression, 'I love you better than my Papa!'" The Duke's prime minister was Sigisbert Count of Briançon, who fell in love with the Duchess, and when his old master left the capital to command the army "he saw her at all times, and made the despatches from the Duke his pretence to come at any hour into her apartment, even to her bedside, where, if ever a clean young lady have any charms, that is certainly the scene wherein they become most conspicuous and dangerous to others." But the Duchess was smitten by the sight of a picture of a young Spanish nobleman, Don Carlos,

Duke of Mendoza, and pined to behold him. Many schemes for accomplishing this purpose were considered; and at last, by the advice of a female *confidante*, she resolved to feign sickness, and make a vow if she recovered to go on a pilgrimage to the shrine of St. Iago de Compostella, in Spain. The plan succeeded, and the Duchess set out on her journey, accompanied by the Lady Isabella, a sister of Don Carlos. When she saw Don Carlos she fell desperately in love with him; but "his modesty was equal to his beauty," and she found him insensible to her charms. She therefore, without bidding him farewell, suddenly left him to go forward to Compostella; but he followed her and overtook her on the road, and avowed that he was "vanquished and irrecoverably lost by the powers of love." She confessed her passion for him, and promised to visit him again on her return from the shrine of St. Iago, when, she said, she should think herself most happy in whatever proofs he could give her of his love, "provided we both may preserve our innocency." In the meantime the Count de Briançon persuaded the Duke of Savoy that it was right to go after his wife, and they both proceeded to Spain. They found her at Compostella, and the Duke knelt beside her at the high

altar of the Cathedral. "Then it was that
she felt the love of God, and the disdain
of her guilty passion filled her heart with
Divine ardour and contempt for her mis-
doings." She resolved to forget Don Carlos
and not see him again, "giving her hand
willingly to the Duke to be conducted back
by sea to Turin." Again her husband left
her in Turin to assume the command of his
troops, and the faithless Count Briançon took
the opportunity of his absence to declare his
passion.

The Duchess received the avowal "with a
sweet disdain, which was more tempered by
sorrow than scorn;" but firmly repulsed the
Count's advances. He persisted in his suit,
and one morning "bringing letters from her
lord to her bedside, which he said required an
immediate answer and consultation, he bade
her women retire, and had the boldness not
only to kiss the Duchess by force but was
proceeding to greater liberties," when he was
compelled to desist by her stern rebuke. The
Count now saw that his own ruin was in-
evitable unless he could first procure that of
the Duchess, and his guilty passion was changed
into hatred and a burning desire for revenge.
He feigned penitence and remorse, and the

fair authoress says, " It may be a proper question whether any woman was ever truly enraged at seeing the effects of her beauty when
she had not suffered much by it. Her High-
ness's wrongs were only imaginary ; a kiss or
two with the aspect of a greater force might
be easily forgiven to a true penitent who was,
perhaps by his death, to expiate his offence.
Add to this the softness and good-nature
which are usually lodged in ladies' breasts ; the
Duchess was so far influenced by them that
she easily came to a composition with the
criminal." He promised not to offend again,
and she promised not to inform the Duke, " if
he never fell into a relapse." The Count had a
young nephew named Lotharius, whom he now
resolved to use as the instrument of his vengeance. He pretended illness, and sending for
his nephew told him that he had made his will
and named him as his heir. His ambition, he
said, was to marry him to the Duchess if the
Duke should die in the campaign, and he advised him to do all in his power to ingratiate
himself with her ; and as he had observed that
she had often cast upon him eyes of affection,
Lotharius willingly entered into the scheme,
and began to pay assiduous court to his
princely mistress, who received him graciously.

At last his uncle told him that he must take steps to assure himself of her sincerity, and suggested that he should get that night into her chamber, and himself under the bed, and " an hour after midnight, when the bed-chamber lady is retired to her own bed in the little room adjoining, who happens to be the Countess of Briançon, of whom thou needest not stand so much in fear, thou mayest come softly out and satisfy her of thy fidelity and discretion." The poor youth fell into the trap and hid himself under the bed, but after the Duchess had got into it, in rushed the Count with his sword drawn, and followed by three great officers of the Court, crying out, " Traitor, I shall certainly find thee here." The scene reminds one of Don Juan—

> They looked beneath the bed, and there they found

—the unhappy Lotharius, who was pulled out by his hair and stabbed to the heart by his treacherous uncle. It was the stratagem of Tarquin to destroy the reputation of Lucretia. A courier was despatched to the Duke with the fatal news, and he sent orders that the law should be put in force against his wife as an adulteress. The judges seem to have been rather at a loss to know what the law was, for they caused the records to be searched, and there they found that according to ancient precedents a pillar of marble was to be erected between the bridge of the Po and the city, on which was to be engraved the accusation against the Duchess and a summons to her champion to enter the lists on her behalf against the Count de Briançon, within twelve months and a day, or else she was to die by fire. To make the rest of the story short, Don Carlos accepted the challenge, and in single combat overthrew the Count. When he had unhorsed him he put his sword to his throat and made him confess his villany, after which the people rushed upon the traitor and tore him to pieces. The Duke died at the right moment, and Don Carlos married the Duchess. "No words can describe the happiness of the two lovers when the close-drawn curtains left them to whisper to each other's souls their mutual desires: Venus blessed their bed, and from this beauteous pair descended a race of heroes worthy of their illustrious extraction."

This will be a sufficient specimen of the seven stories of the 'Power of Love,' and Mrs. Manley's style. It is far less objectionable than that of the 'New Atalantis,' and hardly worse than that of Mrs. Behn, which is certainly not saying much for it.

We now come to Mrs. Heywood, or Haywood, who died in 1756. She figures prominently in the 'Dunciad,' under the name of Eliza, and is represented

With cow-like udders and with ox-like eyes,

as one of the prizes to be contended for in the 'Games of the Dunces.'

See in the circle next Eliza placed,
Two babes of love close clinging to her waist ;
Fair as before her works she stands confessed,
In flowers and pearls by bounteous Kirkall dressed.

The rest of the passage is in Pope's coarsest style. Besides the 'History of Miss Betsy Thoughtless,' she wrote the 'Court of Caramania,' the 'New Utopia,' and several other tales, such as the 'Fortunate Foundling,' and 'Jenny and Jemmy Jessamy.'* 'Miss Betsy Thoughtless' is rather a clever work and interesting, as the first really domestic novel according to modern ideas, that exists in the language. It has been supposed that Miss Burney took it as the model of her 'Evelina,' and it is the only novel I know which could

* She also conducted a monthly periodical called 'The Female Spectator,' from April, 1744, to March, 1746. See Drake's 'Essays,' vol. iv. p. 92.

have served for the purpose. As although
once celebrated it is now almost entirely forgotten, I will give a short sketch of the plot.

Betsy Thoughtless gets into several com-
promising scrapes, not from any vicious pro-
pensities, from which she is absolutely free,
but owing to that feature in her character which
is expressed by her name. Her worst fault is
vanity, and her head is turned by the multiplicity of her admirers, of whom only one,
named Trueworth, is able at all to touch her
heart, and she loses him by her foolish in-
attention to appearances, and her impatience
of the least remonstrance which implies an
imputation upon the correctness of her behaviour. She is left motherless while a child,
and her father dies before she has attained her
fifteenth year. She has two brothers, the eldest
of whom, Thomas, is then abroad, and the
other, Francis, a student at Oxford. She comes
up from the country and is placed in London under the care of one of her guardians,
an elderly merchant named Goodman, who has
married a young widow, Lady Mellasin, who
under the mask of simulated affection entirely
governs him. Lady Mellasin has a daughter
named Flora, an abandoned young lady, who
makes no scruple to sacrifice her honour to her

passions, and who is detected by Miss Betsy in
an intrigue, seen through a chink in the panel
of her bedroom. The secret, however, is kept,
and the young ladies continue to sleep together
as if nothing had happened. Miss Betsy has
also the misfortune to have made friends with
a school-fellow in the country, a Miss Forward,
who falls an easy victim to the arts of a seducer,
and coming up to town imposes upon Betsy's
simplicity as to her position and character and
involves her in embarrassments which make
Trueworth believe that she is wholly unworthy
of his love. This is aided by the unscrupulous
use of anonymous letters, in which her reputation is slandered by Miss Flora. The result is
that he withdraws from his attentions to her
and afterwards falls in love with and marries
Harriet Loveit, the amiable sister of Sir Basil
Loveit. In the meantime Lady Mellasin has
been carrying on an intrigue with an old lover
named Marplus, to whom before her marriage
with Mr. Goodman she was by a trick induced
to give her hand for two thousand five hundred
pounds, and whose rapacious demands upon
her purse she had great difficulty in satisfying
so as to conceal her infamy from her husband.
He, however, is at last arrested for the amount
of the bond, for which by his marriage he had

become liable, and then all the wickedness of his wife becomes known to him. This has such an effect upon him that before he is able to get a divorce he dies, having by his will left only a small provision for his widow; but a forged will is set up by her. While all this is going on Miss Betsy has removed from Mr. Goodman's house and taken lodgings in Jermyn Street, where she lives upon a sufficient income and receives her admirers, whose visits to an unmarried young lady living alone do not seem in the opinion of the authoress to be at all inconsistent with strict propriety. Amongst these are a *soi-disant* baronet, Sir Frederick Fineer, and a Mr. Munden. The Baronet, however, is in reality a discarded valet, who succeeds in forcing her into a sham marriage at the house of her milliner, Mrs. Modeley, by the aid of a mock clergyman; and we have a scene which reminds us of that in 'Sir Charles Grandison,' where Harriet Byron more successfully resists the attempt of Sir Hargrave Pollexfen to compel her to become his wife, when she dashes the Prayer-book on the ground. At the proper moment, however, Miss Betsy is rescued from the villain by her former lover, Mr. Trueworth, just before he becomes the husband of Miss Loveit. She then is persuaded by her brothers and her other guardian, Sir Ralph Trusty, who with his wife has always acted the part of a kind friend to her, to accept the addresses of Mr. Munden, and she becomes his wife, although she cares little for him, and he is very unworthy of her. The marriage turns out unhappily. Her husband is stingy and selfish and a libertine; but she herself endeavours to do her duty, and under the chastening discipline of matrimonial trials she gains sedateness and strength of character.

At the house of a nobleman from whom her husband expects some appointment she is in great danger from his libertine advances, and with great difficulty escapes; but soon after her return home is driven from it by the misconduct of Mr. Munden, who gives loose to his passion for a French woman, the discarded mistress of her eldest brother. She quits his house and takes refuge with her brother. Her husband tries to force her to return to him, but she withdraws from his pursuit, and, while matters are in this state, he falls suddenly ill and she comes to his death-bed to perform her duty to the last. She then retires to pass the first year of her widowhood with Sir Ralph and Lady Trusty in the country; and as in the meantime Trueworth's wife has died, all his old love for Betsy revives, and the story ends when they are happily married.

Trueworth pays a visit to the fair widow at the expiration of a year's mourning, and she becomes aware of his arrival by "a very neat running footman, who, on the gate being opened, came tripping towards the house, and was immediately followed by a coach, with one gentleman in it, drawn by six prancing horses" —people in those days seem never to have travelled with less than six horses—"and attended by two servants in rich liveries, and well mounted. . . . . Prepared as she was by the expectation of his arrival, all her presence of mind was not sufficient to enable her to stand the sudden rush of joy which on the sight of him burst in upon her heart ; nor was he less overcome ;—he sprang into her arms, which of themselves opened to receive him, and while he kissed away the tears that trickled from her eyes, his own bedewed her cheeks. 'Oh ! have I lived to see you thus,' cried he, 'thus ravishingly kind !' 'And have I lived,' rejoined she, 'to receive these proofs of affection from the best and most ill-used of men. Oh ! Trueworth ! Trueworth !' added she, 'I have not merited this from you.' 'You merit all things,' said he; 'let us talk no more of what is past, but tell me that you now are mine; I came to make you so by the irrevocable ties of love and law, and we must now part no more! Speak, my angel,—my first, my last charmer!' continued he perceiving she was silent, blushed, and hung down her head. 'Let those dear lips confirm my happiness, and say the time is come, that you will be all mine.' The trembling fair now having gathered a little more assurance, raised her eyes from the earth and looking tenderly on him, 'You know you have my heart,' cried she, 'and cannot doubt my hand.'"

Such is a meagre sketch of the plot of this once popular novel, omitting numerous episodes which at the present day would be deemed very unfit for the perusal of those for whom it is professedly designed. But, notwithstanding these, it is obvious throughout that it is the honest purpose of the writer to promote the cause of innocence and virtue. In no one of her characters does immorality go unpunished — and, if vicious scenes are too nakedly described, she cannot be accused of making them alluring and attractive. In that age it was taken for granted that they must occur in the so-called journey of life, as much as dirty puddles must be met with in an actual road.

Beyond the risks which every young lady was then supposed to run of becoming the object of licentious addresses, such as would be impossible in good society now, there is not much in this novel that is characteristic of a different state of manners from those of the present day. But a few little touches may be noticed : It seems that it was not thought indecorous for a young woman to receive male visitors in her dressing-room while performing her toilet. The usual mode of conveyance was a chair, and ladies when they wished to preserve an *incognito*, went abroad in masks. It is in this disguise that Flora Mellasin meets Trueworth by appointment "at General Tatten's bench, opposite Rosamond's pond, in St. James's Park." Rosamond's pond had rather a bad reputation, both as the scene of assignations and a place for suicide. In Southern's play of the *Maid's Last Prayer*, acted in 1693, when Granger says to Lady Trickett that he did not see her at Rosamond's pond, she exclaims, "Me! fie, fie, a married woman there, Mr. Granger!" What has become of General Tatten's bench I know not, but Rosamond's pond was filled up in 1770 by "Capability" Brown.

The fashionable dinner hour was then three o'clock.* Knockers were so constructed that they could be removed from the front door at night when the inmates went to bed. At least so I gather from the following passage : " She came not home till between one and two o'clock in the morning, but was extremely surprised to find that when she did so the knocker was taken off the door: a thing which in complaisance to her, had never before been done till she came in, how late soever she stayed abroad."

The passion of love is the same in all ages, but the style of love making is very different.

One of Miss Betsy Thoughtless's lovers thus addresses her :—

" The deity of soft desires flies the confused glare of pomp and public shows ;—'tis in the shady bowers, or on the banks of a sweet purling stream, he spreads his downy wings, and wafts his thousand nameless pleasures on the fond—the innocent and the happy pair.

* In 1725, the time of dinner at Merton College, Oxford, was altered from twelve o'clock to one : and was altered soon afterwards to twelve o'clock again, " for weighty reasons."—Rawlinson's MSS., quoted in ' Oxoniana.'

" He was going on, but she interrupted him with a loud laugh. 'Hold, hold,' cried she; 'was there ever such a romantic description ? I wonder how such silly ideas come into your head—'shady bowers! and purling streams!— Heavens, how insipid! Well' (continued she), 'you may be the Strephon of the woods, if you think fit; but I shall never envy the happiness of the Chloe that accompanies you in these fine recesses. What! to be cooped up like a tame dove, only to coo, and bill, and *breed?* O, it would be a delicious life, indeed!"

CHAPTER VII.

RICHARDSON. — 'CLARISSA HARLOWE.' — 'PAMELA.' — 'SIR CHARLES GRANDISON.' — RICHARDSON'S CORRESPONDENCE. HIS PORTRAIT DRAWN BY HIMSELF.

IF my object were to give a history of fiction in the eighteenth century, there is hardly any name which would more deservedly claim our attention than the name of Defoe, who, of all novelists, is the one who has given the most lifelike reality to his stories, and cheats his readers most easily into the belief that imaginary scenes are the narratives of actual fact. But my purpose is different, and the works of Defoe throw little or no light upon the social manners of the age with which we have to deal, not to mention the difficulty there would be in conveying, without offence, an idea of such heroes and heroines as Captain Single-ton, Roxana, Moll Flanders, and Colonel Jack. We may therefore dismiss from our notice the immortal author of 'Robinson Crusoe,' and turn to the next chief figure amongst the novelists of the century, I mean Richardson, the author of

'Pamela,' 'Clarissa,' and 'Sir Charles Grandison.'

And what are we to say of these famous novels which stirred to their inmost depths the hearts of a bygone generation, and were regarded as the great literary feats of the age in which they appeared? Few, very few, read them now, but there are some minds for which they have attractions still. Lord Macaulay told Thackeray that when he produced 'Clarissa' one hot season at the hills in India, "the whole station was in a passion of excitement. . . . . . the Governor's wife seized the book, and the Secretary waited for it, and the Chief Justice could not read it for tears." One enthusiastic admirer in the last century went so far as to say, that if all other books were to be burnt, 'Pamela' and the Bible should be preserved; and ladies at Ranelagh used to hold up the book in triumph to show that they were lucky enough to possess a copy. One of Richardson's correspondents, however, wrote to him that ladies complained that they could not read the letters of Pamela without blushing,—and well they might.

Sir John Herschel tells an anecdote of a blacksmith at a much later period, who used to read the book to his village neighbours col-

lected round his anvil, and when, at the end of
the story, it turned out that Pamela and her
master were happily married, the unsophisti-
cated rustics shouted for joy, and procuring the
keys of the church set the bells ringing. Mrs.
Barbauld says that she well remembered a
Frenchman who paid a visit to Hampstead, for
the sole purpose of finding out the house in the
Flask Walk where Clarissa lodged, and was
surprised at the ignorance or indifference of the
inhabitants on the subject. The Flask Walk
was to him what the Rocks of Meillerie, on the
Lake of Geneva, were to the worshippers of
Rousseau.

But *de gustibus haud disputandum*, and every
one must judge for himself,

> Nullius addictus jurare in verba magistri.

To me, I confess, 'Clarissa Harlowe' is an
unpleasant, not to say odious, book.

I read it through once, many years ago, and
I should be sorry to do so again. As to the
plot of the story, there is really almost none.

> Story? God bless you, I have none to tell, sir!

A young lady leaves her father's house to
avoid a distasteful marriage, and throws herself
upon the protection of her lover, who, after
in vain attempting to seduce her, succeeds in

effecting her ruin by an act for which he might have been hanged. He afterwards offers to marry her, but she refuses, and retiring to solitary lodgings, dies broken-hearted, while the villain is killed abroad in a duel by a relative of the lady. Upon this foundation Richardson has built up seven or eight tedious volumes, consisting of letters between "two young ladies of virtue and honour," Miss Clarissa Harlowe and Miss Howe, and "two gentlemen of free lives," Mr. Lovelace and Mr. Belford, besides others.* The key-note of the whole composition is libertine pursuit, and we are wearied and disgusted by volume after volume devoted to the single subject of attack on a woman's chastity. It would be bad enough to read this if compressed into a few chapters, but it becomes intolerably repulsive when spun out in myriads of letters. If any book deserved the charge of "sickly sentimentality," it is this, and that it should have once been so widely popular, and thought admirably adapted to instruct young women in lessons of virtue and religion, shows a strange and perverted state of the public taste, not to say public morals.†

---

* Clarissa's will occupies nineteen closely printed pages.

† Two ladies, without the knowledge of each other, wrote to

Richardson, in his preface, thinks that he deserves credit for not making his libertines infidels. He says, " It will be proper to observe, for the sake of such as may apprehend hurt to the morals of youth from the more freely written letters, that the gentlemen, though professed libertines as to the female sex, and making it one of their wicked maxims to keep no faith with any of the individuals of it who are thrown into their power, are not, however, either infidels or scoffers, nor yet such as think themselves freed from the observances of those other moral duties which bind man to man." And, apologising for not making Clarissa Harlowe herself "perfect," he adds, " To have been impeccable must have left nothing for divine grace and a purified state to do, and carried our idea of her from woman to angel." It is nauseous to find religion thus mixed up with such a story; and as to the plea that Lovelace is not an atheist, Richardson forgets the Book where the converse case is put, and we are told that " He that said Do not commit adultery said also, Do not kill. Now if thou commit no adultery, yet if thou kill thou art become a transgressor of

Richardson, the one blaming Clarissa as a coquette, and the other blaming her as a prude. He sent to each the letter of the other by way of an answer to both.—See his ' Correspondence,' vol. vi. p. 82.

the law." As well might a highwayman in the dock urge in his defence that he had not committed arson or forgery.

What has been said of 'Clarissa' applies almost equally to 'Pamela,' which was Richardson's first novel. It is the story, told in interminable letters, of a servant-girl who resists the attempts of her master to triumph over her virtue, and finally marries him. This, however, may be said for 'Pamela,' that the letters, although full of tedious gossip, are written in an artless natural style ;* and if we except one or two scenes, in which the peril of the heroine is too vividly and broadly detailed—witness that in the lonely house in Lincolnshire—they contain little that need offend modern delicacy. It is impossible not to sympathise with the poor girl who so courageously resists every effort to effect her ruin, and not to rejoice in the happiness which is afterwards her lot. But after all, it is only harping upon one string—page after page and letter after letter—and that string is

---

* Richardson had early experience in *affaires de cœur* of the humbler classes, for, when he was a mere boy, he was employed by some young women "who had a high opinion of his taciturnity," to write love-letters for them. If they were at all in his later style, they must have been terribly long-winded, and taxed not a little the patience of the rustic swains to whom they were addressed.

what Charles Lamb calls "the undivided pursuit of lawless gallantry."

Dr. Johnson said that there is more knowledge of the heart in one letter of Richardson than in all 'Tom Jones;' and when Erskine remarked to him, as well he might, "Surely, sir, Richardson is very tedious," Johnson answered, "Why, sir, if you were to read Richardson for the story, your impatience would be so much fretted that you would hang yourself; but you must read him for the sentiment, and consider the story as only giving occasion to the sentiment." If the tediousness of the story would induce a reader to hang himself, I do not think that the sentiment, or rather sentimentality, would prevent him. A great part of it is twaddle, and one cannot help agreeing with D'Alembert, who said with reference to Richardson, "La nature est bonne à imiter, mais non pas jusqu'à l'ennui."

In 'Sir Charles Grandison' we have a story to which the objection of immorality does not apply; and as it was once so celebrated, and is now so seldom read, some account of it may be interesting. Richardson tells us that he was persuaded by his friend "to produce into public view the character and actions of a man of

TRUE HONOUR."* And he presents to the
reader, "in Sir Charles Grandison, the example
of a man acting uniformly well through a
variety of trying scenes because all his actions
are regulated by one steady principle. A man
of religion and virtue, of liveliness and spirit,
accomplished and agreeable, happy in himself,
and a blessing to others." And however much
we may quarrel with the tedious length of the
interminable letters that comprise the work,
and sicken at the sentiment which forms the
staple of most of them, it must be admitted
that, beyond the drawback of too stiff and
ceremonious a politeness, the character of Richardson's hero fully comes up to his ideal. He
is, in fact, "the faultless monster whom the
world ne'er saw!" Young, rich, graceful, and
accomplished, he is not only absolutely free
from vice, but all his actions are governed by
high religious principle. He is romantically
generous and yet perfectly prudent, and his
behaviour toward the fair sex is marked with
all that chivalrous delicacy and respect which,
since the novel was written, has passed into a
proverb, and to be a Sir Charles Grandison to

---

* In one of his letters, in 1756, he says, " I am teased by a
dozen ladies of note and virtue to give them a good man, as they
say I have been partial to their sex and unkind to my own."

the ladies, is supposed to be a modern lady's perfect Knight.

The heroine of the story, and the principal writer of the long-winded letters, is Harriet Byron, an orphan girl, brought up by an uncle and aunt, Mr. and Mrs. Selby, and a grandmother, Mrs. Shirley, who live near one another in easy circumstances, in Northamptonshire. Miss Byron is, of course, beautiful, although rather short, and at the age of twenty, when the letters begin, has three passionate admirers in the country, Mr. Greville, Mr. Fenwick, and Mr. Orme. Greville is a man of no principle, and no self control, full of self conceit; an obstinate lover, who tries to carry her affections by storm, and will take no repulse or denial. Fenwick and Orme are much more amiable, but neither has been able to make any impression on Harriet's heart. Both are kept much in the background of the story, and, indeed, all we know of Orme is that he continues sighing in a state of bashful silliness at his country seat; and when Miss Byron passes in her carriage by the gates of his park, "there was he on the very ridge of the highway. I saw him not till it was near him. He bowed to the very ground with such an air of disconsolateness! Poor Mr. Orme!" Greville and

Fenwick, however, although rivals for her hand, have entered into an armed neutrality together, and each is to try to win the prize without quarrelling with the other. Miss Byron goes up to town to visit her cousins, Mr. and Mrs. Reeves, and is attended by her two lovers Greville and Fenwick to the first "baiting," when they had "a genteel dinner" ready provided for them, and then took leave. "Fenwick, you dog, said Mr. Greville," it is Miss Byron who writes, "we *must* return. Miss Byron looks grave . . . . And in the most respectful manner they both took leave of me, insisting, however, on my hand that I would wish them well."

No sooner has Miss Byron arrived in London than she is instantly beset by lovers; one of them is Mr. Fowler, the nephew of a Welsh knight, Sir Rowland Meredith, an old bachelor, with "a gold button and button-hole coat, and full buckle and wig," whose great object in life is to see his nephew well married. Mr. Fowler falls in love with Harriet at first sight, when he meets her at a dinner-table, and comes the next day to beseech Mr. Reeves "to give him his interest" with her "without asking any questions about her fortune." He is followed next morning by Sir Rowland, who breakfasts with the family, and besides Miss Byron and her uncle and aunt, three young ladies are present.

But he proceeds at once to business, and pleads the cause of his nephew with high-flown compliments to the charmer—and talking nonsense like a silly old fool—which character he sustains throughout, although I believe Richardson intends the reader to regard him as a kind-hearted generous gentleman, whose whole soul is wrapped up in the happiness of his nephew and who acts as proxy in the love-making. He tries hard to soften Harriet's heart, but in vain.

"He met me, and taking my not-withdrawn hand and peering in my face, 'Mercy,' said he, 'the same kind aspect! the same sweet and obliging countenance! How can this be? But you *must* be gracious! You *will!* Say you will.'

"'You must not urge me, Sir Rowland. You will give me pain if you lay me under the necessity to repeat——'

"'Repeat what? Don't say a refusal. Dear madam, don't say a refusal! Will you not save a life? Why, madam, my poor boy is absolutely and *bonâ fide* broken-hearted. I would have had him come with me; but no, he could not bear to leave the beloved of his soul!

Why, there's an instance of love now! Not for all his hopes, not for his life's sake, could he bear to tease you! None of your fluttering Jack-a-dandies, now, would have said this! and let not such succeed where modest merit fails! Mercy! you are struck with my plea! Don't, don't, God bless you now, don't harden your heart on my observation. . . . . Come, come, be gracious! be merciful. Dear lady, be as good as you look to be. One word of comfort for my poor boy; I could kneel to you for one word of comfort—nay, I *will* kneel;' —taking hold of my other hand as he still held one; and down on his knees dropped the honest knight."

The matter is at last compromised by an agreement that Miss Byron is to call the old gentleman Father, and his nephew Brother.

Another advance of a very different stamp is 'Sir Hargrave Pollexfen,' a young baronet, " handsome and genteel, pretty tall, about twenty-eight or thirty." He is a libertine, and a scoundrel, and falls desperately in love with Harriet Byron, whom he persecutes with offers of marriage, which she steadily rejects.

The following is a specimen of the mode in which he makes love :—

" I made an effort to go. He caught my

hand and arose, then kissed it and held it between both his.

"'For God's sake, madam——'

"'*Pray*, Sir Hargrave——'

"'Your objections? I insist upon knowing your objections. My *person*, madam—forgive me, I am not used to boast — my *person*, madam——'

"'*Pray*, Sir Hargrave——'

"'—Is not contemptible. My *fortune*——'

"'God bless you, sir! with your fortune.'

"'—Is not inconsiderable. My *morals*——'

"'Pray, Sir Hargrave! why this enumeration to me?'

"'—Are as unexceptionable as those of most young men of fashion in the present age.'

"'I am sorry if this be true,' thought I to myself. 'You have reason, I hope, sir, to be glad of that.'

"'My *descent*——'

"'Is honourable, sir, no doubt.'

"'My *temper* is not bad. I am thought to be a man of vivacity and cheerfulness. I have *courage*, madam—and this should have been seen, had I found reason to dread a competitor in your favour.'"

At last Sir Hargrave, aided by the treachery of her man-servant, carries Miss Byron off in her sedan chair from a masquerade, to a house in Lisson Green (now Lisson Grove), where he tries to force her into a marriage. It may interest female readers to know how she was dressed for the ball at which this happened. A white Paris net sort of cap, glittering with spangles, and encircled by artificial flowers, "with a little white feather perking from the left ear," a Venetian mask, tucker and ruffles, and blond lace, a waistcoat of blue satin, trimmed with silver point d'Espagne, the skirts edged with silver fringe, so as to sit close to the waist by double clasps, all set off with bugles and spangles, "which made a mighty glitter," a petticoat of blue satin, trimmed and fringed as the waistcoat.

The house in Lisson Green, to which Miss Byron is taken, is kept by a widow with two daughters, who has agreed to assist Sir Hargrave in his project of marrying her, but nothing more. She tells our heroine, " These young women *are* my daughters. They are sober and modest women. No ruin is intended you. One of the richest and noblest men in England is your admirer; he dies for you; he assures me that he intends honourable marriage to you. You are not engaged, he says, and you must and you shall be his. You may save murder, madam, if you consent. He resolves to be the death of any lover whom you may encourage."

A clergyman now appears upon the scene, a description of whose figure and appearance I have already quoted.*

"'*Dearly beloved,*' began to read the snuffling monster. 'Read no more!' said I, and in my frenzy dashed the book out of the minister's hand, if a minister he was. . . . . '*Dearly beloved,*' again snuffled the wretch. O! my Lucy, I shall never love these words. Sir Hargrave still detained my struggling hand. I stamped and threw myself to the length of my arm as he held my hand. '*No dearly beloveds,*' said I. I was just beside myself. What to say, what to do, I knew not."

The whole scene is powerfully drawn, and is one of Richardson's best. Miss Byron's passionate resistance succeeds in stopping the performance of the ceremony, and Sir Hargrave, unable to accomplish his purpose of a forced marriage at Lisson Green, resolves to carry her to a country-house he has near Windsor, and compels her, still in her masquerade dress, to accompany him, attended by his servants on horseback, in a chariot and six,

* *Ante*, p. 127.

with a handkerchief tied over her face, and
muffled up in a scarlet cloak.   But beyond
Hounslow, they are met by another coach and
six, and Miss Byron's cries for help bring to
her rescue Sir Charles Grandison, who happens
to be travelling to town.   A scuffle takes
place, and Sir Hargrave Pollexfen, who pretends that he is conveying a fugitive wife,
who was going to elope from him at a "damned
masquerade," is flung under the wheels in
a dilapidated state, while Sir Charles places
the lady in his own carriage, and takes her
to the house of his brother-in-law the Earl
of L.

He has two sisters, one married, Lady
L., and the other unmarried, Miss Charlotte Grandison.   She is meant by Richardson
to be witty or "whimsical," as the word was
then used, and sprightly, but her wit and
sprightliness sound strangely in the ears of the
present generation.   Her favourite expressions
are " deuced," " deuce take it," and " what
a deuce," and when she does marry at last,
she treats her husband with a petulance and
insult for which, if he had boxed her ears,
instead of humouring her, one would have been
inclined to excuse him.

Harriet Byron falls in love with Sir Charles

Grandison, and Sir Charles falls in love with her—or rather *would* fall in love and declare himself, but for an entanglement, owing to which he is not altogether a free man. He has a mystery which his sisters have been unable to unravel, for it is connected with his absence abroad during his father's life. His father, Sir Thomas Grandison, was a profligate spend-thrift, who, after the death of his wife, seduced the governess of his daughter, a Mrs. Oldham, and by her he had two children. He kept her at his country-house, where his daughter re-sided, and had another mistress in town, who died of the small-pox, caught at the opera, where she was taken ill "on seeing a lady of her acquaintance there, whose face bore too strongly the marks of the distemper." Sir Thomas behaved like a brute to his two daughters, and forbade the eldest to receive the addresses of Lord L. One of the most painful scenes in the story is that in which he summons them both into the dining-room, and commands Caroline to give up her lover. He thus addresses her—"And what cries the girl for? Why, Caroline, you *shall* have a husband, I tell you. I will hasten with you to the London market. Will you be offered at Ranelagh market first? the concert or break-

fasting? or will I show you at the opera or
at the play? Ha, ha, hah! Hold up your
head, my amorous girl! You shall stick some
of your mother's jewels in your hair and in your
bosom, to draw the eyes of fellows. You must
strike at once, while your face is new, or you
will be mingled with the herd of women who
prostitute their faces at every polite place.
Look at me, Caroline."

And yet Sir Charles Grandison, who knows
his father's cruelty and worthless character,
addresses him from abroad as " Dear and ever
honoured Sir! " and after his death always
speaks of him in terms of affection and respect.

Sir Thomas afterwards entered into a bargain
with her relations for the ruin of a young Irish
girl—the details of which nefarious scheme are
minutely given by Miss Byron in her letters to
her cousin, Lucy Selby—when he was sud
denly cut off by a fever. His son then returned to England, "the graceful youth of
seventeen, with fine curling auburn locks
waving upon his shoulders; delicate in complexion; intelligence sparkling in fine free
eyes, and good humour sweetening his lively
features." When he first met his sisters, "'O
my brother,' said Caroline, with open arms,
but shrinking from his embrace, '*may* I say

my brother ?' and was just fainting. He
clasped her in his arms to support her."

He astonished his sisters, as he well might,
by his courteous politeness to his father's late
mistress, Mrs. Oldham, in his own house, and
the account given to Miss Byron of his generosity and kindness on the occasion, so overpowers her that she exclaims to her correspondent—

"Lord bless me, my Lucy! what shall I do
about this man? . . . . Here (would you believe it?) I laid down my pen, pondered and
wept for *joy*; I think it *was* for joy, that there
is such a young man in the world; for what
else could it be? And now, with a watery eye,
twinkle, twinkle, do I resume it." And again—

"O my Aunt! be so good as to let the servants prepare my apartments at Selby House.
There is no living within the blazing glory of
this man."

Of course such a phenomenon as Sir Charles
is adored by the sex. Lady Ann S., the only
daughter of an Earl with "a vast fortune," is
in love with him. Miss Jervis, a young girl
and sort of ward of his, not sixteen years old,
is unconsciously in love with him, and the Lady
Olivia, an Italian whom he has met abroad, is
so madly in love that she follows him to Eng-

land, and threatens his life if he will not marry
her! But he has another and more serious
affair. While in Italy he had saved the life of
one of the sons of the Marchese della Porretta,
when he was attacked by assassins, and this led
to an intimacy with the family. The only
daughter was the Lady Clementina, and she
and Sir Charles Grandison fell in love with
each other. But she was a Roman Catholic
and he was a Protestant, and although passionately devoted to him, she dared not peril
the salvation of her soul by union with a
heretic. I think that the Lady Clementina is
the best drawn character in Richardson's novels,
but the interest of her story is marred and
almost destroyed by the astounding length at
which it is drawn out. Sir Charles tries to
overcome her scruples, and offers her full
liberty to adhere to her own faith, giving a promise, on which she knows that she can rely, that
if she becomes his wife he will make no attempt
to induce her to change her religion; but she
feels that she loves him too well not to fear
that the force of his silent example may be
strong enough to win her over to his creed.
The conflict between her passion for Sir
Charles and what she believed to be her duty
to her God, overthrows her reason, and I know

no author who has more finely touched what I may call the pathos of madness, than Richardson has in the scenes where he describes the struggles of her confused and bewildered intellect.

While she is in this state Sir Charles is summoned home by the news of his father's death, and afterwards meets Miss Byron and falls in love with her, as I have mentioned. But he is the soul of honour, and besides, still retains much of his old feeling for Lady Clementina. In fact, he is in a most perplexing dilemma, being in love with both ladies at once; and conceiving that, he is in duty bound to give the Italian another chance, provided that she recovers her intellect. He therefore leaves Miss Byron in England and goes to Italy to join the Porretta family. Before, however, he goes away, Sir Hargrave Pollexfen sends him a challenge; but instead of accepting it, he invites himself to breakfast with the crest-fallen baronet, at his house in Cavendish Square; and we have a long and prosy account of the conversation at the interview as taken down by a short-hand writer, who was summoned and hid in a closet for the purpose. Lady Clementina has in the meantime been restored to her senses, and her love for Sir Charles burns as strongly as ever.

But the old obstacle remains. She dares not bring herself to marry a Protestant, notwithstanding that her parents and brothers consent, and she tries in vain to persuade Sir Charles to become a Catholic. She, therefore, has but one wish left, and that is to be allowed to enter a convent and take the veil. This, however, is strongly opposed by her relatives, who are bent upon her marrying somebody, and an Italian nobleman is desperately in love with her. Whole chapters of the novel are occupied with the argument on both sides, in which considerable skill and a good deal of theological knowledge are displayed, at the expense, however, of awful prolixity.

As the lady is inflexible in her determination not to marry a heretic, and Sir Charles will not change his religion, she repeatedly urges him to find an English wife, little thinking at the moment that he was already more than half in love with another. In his heart of hearts, therefore, he is not sorry to be released, and he leaves Italy ; and on his arrival in England in true Grandisonian manner, solicits the hand of Harriet Byron. It may amuse the reader to see the mode in which this mirror of chivalry makes love. He pays the most extravagant compliments.

" ' There seems,' said he, ' to be a mixture of generous concern and kind curiosity in one of the loveliest and most intelligent faces in the world.' "

" ' Thus,' resumed he, snatching my hand and ardently pressing it with his lips, ' do I honour to myself for the honour done me. How poor is man, that he cannot express his gratitude to the object of his vows for obligations confessed, but by owing to her new obligations ! ' " What a formal pedant of a lover !

" In a soothing, tender and respectful manner he put his arm round me, and taking my own handkerchief, unresisted, wiped away the tears as they fell on my cheek. ' Sweet humanity ! charming sensibility ! Check not the kindly gush. Dew-drops of Heaven ! (wiping away my tears, and kissing the handkerchief), dew-drops of Heaven, from a mind like that Heaven, mild and gracious.'

" He kissed my hand with fervour ; dropped down on one knee ; again kissed it. ' You have laid me, madam, under everlasting obligations ; and will you permit me before I rise, loveliest of women, will you permit me to beg an early day ? ' "

" He clasped me in his arms with an ardour

that displeased me not, on reflection; but at the time startled me. He then thanked me again on one knee. I held out the hand he had not in his, with intent to raise him; for I could not speak. He received it as a token of favour; kissed it with ardour; arose, *again* pressed my cheek with his lips. I was too much surprised to repulse him with anger; but was he not too free? Am I a prude, my dear?"

Yes! Miss Byron, I am afraid you are a prude, to feel such surprise and doubt at an innocent kiss after a formal engagement.

After Sir Charles has prevailed over the coy reluctance of Miss Byron to "name the day," about which she makes a most absurd difficulty, he thus writes to her :—

"Receive, dearest, loveliest of women, the thanks of a most grateful heart, for your invaluable favour *of* Wednesday last. Does my *Harriet* (already, methinks, I have sunk the name of Byron into that of Grandison), do Mrs. Shirley, Mrs. Selby, think that I have treated one of the most delicate of female minds indelicately in the *wish* (not the *presumption*) I have presumed to signify to the beloved of my heart, that within three days, after my *permitted* return to Northamptonshire, I may be allowed to receive at the altar the greatest bless-

ing of my life ? I would not be thought un-
generous. I signified my wishes ; but I told
you in the same letter that your *cheerful* compliance was to me the great desirable . . . If
I have not your commands to the contrary,
Tuesday morning, then, if not Monday night,
shall present to you the most ardent and sincere of men, pouring out in your hand his
grateful vows for the invaluable favour of Wednesday's date, which I considered in the sacred
light of a plighted love, and, as such, I have
given it a place near my heart. . . . . . Conclude me, dearest madam, your most grateful,
obliged and ever affectionate

"CHARLES GRANDISON."

It seems to have been the custom for the
bridegroom, after the ceremony of marriage had
been performed, to wait upon the bride and the
guests at table ; and Sir Charles, on the day of
his wedding, takes a napkin from the butler, and
"was the modestest servitor that ever waited at
table while his napkin was under his arm ; but
he laid it down while he addressed the company, finding something to say to each, in his
pithy, agreeable manner, as he went round the
table."

The banquet was followed by a dance, as

usual, and the ceremony of throwing the stocking was on this occasion dispensed with. " Lord L. undertook to make the gentlemen give up form ; which, he said, they would the more easily do, as they were set into dancing." *

The story ought to have ended here, but it is spun out to a considerable length. Lady Clementina, distracted between love and religion, quits Italy clandestinely, and, attended only by a page, comes to England and hides herself in London. At last Sir Charles Grandison finds her out, and her parents follow her. They all go down to Grandison Hall, where she is followed by the Count Belvedere, the Italian nobleman who is in love with her and wishes to make her his wife. There infinite palaver takes place after formal " articles of accommodation " have been drawn up and

---

* It was while Richardson was writing one of the letters which describes the wedding that the incident occurred mentioned in his 'Correspondence.' He was seated in his room in Salisbury Square, where he carried on his printing business, when he was disturbed by a loud cry. "Oh ! my nerves, my nerves !" he exclaimed, and rang the bell. It turned out that the 'prentices were " cobbing" wall-eyed Tom, for watering a can of porter after drinking some of it himself, for which he had been sent to the Barley Mow. It was contrary to rules to have beer in the office before noon, but the pressmen pleaded that they had been working all night upon 'Moore's Almanac,' of which the Treasurer wanted "ten thousand perfect, a week before publishing day," and they required some refreshment.

signed, whereby the Lady Clementina engages to give up all thoughts of entering a convent; and her parents and family promise that they will "never with earnestness endeavour to persuade, much less compel, her to marry any man whatever." The last interview between the parties, before Lady Clementina leaves Grandison Hall to return with her parents to Italy, takes place in the garden—present, Sir Charles, Lady Grandison, and the Lady Clementina.

"When we saw Sir Charles enter the garden we stood still, arm in arm, expecting and inviting his approach. 'Sweet sisters! lovely friends!' said he, when he came up to us, taking a hand of each and joining them, bowing on both; '*let* me mark this blessed spot with my eye,' looking round him, then on me. 'A tear on my Harriet's cheek!' He dried it off with his own handkerchief. 'Friendship, dearest creatures, will make at pleasure a safe bridge over the narrow seas. . . . Kindred souls are always near.' . . . 'Promise me again,' said the noble lady. 'I, too, have marked the spot with my eye' (standing still, as Sir Charles had done, looking round her). 'The orangery on the right hand; that distant clump of oaklings on the left; the villa, the rivulet before us; the cascade in view; that obelisk behind us. Be *this* the spot to be recollected as witness to the promise (that the Grandisons will visit her in Italy) when we are far, far distant from each other.'

"We both repeated the promise; and Sir Charles said (and he is drawing a plan accordingly) that a little temple should be erected on that little spot, to be consecrated to our friendship; and since she had so happily marked it, to be called after her name."

There only remains to add that Sir Hargrave Pollexfen dies a penitent sinner, and leaves by his will a very large legacy to Lady Grandison, and another to Sir Charles, whom he had made his sole executor.

Miss Grandison, Sir Charles's sister, is intended to be sprightly and witty; but Richardson had no conception of either sprightliness or wit; and as to humour, he had not a particle of it in his composition. I will give one or two specimens of her talk.

"*Harriet.*—My lord is nothing to me. I *have* answered. I have given my negative.

"*Miss Grandison.*—The deuce you have! Why the man has a good 12,000*l.* a-year.

"*Harriet.*—I don't care.

"*Miss G.*—What a deuce ails the girl?

" Then humorously telling on her fingers— 'Orme, one; Fenwick, two; Greville, three; Fowler, four :—I want another finger ; but I'll take in my thumb—Sir Hargrave, five ; and now' (putting the forefinger of one hand on the thumb of the other), ' Lord D., six! And none of them the man !—Depend upon it, girl, pride will have a fall.' "

Two days after marriage Charlotte quarrels with her husband, and concludes a note to Miss Byron thus : " Hang me, if I sign by any other name while this man is in his fits than that of CHARLOTTE GRANDISON." Certainly no other husband would have put up with such disgusting petulance as she showed, which Richardson designed as a proof of her " humorous " character. Her husband makes her a present of some old china, " And when he had done," says his wife, " taking the *liberty* as he phrased it, half fearful, half resolute, to salute his bride for his reward, and then pacing backwards several steps with such a strut and crow—I see him yet—indulge me, Harriet ! I burst into a hearty laugh ; I could not help it ; and he reddening looked round himself and round himself to see if anything was amiss on his part. ' The *man*, the *man*, honest friend,' I could have said, but had too much reverence for my husband, 'is the oddity! nothing amiss in the garb.'" And when to play him a trick, or as she says, to give him a hint, she pins her apron to his coat and the apron is torn, she calls out, "You are always squatting upon one's clothes in defiance of hoop or distance."

We must not however suppose that the style of conversation which Richardson puts into the mouths of his characters in 'Sir Charles Grandison,' represents the style prevalent in his time amongst the higher classes of society. Of this he knew personally little or nothing, and he must have consequently evolved it, in the same way that the German writer is said to have evolved his description of a camel, "from his own consciousness."* Cooped up in a small room in Salisbury Court during the day, and spending his evenings and holidays at Parson's Green, he was not likely to have many opportunities of seeing fashionable life, and he was much more at home in writing the letters of a servant girl like Pamela, or of a young lady of the middle class like Clarissa

---

* "I am apt to conceive, that one reason why many English writers have totally failed in describing the manners of upper life, may possibly be that in reality they know nothing of it. . . . . A true knowledge of the world is gained only by conversation, and the manners of every rank must be seen in order to be known."—Fielding in 'Tom Jones,' book xiv. chap. i.

Harlowe, than in imitating the language and describing the manners of Charlotte Grandison and her sister, Lady L——.

The last specimen I will give of Richardson's style is the scene in which Miss Byron relates her meeting with her despairing lover, Mr. Orme, on her way home from town. "Mr. Orme, good Mr. Orme, when we came near his park, was on the highway side. Perhaps near the very spot where he stood to see me pass to London so many weeks ago. Poor man! when I first saw him he looked with so disconsolate an air and so fixed, that I compassionately said to myself, 'Surely the worthy man has not been there ever since!'

"I twitched the string just in time: the coach stopped. 'Mr. Orme,' I said, 'how do you? Well, I hope? How does Miss Orme?'

"I laid my hand on the coach-door. He snatched it. It was not an unwilling hand. He pressed it with his lips. 'God be praised,' said he (with a countenance, O! how altered for the better!) 'for permitting me once more to behold that face—that *angelic* face!' he said.

"'God bless you! Mr. Orme,' said I, 'I am glad to see you. Adieu.'"

Richardson intended this as serious sentiment; but the scene is, I think, rather comic
than serious. The poor rejected lover stands,
and may have stood for weeks, behind his
park palings watching for the carriage, and
then when it comes up thanks Heaven for
allowing him to see the angelic creature whom
he knows it is in vain to adore.

I have heard Sir Charles Grandison called
a "solemn fop;" but, I think, this is to mistake his real character. Solemn enough he is
beyond all doubt, but there is nothing foppish
in his manner or talk. It is true that one feels
often inclined to kick him; but this is because
one feels bored by his overstrained courtesy
and elaborate politeness.* He is too much
of a paragon—too much praised by everybody.
We sympathize with the man who was tired
of always hearing Aristides called the Just;
and we sympathize with Harriet Byron, who
when she was in love with Sir Charles was half
inclined to wish that he were not such an angel.
"A most intolerable superiority! I wish he
could do something wrong; something cruel;

---

* In his 'Sketches by Boz,' Dickens describes Mr. Watkins
Tottle as having " a clean-cravatish formality of manner, and a
kitchen-pokerness of carriage, which Sir Charles Grandison himself might have envied."

if he would but bear malice, would but stiffen his air by resentment, it would be something." He is worshipped by his two sisters, with an idolatry which is almost childish, and we are cloyed by the treacle of their panegyrics and compliments.

"O my brother! O my brother! said both ladies at one time—half in admiration, though half concerned, at a goodness so eclipsing."

"You, my brother, who in my eye are the first of men, must not let me have cause to dread that your Caroline is sunk in yours."

M. Taine says, and I agree with him, "Nothing is so insipid as an instructive hero. This one is as correct as an automaton; he passes his life in weighing his duties and making salutations . . . . He is great, he is generous, he is delicate, he is pious, he is irreproachable, he has never done a dirty action nor made a false step. His conscience and his periwig are intact. Amen. We must canonise him, and stuff him with straw."*

---

* 'Histoire de la Littérature Anglaise,' vol. iii. 299-302. I have before me a curious pamphlet, published in 1754, and styled 'A candid examination of the History of Sir Charles Grandison in a Letter to a Lady of Distinction.' The writer complains of the length of the novel and its enhanced price, "as if Mr. R——n began to consider himself as a bookseller as well as an author." The criticism of the novel is not worth much, and need not be

The abduction of Harriet Byron by Sir Hargrave Pollexfen is a fiction, but in those times such an adventure might easily have happened. At an earlier period in France, it did befal a once celebrated lady, Madame de Miramion, who for her piety was entitled by Madame de Sévigné " one of the mothers of the church," and whose benevolence and charity made the Duc de St. Simon say that " her death was considered a public loss." *

The scene, also, of the attempt to force Miss Byron into a marriage at Lisson Green very much resembles what actually occurred in Ireland in the last century, when a Miss M'Dermott was carried off by Mr. Flinn, who tried to compel her to marry him in a wayside cabin. The story is told by Mrs. Delany, as related to her by Miss M'Dermott herself.† " Finding she was resolute in not complying with his

quoted ; but such a passage as the following would be thought strange in a letter addressed now-a-days to a " Lady of Distinction." " I think Mr. R——n makes a great deal too much of the terrible apprehensions of matrimony, and of Miss Byron's almost fainting, dying : but as I hear, your ladyship felt something of these palpitations on the approach of the awful day, the solemn rite, the fearful night, I must not take the liberty to be so full as I should be on this occasion."

* The story is told in the ' Life of Madame de Miramion,' by M. Bonneau, edited by Lady Herbert.

† ' Mrs. Delany's Autobiography,' vol. iii. p. 348.

request, but vehemently asserted that she would rather die than be united to such a monster, on their laying hold of her to put the ring on her finger, she threw it off whilst the priest was muttering over the marriage ceremony, and springing from them, snatched up a mug of milk which she had accidentally laid her eyes on, standing by the fire, and threw it full in the priest's face." Happily the lady was rescued from the ruffians after having been badly wounded, and plunged in a bog up to her shoulders in mud.

It is very curious and amusing to read ' Richardson's Correspondence,' in six volumes, and see the old gentleman, in his house at North End, Hammersmith, or Parson's Green, between Chelsea and Fulham, writing to and receiving letters from ladies—"my ladies," as he calls them, or " dear girls "—who smother him with compliments, and interest themselves about the fate of his heroes and heroines, Sir Charles Grandison, Harriet Byron, and Clarissa Harlowe, as if they were friends and acquaintances. But amongst his correspondents is Colley Cibber, who makes himself a conspicuous ass. He writes to Richardson, in 1748, and prays that the Lord grant he may be disappointed in his apprehension of meeting in the course of

the story of ' Clarissa,' something to displease
him. "O Lord, Lord! can there be anything
yet to come that will trouble this smooth stream
of pleasure I am bathing in? But the book
again lies open before me? I have just finished
this letter of Miss Howe's (Clarissa's correspondent); with that charming chicken's neck
at the end of it. What a mixture of lively
humour, good sense, and wanton wilfulness
does she conclude it with! How will you be
able to support this spirit?" Again, "Ah! ah!
you may laugh if you please; but how will you
be able to look me in the face if the lady (Clarissa) should ever be able to show *hers* again?
What piteous, d——d disgraceful pickle have
you placed her in? For God's sake send me
the sequel, or—I don't know what to say! . . .
My girls are all on fire and fright to know what
can possibly have become of her. Take care.
If you have betrayed her into any shocking
company, you will be as accountable for it as if
you were yourself the monster that took delight
in her calamity." In 1750, he writes, with disgusting levity, " Though Death has been cool-
ing his heels at my door these three weeks, I
have not had time to see him. . . . . If you
have a mind to make one among us, I will
order Death to come another day. To be

serious, I long to see you, and hope you will take the first opportunity." In 1753, "The delicious meal I made of Miss Byron on Sunday last, has given me an appetite for another slice of her, off from the spit, before she is served up for the public table. If about five o'clock to-morrow afternoon will not be inconvenient, Mrs. Brown and I will come and piddle upon a bit more of her." He raved when he heard that Clarissa was destined to have an unhappy end, and said, " God d——n him, if she should ! "

Dr. Young, the author of the ' Night Thoughts,' approved of the portrait of the scoundrel libertine Lovelace, on account of its fidelity, but we should hardly expect the following criticism from a divine. " Be not concerned about Lovelace ! 'tis the likeness, not the morality of a character we call for. A sign-post angel can by no means come into competition with the devils of Michael Angelo." And again, " Believe me, Christians of taste will applaud your plan, and they who themselves would act Lovelace's part, will find the greatest fault with it." But Richardson himself seems to have had a more just idea of the character he was drawing. He answers one of Dr. Young's letters with a promise to send two more of his volumes, and adds, " Miss Lee may venture (if you and she have patience) to read these two to you. But Lovelace afterwards is so vile a fellow, that if I publish any more (so much have some hyper-critics put me out of conceit with my work) I doubt whether she, of whose delicacy I have the highest opinion, can see it as from you or me." Dr. Young assured him, after the appearance of 'Sir Charles Grandison,' that he looked upon him " as an instrument of Providence." In one of the letters to Richardson, the writer, after mentioning that a lady of very high rank (but bad character) had declared that Lovelace was a charming young fellow, and owned that she liked him excessively, says that the anecdote is an instance of what " you have reason to say you too often meet with, namely, the fondness most women have for the character of Lovelace."

As to the ladies, they could hardly find words strong enough to express their admiration of the novels. Miss Fielding, in 1749, wrote of ' Clarissa ' to the author, " When I read of her I am all sensation ; my heart glows. I am overwhelmed, my only vent is tears, and unless tears could mark my thoughts as legibly as ink, I cannot speak half I feel." Miss Collier said that her " good old folks " believed

both 'Clarissa' and 'Sir Charles' to be real
stories, and no work of imagination, and she
did not care to undeceive them. Poor Mrs.
Pilkington, who was reduced so low as to be
obliged to issue the following advertisement
—"At the sign of the Dove in Great White
Lion Street, near the Seven Dials, letters are
written on any subject (except the law) by
Letitia Pilkington, price one shilling,"—prayed
Richardson to save Clarissa from dishonour :
" Spare her virgin purity, dear sir, spare it !
Consider if this wounds both Mr. Cibber and
me (*who neither of us set up for immaculate
chastity*), what must it do with those who
possess that inestimable treasure ? "

In a letter written in 1750, Richardson says
that he had just had a breakfast visit at North
End, from two very worthy ladies recommended
by Mrs. Delany, who were both extremely
earnest with him to give them *a good man*, that
is, draw a good character, and he asks the
young lady who is his correspondent, " How
can we hope that ladies will not think a good
man a tame man ? "

Amongst the correspondents of Richardson
was Klopstock's first wife, who lived at Ham-
burg, and wrote very good English. She gives
an account of how she fell in love with the

poet on reading his ' Messiah,' before she ever saw him, how she afterwards married him, and how happy she was. Poor thing! her last letter expresses her joy in the prospect of becoming a mother, and then comes another from a stranger, dated a week later, telling him that Mrs. Klopstock had just died "in a very dreadful manner" in childbed.*

But all these ladies are eclipsed by Lady Bradshaigh, who, under the name of Belfour, carried on a long correspondence with Richardson, which began in the following manner. A lady calling herself Belfour, after reading the first four volumes of ' Clarissa,' which came out in parts, wrote to him, in 1748, telling him that a report prevailed that the history of Clarissa was to end in a most tragical manner, and expressing her abhorrence of such a catastrophe, she begged to be satisfied of the truth by a few lines inserted in the ' Whitehall Evening Post.' This led to the letters which passed between them, and very curious they are. I can only give a few extracts, which will be enough to show the earnestness of the lady in pleading for a happy conclusion to ' Clarissa.'

---

* When I was at Altona, I read on Klopstock's tomb, a copy of verses addressed by his second wife to the memory of the first.

" You must know (though I shall blush again) that if I was to die for it, I cannot help being fond of Lovelace. A sad dog! why would you make him so wicked and yet so agreeable ? . . . . If you disappoint me, attend to my curse :—May the hatred of all the young, beautiful, and virtuous, for ever be your portion! and may your eyes never behold anything but age and deformity ! May you meet with applause only from envious old maids, surly bachelors, and tyrannical parents! May you be doomed to the company of such, and after death may their ugly souls haunt you !

" Now make Lovelace and Clarissa unhappy if you dare."

" Do, dear sir (it is too shocking and barbarous a story for publication—I wish I could not think of it) blot out but one night, and the villanous laudanum, and all may be well again. . . . . I am as mad as the poor injured Clarissa, and am afraid I cannot help hating you, if you alter not your scheme."

" When alone, in agonies would I lay down the book, take it up again, walk about the room, let fall a flood of tears, wipe my eyes, read again, perhaps not three lines, throw away the book, crying out, Excuse me, good Mr. Richardson, I cannot go on ; it

is your fault, you have done more than I can
bear."

"A lady was reading to two or three others
the seventh volume of 'Clarissa,' whilst her
maid curled her hair, and the poor girl let fall
such a shower of tears upon her lady's head
that she was forced to send her out of the room
to compose herself, asking her what she cried
for.   She said, to see such goodness and innocence in distress ; and a lady followed her out
of the room, and gave her a crown for that
answer."

These passages will give some idea of the
extraordinary interest which Richardson's novels
excited in the hearts of the fair sex, and the
way in which they made the woes of Clarissa
their own.

Lady Bradshaigh kept up for a long time her
incognita of Belfour, and many were the contrivances which she and Richardson adopted,
she to see him without being known, and he to
discover his admirer.   He walked in the Park,
"up the Mall and down the Mall," having sent
her a description of himself which I will quote
by-and-by, and hoping that she would reveal
herself, as she said that she would look for him
in the Park.   She once ventured to go to
Salisbury Court, where he carried on his busi-

ness of a printer, and got as far as his door, when her courage failed her. At last she wrote in her real name, and told him that she had walked for an hour in the Park, in the vain hope of seeing him, and would try her fortune again next Saturday. Then comes a letter telling him that her curiosity was satisfied as to a distant view. " I passed you four times last Saturday in the Park ; knew you by your own description at least three hundred yards off; walking in the Park between the trees and the Mall. . . . . You looked at me every time we passed, but I put on so unconcerned a countenance, that I am almost sure I deceived you." She feared that she would find something in his person stern and awful, but it turned out "quite the contrary." The comical pair, however, at last put an end to this game of hide and seek, and Lady Bradshaigh made the personal acquaintance of the author who had so bewitched her.

Let us now see what manner of man in the flesh this petted and spoiled favourite of the ladies was. He has twice given us his own portrait, and described himself to the life. First as he walks on the pantiles at Tunbridge Wells. " A sly sinner, creeping along the very edges of the walks, getting behind benches ; one hand in his bosom, the other held up to his chin, as if to keep it in its place; afraid of being seen as a thief of detection . . . . stealing in and out of the bookseller's shop, as if he had one of their glass-cases under his coat. Come and see this odd figure!" *

And at a later period in St. James's Park— "Short, rather plump than emaciated, notwithstanding his complaints; about five feet five inches; fair wig, lightish cloth coat, all black besides; one hand generally in his bosom, the other a cane in it, which he leans upon under the skirts of his coat usually . . . . of a light brown complexion, teeth not yet failing him, smoothish face and ruddy cheeked; at some times looking to be almost sixty-five, at other times much younger, a regular even pace, stealing away ground rather than seeming to rid it; a grey eye too often overclouded by mistiness from the head; by chance lively—very lively it will be if he have hopes of seeing a lady whom he loves and honours; his eye always on the ladies; if they have very large hoops he looks down and supercilious, and as if he would be thought wise, but perhaps the sillier for that."† Yes, we see the sentimental little prig

* 'Correspondence of Richardson,' vol. ii. p. 206.
† Ibid. vol. iv. p. 290.

before us to the life, with his head turned by all the compliments paid to him by the ladies, and thinking that every woman whom he meets is conscious that she looks upon the author of 'Clarissa Harlowe' and 'Sir Charles Grandison.'

CHAPTER VIII.

FIELDING.—'TOM JONES,' A FAVOURITE OF THE LADIES.—
'JOSEPH ANDREWS.'—'AMELIA.'

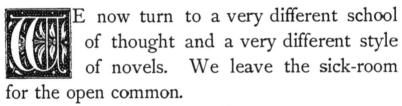E now turn to a very different school of thought and a very different style of novels. We leave the sick-room for the open common.

A lady once asked me why she might not read 'Tom Jones.' It seemed hard, she thought, that so famous a work which was praised by everybody—that is, by every *man* who had read it—should remain a sealed book to her; and she inquired whether I could not give her an idea of its merits and an inkling of the story without sinning against decorum. The question was a delicate one, and I cannot pretend that I answered it satisfactorily. The truth is, that it would be impossible to give an analysis of the novel, or even describe the plot except in the most meagre terms, without offending against the respect due to female delicacy now. And such a description as could be given *salvo*

pudore would be worthless. It would be like producing a bony skeleton as the representative of the human form. What idea would a listener have of the mirth and fun and fulness of life in ' Tom Jones,' if he were merely told that it is the story of a young man, a foundling, brought up as a dependent in a gentleman's family, who falls in love with Sophia, the daughter of Squire Western, and with whom Miss Western falls in love, running after him from place to place, accompanied only by her maid ; who is exposed to the mean hatred of a wretch called Blifil, the nephew of an excellent gentleman named Allworthy, who befriends Tom until his patience is exhausted by the tales he hears of his unworthy conduct; and who, after many vicissitudes of fortune and many diverting but wicked scrapes, is discovered at last to be the natural son of Mr. Allworthy's maiden sister ; and Blifil's villany being now exposed and discomfited, is made Mr. Allworthy's heir, and marries the fair Sophia ? And yet this is the main plot of the story, or at all events it was all I could tell my inquirer. But her grandmother, no doubt, had read ' Tom Jones,' and was as modest and virtuous a lady as herself.*

* Mrs. Delany says in one of her letters (1749) : " Unluckily for ' Gaudentio'" a book attributed to Bishop Berkeley, " I had

Lady Bradshaigh, writing to Richardson in 1749, says, " As to ' Tom Jones,' I am fatigued with the name, having lately fallen into the company of several young ladies who had each a ' Tom Jones ' in some part of the world, for so they called their favourites ; and ladies, you know, are ever talking of their favourites. Last post I received a letter from a lady who laments the loss of her ' Tom Jones ;' and from another who was happy in the company of her ' Tom Jones.' " And again, " The girls are certainly fond of ' Tom Jones,' as I told you before ; and they do not scruple declaring it in the presence of your *incognita.*"

We cannot but regret that the coarseness of the age and his own natural instincts led Fielding to choose for the hero of his novel a young libertine, whose adventures are only fit for the ale-house or a worse place ; while he has lavished upon it a skill of construction and artistic development of plot such as have never been surpassed. In these respects it well deserves the title of a prose epic. Coleridge says, " Upon my word, I think the ' Œdipus

just been reading ' Clarissa,' and it must have been an extraordinary book that would have been relished after that ! ' Tom Jones ' in his married state, is a *poor thing*, and not written by Fielding."

Tyrannus,' ' The Alchymist,' and ' Tom Jones '
the three most perfect plots ever planned." *
But the coarseness and licentiousness in which
it abounds admit of no defence, however much
some writers may say the contrary.

> If lowsie is Lucy as some volke miscall it,
> Then Lucy is lowsie whatever befall it.

It is all very well for Charles Lamb to say
that the hearty laugh of ' Tom Jones ' " clears
the air ; " and no doubt it is refreshing as contrasted with the sentimentality of Richardson,
whose style was Fielding's special aversion ;
but we must remember that it is the horse-
laugh of a youth full of animal spirits and
rioting in the exuberance of health, who *sells*
himself to Lady Bellaston as her paramour,
while all the time he is described as being desperately in love with Sophia Western.

I know no writer more likely than Thackeray
to have given unqualified praise to ' Tom Jones,'
and certainly none more fitted to appreciate the
character ; for the robust nature of his intellect
made him by no means squeamish, and no
man was more disposed to look kindly upon
the frailties of others, whether heroes of fiction
or persons in real life. But what does he say

* ' Table Talk,' p. 332.

about Fielding's hero ?   I am glad to quote the passage, for it shows Thackeray's sound sense and right feeling.

" I can't say that I think Mr. Jones a virtuous character ; I can't say but that I think Fielding's evident liking and admiration for Mr. Jones shows that the great humourist's moral sense was blunted by his life, and that here, in ' Art and Ethics,' there is a great error.   If it is right to have a hero whom we may admire, let us at least take care that he is admirable ; if, as is the plan of some authors (a plan decidedly against their interests, be it said), it is propounded that there exists in life no such being, and therefore that in novels, the picture of life, there should appear no such character ;   then Mr. Thomas Jones becomes an admirable person, and we examine his defects and good qualities, as we do those of Parson Thwackum or Miss Seagrim. But a hero with a flawed reputation ; a hero spunging for a guinea ; a hero who can't pay his landlady and is obliged to let his honour out to hire, is absurd, and his claim to heroic rank untenable.   I protest against Mr. Thomas Jones holding such rank at all.   I protest against his being considered a more than ordinary young fellow, ruddy-cheeked, broad-shouldered, and fond of wine and pleasure.   He would not rob a church, but that is all; and a pretty long argument may be debated as to which of these old types—the spendthrift, the hypocrite, Jones and Blifit, Charles and Joseph Surface—is the worst member of society, and the most deserving of censure. . . . I am angry with Jones. Too much of the plum-cake and rewards of life fall to that boisterous, swaggering young scapegrace. Sophia actually surrenders without a proper sense of decorum, the fond, foolish, palpitating little creature."* Coleridge might have been expected to be at least equally sensitive to the tainted atmosphere of the work; but, strange to say, he is more than indulgent to it, and can discover no fault at all. He says, " I do not speak of young women; but a young man, whose heart or feelings can be injured, or even his passions excited by this novel, is already thoroughly corrupt. There is a cheerful, sunshiny, breezy spirit that prevails everywhere, strongly contrasted with the close, but day-dreamy continuity of Richardson."† Who that has read ' Tom Jones' can read this passage without amazement? If no young man's heart or feelings can be injured, or even his passions be excited, by the novel unless

* ' English Humourists,' pp. 276-7.
† ' Literary Remains,' ii. p. 374.

he is "already thoroughly corrupt," why in the name of common sense does Coleridge imply that young women can be injured by its perusal? What he says of 'Tom Jones' is undoubtedly true of Shakspeare; and therefore it is that we allow our wives and sisters and daughters to read him without fear or scruple. Coleridge adds that he "loathes the cant which can recommend 'Pamela' and 'Clarissa Harlowe' as strictly moral, while 'Tom Jones' is prohibited as loose." But this is really a false issue. It would indeed be grossly inconsistent to recommend 'Clarissa Harlowe' as moral and condemn 'Tom Jones' as loose; but of such inconsistency we are not likely to find examples —at all events not now; but it is not a logical consequence that because some men may mistake grey for white, they are therefore wrong when they call black by its real name. Coleridge further says that this novel is, and indeed pretends to be, no example of conduct. But this is a poor and weak defence. There is nothing to show that the author had any such idea; on the contrary, he does all in his power to make his readers admire his hero; and he therefore invests him with the qualities of courage, generosity and kindness.*

* "'Tom Jones' is Fielding himself, hardened in some places,

The real defence which Fielding himself makes for what he calls "the wit and humour" of his novel—and that it abounds in wit and humour no reader of it can deny, only it must be admitted to be of the broadest kind—is that he has "endeavoured to laugh mankind out of their favourite follies and vices." But I fear the attempt has been as little successful as that of trying to put burglary out of fashion by making it ridiculous. We laugh *with* the author, and not *at* the folly or the vice.

In his dedication of 'Tom Jones' to the Hon. George Lyttelton, Fielding says : " I hope any reader will be convinced at his very entrance on this work, that he will find in the whole course of it nothing prejudicial to the cause of religion and virtue ; *nothing inconsistent with the strictest rules of decency nor which can offend even the chastest eye in the perusal.*" The italics are my own, and the passage marked shows that Fielding believed, or pretended to believe, that the purest maiden might read his novel without offence. And this, with the scene of Partridge's trial for incontinency, the scene be-

softened in others. His Lady Bellaston is an infamous woman of his former acquaintance. His Sophia is again his first wife." Letter from Richardson to Mrs. Donnellan in his 'Correspondence,' vol. iv. p. 60. But we must remember that Richardson hated Fielding.

tween Philosopher Square and Molly Seagrim, the scenes between Tom Jones and Mrs. Waters in the inn at Upton, between him and Lady Bellaston in London, to say nothing of the language of Squire Western and others!

The same insensibility to what is indecent and immodest is shown by Defoe; for he, like Fielding, thought that in some of his most offending novels there was nothing improper. In his preface to 'Roxana, or The Fortunate Mistress,' he says, "If there are any parts in her story which, being obliged to relate a wicked action, seem to describe it too plainly, the writer (Defoe pretends that the story was written by Roxana herself) says all imaginable care has been taken to keep clear of indecencies and immodest expressions; and it is hoped you will find nothing to prompt a vicious mind, but everywhere much to discourage and expose it." And this with the conversations between Roxana and her maid Amy, and the scenes before his eyes, in which they both are actors! It only shows how the moral sense may be blunted in a corrupt period, and how men can put bitter for sweet even if they do not put sweet for bitter.

In 1787, Canning, then a boy at Eton, asks, in the 'Microcosm,' "Is not the novel of 'Tom

Jones,' however excellent a work of itself, generally put too early into our hands, and proposed
too soon to the imitation of children ?" This
shows what different ideas prevailed even then
from those which prevail now on such a question.   No parent nor schoolmaster would dream
of putting 'Tom Jones' into the hands of a
mere boy in the hope (as the practice was
formerly defended) that he would be attracted
by the manliness of the hero's character, and
draw for himself the line—which certainly is
not drawn by Fielding—where virtue ends and
vice and immorality begin.

The book is so full of wit and fun that it is pro-
voking not to be able to give specimens without
the risk of offending against decorum.   Perhaps
the following passage will bear quotation, where,
after Tom Jones has been detected with Molly
Seagrim, like Æneas and Dido in their cave,
by Thwackum and Blifil, and a battle royal has
been fought between them, Squire Western,
who comes up and separates the combatants,
exclaims, "'But where is she ? Prithee, Tom,
show me.' He then began to beat about, in the
same language and in the same manner as if he
had been beating for a hare ; and at last cried
out, 'Soho ! Puss is not far off. Here's her
form, upon my soul ! I believe I may cry, 'Stole

away!' And indeed so he might; for he had now discovered the place whence the poor girl had at the beginning of the fray stolen away, upon as many feet as a hare generally uses in travelling."

When the Squire's sister says to him "Your ignorance, brother, as the great Milton says, almost subdues my patience," he answers, "D—n Milton, if he had the impudence to say so to my face, I'd lend him a douse, thof he was never so great a man."

Fielding is fond of what may be called Homeric similes, and several occur in 'Tom Jones,' of which the following is a good example. He is describing the attack made by Mrs. Partridge upon her husband :—

"As fair Grimalkin, who, though the youngest of the feline family, degenerates not in ferocity from the elder branches of her house ; and though inferior in strength, is equal in fierceness to the noble tiger himself ; when a little mouse, whom it hath long tormented in sport, escapes from her clutches, for a while frets, scolds, growls, swears ; but if the trunk or box behind which the mouse lay hid be again removed, she flies like lightning on her prey, and with envenomed wrath bites, scratches, mumbles, and tears the little animal—

" Not with less fury did Mrs. Partridge fly on the poor pedagogue. Her tongue, teeth and hands fell all upon him at once. His wig was in an instant torn from his head, his shirt from his back, and from his face descended five streams of blood, denoting the number of claws with which nature had unhappily armed the enemy."

And again, when the Somersetshire mob rushes forward to assault Molly Seagrim :—

" As a vast herd of cows in a rich farmer's yard, if, when they are milked, they hear their calves at a distance lamenting the robbery which is then committing ; so roared forth the Somersetshire mob an halloo. . . . "

But having quoted the prologue to the fight, I cannot resist the temptation of quoting also the prowess of the victorious Molly :—

" Molly, then, taking a thigh-bone in her hand, fell in among the flying ranks, and dealing her blows with great liberality on either side, overthrew the carcass of many a mighty hero and heroine.

" Recount, O Muse, the names of those who fell on that fatal day. First, Jemmy Tweedle felt on his hinder head the direful bone. Him the pleasant banks of sweetly-winding Stour had nourished, where he first learnt the vocal art, with which, wandering up and down, at wakes and fairs, he cheered the rural nymphs and swains, when upon the green sward they interweaved the sprightly dance ; while he himself stood fiddling and jumping to his own music. How little now avails his fiddle ! He thumps the verdant floor with his carcass. Next, old Echepole, the sow-gelder, received a blow on his forehead from our Amazonian heroine, and immediately fell to the ground. He was a swingeing fat fellow, and fell with almost as much noise as a house. His tobacco-box dropped at the same time from his pocket, which Molly took up as lawful spoils. Then Kate of the mill tumbled unfortunately over a tombstone, which, catching hold of her ungartered stocking, inverted the order of nature, and gave her heels the superiority to her head. Betty Pippin, with young Roger her lover, fell both to the ground, where, oh perverse fate ! she saluted the earth and he the sky. . . . ."

The following burst of eloquence ushers in the first appearance of Sophia Western :—

" Hushed be every ruder breath. May the heathen rulers of the winds confine in iron chains the boisterous limbs of noisy Boreas, and the sharp-pointed nose of bitter-biting Eurus. Do thou, sweet Zephyrus, rising from thy fragrant bed, mount the western sky, and lead on those delicious gales, the charms of which call forth the lovely Flora from her chamber, perfumed with pearly dews, when on the 1st of June, her birthday, the blooming maid, in loose attire, gently trips it o'er the verdant mead, where every flower rises to do her homage, till the whole field becomes enamelled, and colours contend with sweets, which shall ravish her most.

" So charming may she now appear ! And you the feathered choristers of nature, whose sweetest notes not even Handel can excel, tune your melodious throats to celebrate her appearance. From love proceeds your music, and to love it returns. Awaken therefore that gentle passion in every swain ; for lo ! adorned with all the charms in which Nature can array her ; bedecked with beauty, youth, sprightliness, innocence, modesty, and tenderness ; breathing sweetness from her rosy lips, and darting brightness from her sparkling eyes, the lovely Sophia comes ! "

The next most celebrated novel of Fielding, although earlier in point of time, is ' Joseph Andrews,' with the immortal character of Parson Adams ; a rare compound of simplicity, benevolence and goodness. Fielding tells us

in his preface that in Parson Adams he
designed a character of perfect simplicity and
hopes his goodness will excuse the author
" to the gentlemen of his cloth, as no other
office could have given him so many opportunities of displaying his worthy inclinations
notwithstanding the low adventures in which
he is engaged."*

And the adventures are low indeed. In one
of them at a village ale-house Parson Adams,
to defend Joseph Andrews, hits the landlord
on the face with his fist, when Mrs. Tow-
wouse, the landlady, rushes to the rescue,
" when lo! a pan full of hog's blood, which
unluckily stood on the dresser, presented itself
first to her hands. She seized it in her fury,
and without any reflection discharged it into
the parson's face; and with so good an aim,
that much the greater part first saluted his
countenance, and trickled thence in so large a
current down to his beard, and all over his

* " Parson Young sat for Fielding's Parson Adams, a man he
knew, and only made a little more absurd than he is known to
be." Letter from Richardson to Mrs. Donnellan, vol. iv. p. 60.
Fielding says of the characters in this novel : " I declare here,
once for all, I describe not men but manners ; not individuals,
but a species. Perhaps it will be answered—are not the characters then taken from life ? To which I answer in the affirma-
tive ; nay, I believe I might aver that I have writ little more than
I have seen."

garments, that a more horrible spectacle was hardly to be seen, or even imagined." In another scene, having by mistake taken a wrong turn, he enters Fanny's bedroom and laying himself down beside her in utter unconsciousness of her presence falls fast asleep, " nor could the emanation of sweets which flowed from her mouth overpower the fumes of tobacco which played in the parson's nostrils." Joseph comes in the morning to the bedroom-door to awaken the fair Fanny, and we may imagine the confusion that follows.

The object of Parson Adams's journey is to have a volume of his sermons published, and at an inn, when his money had run short, he wants to borrow from the landlord three guineas on the security of the manuscript. Pointing to his saddle-bag he told him, " with a face and voice full of solemnity, that there were in that bag no less than nine volumes of manuscript sermons, as well worth a hundred pounds as a shilling was worth twelve pence, and that he would deposit one of the volumes in his hands by way of pledge." But the landlord did not like the security—and shortly afterwards, when the saddle-bags are opened by Joseph to look for the sermons he

can find none.   " 'Sure, sir,' says Joseph,
'there is nothing in the bags.'   Upon which
Adams, starting and testifying some surprise,
cried, ' Hey! fie, fie upon it! they are not
here sure enough.   Ay, they are certainly left
behind.' "

The least objectionable, according to modern
notions, of Fielding's novels, is ' Amelia.'
There is much less coarseness, and also *less*
licentiousness.   His object is to portray the
conduct of a virtuous wife, who adores her
husband and children ; and she is really a
charming character.   Scenes of course are
introduced in which the old, old story of
illicit love goes on ; but they are wholly
unknown to her, and they serve only to en-
hance, by the force of contrast, the innocence and purity of her mind.   M. Taine
says, " ' Amelia' is the perfect model of an
English wife, excelling in the kitchen, devoted
to her husband, even so far as to pardon
his accidental infidelities ; *toujours grosse*.   She
is modest in excess, always blushing and
tender." *

---

* ' Histoire de la Littérature Anglaise,' vol. iii. p. 33.   I hardly
know what M. Taine means by applying the terms " *toujours
grosse*" here, for Amelia is not once represented as being in that
interesting situation.

She is no doubt intended to represent the character of Fielding's first wife, as her husband, Captain Booth, is, in some points, intended to represent his own. But he is, upon the whole, a poor creature, if not what Lady Mary Wortley Montague called him, "a sorry scoundrel"—hardly ever proof against temptation, and getting constantly into debt. He, however, fully appreciates the value of the treasure he has got in his wife; and in the midst of his frailties has the merit of feeling repentance and remorse.

'Amelia' is not a comic novel. There are no ludicrous scenes like those in 'Tom Jones,' 'Joseph Andrews,' and 'Peregrine Pickle;' and yet there is sufficient incident and variety in the plot to interest and amuse the reader. We are introduced into the interior of a prison, and have a vivid picture of all its abominations in those days—to Vauxhall, where Amelia is insulted by libertine advances—to a masquerade, with its intrigues and loose talk—and to domestic scenes of profligate noblemen and colonels, and conversations where Mrs. Atkinson quotes Virgil and Horace as familiarly as if they had been written in her mother tongue.

If we may believe Richardson, who had a

spite against Fielding for representing Pamela
as the sister of Joseph Andrews, and ridiculing
her, the novel of 'Amelia' was not successful.
He says in one of his letters in 1752, " Mr.
Fielding has met with the disapprobation you
foresaw he would meet with in his 'Amelia.'
He is, in every paper he publishes under the
title of the Covent Garden, contributing to his
own overthrow.   He has been overmatched
in his own way by people whom he had de-
spised, and whom he thought he had vogue
enough from the success his spurious brat
'Tom Jones' so unaccountably met with, to
write down."*   And again, "Captain Booth
(Amelia's husband), madam, has done his own
business. . . . . The piece, in short, is as dead
as if it had been published forty years ago,
as to sale. You guess that I have not read
'Amelia.'   Indeed, I have read but the first
volume.   I had intended to go through with
it ; but I found the characters and situations so
wretchedly low and dirty, that I imagined I
could not be interested for any one of them.
. . . . Booth in his last piece again himself.
Amelia, even to her noselessness, is again his
first wife.   His brawls, his jars, his gaols, his

* 'Richardson's Letters,' vol. iii. p. 63.

spunging-houses, are all drawn from what he has seen and known."*

However this may be, I think that of all the novels of that period, 'Amelia' is the one which gives the most generally truthful idea of the manners and habits of middle-class society then. There is little if any exaggeration or caricature, and I have no doubt that Fielding intended faithfully to depict society, such as he knew it, with its merits and its faults,—its licentious manners, and domestic virtues; its brawls, its oaths, its prisons, and its masquerades.

---

* This is bitter spite on the part of Richardson. Fielding describes Amelia as having her nose injured by a fall before her marriage. Dr. Johnson said " Fielding's ' Amelia' was the most pleasing heroine of all the romances, but that vile broken nose, never cured, ruined the sale of perhaps the only book which being printed off betimes one morning, a new edition was called for before night."

CHAPTER IX.

SMOLLETT.—DIFFERENCE BETWEEN HIM AND FIELDING.—
'PEREGRINE PICKLE.'—'HUMPHRY CLINKER.'—'THE
SPIRITUAL QUIXOTE.'

THE jolly, riotous kind of life which I have spoken of as characteristic of one class of novels of the last century is fully displayed in the pages of Smollett. He reflects, in many respects, the character of the age more fully than any other writer,—its material pleasures—its coarse amusements—its hard drinking, loud swearing, and practical jokes. His heroes are generally libertines, full of mirth and animal spirits, who make small account of woman's chastity; and whose adventures are intrigues, and their merriment broad farce. Such are the chief features of 'Roderick Random' and 'Peregrine Pickle' —neither of which, however, is so offensive as the 'Adventures of Ferdinand, Count Fathom,' the hero of which is a blackguard and a scoundrel, without a redeeming virtue.

The French critic, M. Taine, whom I have already quoted, thus speaks of Smollett : "He exaggerates caricature ; he thinks he amuses us in showing us mouths gaping to the ears, and noses half-a-foot long ; he exaggerates a national prejudice or a professional trick until it absorbs the whole character. He flings together personages the most revolting with the most grotesque—a Lieutenant Lismahago, half-roasted by Red Indians ; sea wolves who pass their lives in shouting and travestying all their ideas into a sea jargon ; old maids as ugly as she-asses, as withered as skeletons, and as acrid as vinegar; maniacs steeped in pedantry, hypochondria, misanthropy, and silence. Far from sketching them slightly, like Gil Blas, he brings into prominent relief each disagreeable trait, and overloads it with details, without considering whether they are too numerous, without reflecting that they are excessive, without feeling that they are odious, without seeing that they are disgusting. The public whom he addresses is on a level with his energy and roughness, and in order to shake such nerves a writer cannot strike too hard." *

One of the chief differences between Smollett and Fielding is this—the scenes and adventures

* 'Histoire de la Littérature Anglaise,' vol. iv. p. 323.

in Smollett's novels are laughable and farcical in themselves; but have little or no bearing upon the progress of the story. They are too much like the disconnected slides in a magic-lantern. But Fielding makes each separate adventure, especially in ' Tom Jones,' subservient to the plot, the issue of which is worked out with admirable consistency and skill.

It will be sufficient, for the purpose of giving an idea of Smollett's humour, to take two of his stories, ' Peregrine Pickle' and ' Humphry Clinker.' Peregrine Pickle is the son of Gamaliel Pickle, and at his birth his mother conceived an unnatural aversion to him, which she continued to feel until her death. He is adopted by an uncle, Commodore Trunnion, who, with his friend and companion Lieutenant Jack Hatchway (with a wooden leg), and his former boatswain Tom Pipes, has retired from the navy and ensconced himself not far from his brother's house near the sea-side, in an habitation which is called the Garrison, defended by a ditch, over which he had laid a draw-bridge and planted his courtyard with patereroes continually loaded with shot. There is little doubt that Sterne took the idea of Uncle Toby and Corporal Trim in ' Tristram Shandy' from Commodore Trunnion and Jack Hatchway.

The Commodore gives everything a nautical turn, and hardly ever speaks without uttering a volley of oaths. Smollett himself had been a surgeon's mate, and was perfectly at home in sea phrases. Mr. Gamaliel Pickle has a sister Grizzle, "with a very wan, not to say sallow, complexion," a cast in her eye, and an enormous mouth, and slightly addicted to brandy, who sets her heart on engaging the affections of the Commodore. She is aided in her schemes by Jack Hatchway, who persuaded Pipes to get on the chimney belonging to the Commodore's chamber at midnight, and lower down by a rope a bunch of rotten and phosphorescent whitings, while he put a speaking-trumpet to his mouth and in a voice like thunder shouted out " Trunnion! Trunnion! turn out and be spliced, or lie still and be d—d." This so terrifies the gallant sailor that he yields to the lady's advances, exclaiming, " Well, since it must be so, I think we must e'en grapple. But . . . 'tis a hard case that a fellow of my years should be compelled, d'ye see, to beat up to windward all the rest of my life, against the current of my inclination." I have already described the dress he wore at his wedding, but not the adventure that befel him on the occasion. When he had mounted his horse, attended by his lieutenant, to meet the bride at church, a pack of hounds unluckily crossed his path. Off set the two horses, and Jack Hatchway was soon deposited in a field of clover, while the Commodore was carried past him at a gallop, crying out " O ! you are safe at anchor. I wish to God I were as fast moored." His horse takes a five-barred gate, "to the utter confusion and disorder of his owner, who lost his hat and periwig in the leap, and now began to think in good earnest that he was actually mounted on the back of the devil." After various other mishaps, he is first in at the death of the stag, and, being refreshed by a flask of brandy, explains to the sportsmen the cause of his strange appearance. He says he was bound to the next church on the voyage of matrimony ; but, " howsomever," the wind shifting, blowed directly in their teeth, so that they were forced to tack all the way, and had almost hauled up within sight of port when the two horses luffed round in a trice, and then refusing the helm, drove away like lightning. " I have been carried over rocks and flats and quicksands, among which I have pitched away a special good tie-periwig and an iron-bound hat ; and at last, thank God ! am got into smooth water and safe riding ; but if ever I venture my carcass upon such a hare'um

scare'um . . . again, my name is not Hawser
Trunnion. . . ."

The ceremony of marriage was performed at
a later day in the Garrison, and the wedding
supper consisted of a huge pillau, two dishes of
hard fish flanked by lobscouse and salmagundy,
a goose "of monstrous magnitude," two guinea-
hens, a pig barbacued, a leg of mutton roasted
with potatoes, and another boiled with yams.
Then came a loin of fresh pork with apple-
sauce, a kid smothered with onions, and a
terrapin baked in the shell; and last of all a
prodigious sea-pie "with an infinite volume of
pancakes and fritters." Of liquors there was
abundance in the shape of strong beer, flip,
rumbo and burnt brandy, "with plenty of Bar-
badoes water for the ladies." The happy pair
go to bed in a hammock, which, not being used
to a double weight, tumbles to the ground, and
Mrs. Trunnion screams.

Peregrine is sent by his uncle to a boarding-
school, kept by "an old illiterate German quack,
who had formerly practised corn-cutting among
the quality, and sold cosmetic washes to the
ladies, together with tooth-powders, hair-dyeing
liquids, prolific elixirs, and tinctures to sweeten
the breath." But he has an excellent usher,
who was a man of learning, probity, and good

sense ; but who soon resigned his situation, and "finding interest to obtain holy orders he left the kingdom, hoping to find a settlement in some of our American plantations."

Peregrine now returns to the Commodore at the Garrison, upon whom, in conjunction with Hatchway and Pipes, he plays several practical jokes, and being detected, is sent off with a tutor to Winchester school. Here he meets at a race-ball Miss Emilia Gauntlet, with whom he falls in love, and who is the virtuous heroine of the story. He makes her acquaintance by begging that she would do him the honour to walk a minuet with him, and is introduced to her mother, who lives with her daughter in a small house in a village near Winchester. He writes a copy of verses in praise of his charmer, and enclosing them in a tender epistle, commits it to the care of Pipes, who had accompanied him to Winchester, with directions to deliver it and a present of venison at Mrs. Gauntlet's house. For the sake of safety, Tom Pipes puts the letter between the stocking and sole of his foot, and when he looks for it at the end of his journey finds it torn to tatters. He therefore goes to an inn and composes a love-letter himself to replace the one that was lost, and we may guess the kind of nonsense it contained. He delivers the letter, and Emilia's astonishment on reading it is only equalled by her indignation at what she supposes is meant to be an insult. She dismisses Pipes without an answer; and Peregrine, taking offence at this, resolves to retort her own neglect upon his ungrateful mistress, so that the misunderstanding is complete.

He afterwards goes to the University of Oxford as a student, and happening to meet Emilia, an explanation takes place between them, and they are reconciled. Tom Pipes is interrogated as to the letter. Seizing him by the throat, Peregrine asks him, "Rascal! tell me this instant what became of the letter I entrusted to your care," and Pipes, squirting a collection of tobacco-juice out of his mouth, replies, "Why, burnt it. You wouldn't have me give the young woman a thing that shook all in the wind in tatters, would you?" Peregrine quarrels with his tutor, who writes to Mrs. Trunnion, and informs her of the love-affair, and this leads to a rupture with his uncle, who sends him a letter in which he says, "I am informed as how you are in chase of a painted galley, which will decoy you upon the flats of destruction, unless you keep a better look out and a surer reckoning than you have hitherto done." Jack Hatchway brings the letter, and tries all he can to persuade him to yield to the Commodore's wishes. "Amongst other remonstrances Jack observed that mayhap Peregrine had got under Emilia's hatches, and did not choose to set her adrift; and that if that was the case, he himself would take charge of the vessel, and see her cargo safely de-livered; for he had a respect for the young woman, and his needle pointed towards matri-mony, and as, in all probability, she would not be much the worse for the wear, he would make shift to scud through life with her under an easy sail."

But Peregrine is obstinate, and the two friends get so warm that Hatchway at last says, "You and I must crack a pistol at one another; here is a brace; you shall take which you please." They stand up in the Park, when Tom Pipes interposes with his cudgel, and prevents the duel, saying to Peregrine, "I am your man. Here's my sapling, and I don't value your sap-ling a rope's end." The quarrel is soon made up, and Peregrine goes to pay a visit to Emilia, where he meets a brother, and after fighting a duel with him, becomes his intimate friend. He then returns to the Garrison, and there finds the poor old Commodore sadly hen-pecked by

his wife, " who by the force of pride, religion,
and cognac, had erected a most terrible tyranny
in the house." I should mention that Peregrine
has a younger brother Gamaliel, or Gam, as he
is called, upon whom his mother lavishes all
her fondness, and who is an ugly, deformed
scoundrel, and also a sister Julia, a loving,
charming creature. He now resolves to travel
abroad, and sets off for the Continent, accompanied by Jolter as his tutor or companion.
We need not follow him there, for it is beside
the purpose of this book to give descriptions of
foreign cities and foreign manners. It is
enough to say that Peregrine is not a Joseph,
and if the fair Emilia had known of all his
adventures, she would have been quite justified
in declining further intimacy with such a scapegrace. But I must mention the famous banquet in Paris, which a pedantic doctor "in a
suit of black, and a huge tie-wig," gave in the
manner of the ancients. He had to dismiss
five cooks, who could not prevail upon their
consciences to obey his directions, and the last
whom he engaged begged on his knees to be
released from his contract, but finding this in
vain, " wept, sang, cursed, and capered for two
whole hours without intermission." When the
guests meet, the Doctor apologises for not

having been able to procure for them the exact
triclinia of the ancients, and they have to put
up with couches, where, on settling themselves,
the feet of one come in contact with the head
of another, to the great discomfiture of periwigs. " At each end there are dishes of the
salacacabia of the Romans ; this is made of
parsley, pennyroyal, cheese, pinetops, honey,
vinegar, lime, cucumber, onions, and hen-
livers." But the Frenchman who swallowed
the first spoonful, "made a full pause, his throat
swelled as if an egg had stuck in his gullet, his
eyes rolled, and his mouth underwent a series
of involuntary contractions and dilatations." A
pie follows, and well might the painter exclaim,
" A pie made of dormice and syrup of poppies !
Lord in heaven ! what beastly fellows those
Romans were !" The sow's stomach and fricassee of snails were not more tempting, and
when one of the fowls was opened, the unhappy carver was assaulted by such an irruption
of intolerable smells, that without staying to
disengage himself from the cloth, he sprang
away, with an exclamation ' Lord Jesus ! ' and
involved the whole table in havoc, ruin, and
confusion."

Peregrine returns to England a thorough
libertine, and when he meets Emilia, talks to

her in a strain which keeps barely within the
bounds of decency. His object now is something very different from marriage, but he finds
himself baffled by her prudence and reserve.
He goes back to the Garrison, where he finds
the old Commodore very near his end, but
cheerful to the last. " Swab the spray from
your bowsprit," he cries, " and coil up your
spirits. You must not let the top-lifts of your
heart give way because you see me ready to go
down at these years. . . . . Here has been a
doctor that wanted to stow me chock-full of
physic, but when a man's hour is come, what
signifies his taking his departure with a 'pothe-
cary's shop in his hold ? Those fellows come
alongside of dying men, like the messengers of
the Admiralty, with sailing orders ; but I told
him as how I could slip my cable without his
direction or assistance, and so he hauled off in
dudgeon. . . . . There's your aunt sitting
whimpering by the fire. I desire you will keep
her tight, warm, and easy in her old age ; she's
an honest heart in her own way ; and thof she
goes a little crank and humoursome, by being
overstowed with Nantz and religion, she has
been a faithful shipmate to me. . . . . Jack
Hatchway, you know the trim of her as well as
e'er a man in England, and I believe she has a

kindness for you; whereby if you two will grapple in the way of matrimony, when I am gone, I do suppose that my godson, for love of me, will allow you to live in the Garrison all the days of your life." And so the kind-hearted old gentleman dies—a man whom, with all his failings, it is impossible not to love, and we sympathise with honest Tom Pipes, who exclaims, " Well fare thy soul, old Hawser Trunnion—man and boy I have known thee these five-and-thirty years, and sure a truer heart never broke biscuit. Many a hard gale hast thou weathered ; but now thy spells are all over, and thy hull fairly laid up. A better commander I'd never desire to serve, and who knows but I may help to set up thy standing-rigging in another world ? "

He dies, leaving the bulk of his fortune to Peregrine, who, on the strength of it, goes to town, buys a new chariot and horses, and seeks to distinguish himself in the world of fashion. He now lays a plan for carrying out his in-famous design upon Emilia, whom he meets in London. He persuades her to accompany him to a masquerade in the Haymarket, where he drugs the wine he offers her, and afterwards, instead of conveying her in his carriage to her uncle's house, as she supposes, had her driven elsewhere. But he little knows the character and spirit of Emilia. When she discovers the trick that has been played upon her, she betrays no alarm, but confounds him with the severity of her rebuke. "'Sir,' she said, 'your behaviour on this occasion is in all respects low and contemptible, for ruffian as you are, you durst not harbour one thought of executing your execrable scheme while you knew my brother was near enough to protect or avenge the insult; so that you must not only be a treacherous villain, but also a most despicable coward.'

" Having expressed herself in this manner with a most majestic serenity of aspect, she opened the door, and walking down stairs with surprising resolution, committed herself to the care of a watchman, who accommodated her with a hackney-chair," in which she is safely conveyed to her uncle's house. Peregrine goes to the uncle, an alderman in the city, who shows him the door, and then we have a series of adventures in London, which are neither edifying nor interesting.

It is here that Smollett introduces the long episode called the ' Memoirs of a Lady of Quality,' to which I have before alluded, and which occupy a considerable part of the novel.

There is also a tiresome Welshman, named Cadwallader, who is one of the bores of the story.

Peregrine goes on from bad to worse, sinking lower and lower in fortune, until at last, having taken to authorship and libelled a Minister, he is at his instigation arrested for debt and lodged in the Fleet. Here again we have another long and tedious episode, the 'Memoirs of Mr. M——,' a fellow-prisoner in the Fleet, who no doubt is intended to represent some real character of the time. Hatchway and Pipes come to visit him, and, like Sam Weller in 'Pickwick,' insist upon taking up their quarters in the prison to keep him company. At last better fortune begins to dawn; some money which he thought he had irrevocably lost in an adventure is repaid to him; the fair Emilia, who has in the meantime become a great heiress, relents and offers to forgive the past; his father dies suddenly intestate, leaving Peregrine his heir, and he offers Emilia his hand. In those days, or at all events in the novels of those days, no time was lost in wedding preparations. He falls at her feet and entreats that they may be married at once, " but the bride objects with great vehemence to such precipitation, being desirous

of her mother's presence at the ceremony."
She is however teased into compliance; they
go to Doctors' Commons for a licence, engage
a clergyman, and the ceremony is performed at
Emilia's lodgings. The evening is spent " at
the public entertainments in Marylebone Gardens, which were at that time frequented by
the best company in town," and after Emilia
and her friend Sophy have retired to her
lodging, Peregrine follows her there, " where
he found her dished (!) out, the fairest daughter
of chastity and love."

' Humphry Clinker ' is a very different kind
of novel, in which Smollett gives full play to
his powers of satire; and in which, therefore,
it is necessary to be cautious, before we can
accept any part of his descriptions as true.
It was written by him when he was dying at
Leghorn, and is a proof of the vigour and
fertility of his intellect.

The story consists of the adventures of a
Welsh family of the name of Bramble in
their travels through England and Scotland,
and the wit depends upon the oddity of the
characters introduced.

Mr. Matthew Bramble, a testy but ' kind-
hearted Welsh squire,—whose opinions are
supposed to represent those of Smollett him-

self,—accompanied by his stingy and ugly sister, Miss Tabitha Bramble,—"exceedingly starched, vain and ridiculous," and bent at all cost upon matrimony,—his nephew and his niece—makes a family tour in a coach and six. They are attended by a lady's maid, Mrs. Winifred Jenkins, whose letters to her fellow servants at Brambleton Hall, with their wonderful spelling and "malaprop" words, are the most amusing part of the work. They pick up a postilion named Humphry Clinker, a convert to the new doctrines of Whitfield and Wesley, who afterwards turns out to be a natural son of Mr. Bramble himself, and who, after converting Miss Tabitha and Mrs. Winifred, marries the latter. The niece, Lydia Melford, has a love affair with a young gentleman, whom she first meets in the disguise of a strolling actor and whom she ultimately marries.

A great part of the wit of the novel consists in the ludicrous way in which the language of the Methodists is travestied. But this is, I think, wit of the lowest kind. Nothing is easier than to write a parody, and of all parodies those which turn sacred things into ridicule are the easiest and the most reprehensible. It is but poor jesting to make a maid servant

write " grease " for " grace," and " pyebell " for
" Bible ;" to " pray constantly for grease that
I may have a glimpse of the new-light to
show me the way through the wretched veil
of tares ;" and say, " Mr. Clinker assures me
that by the new light of grease I may deify
the devil and all his works ;" or, " Sattin has
had power to temp me in the shape of Van
Ditton, the young squire's wally de shamble,
but by God's grease he did not perrvail." " O !
Mary Jones, pray without seizing for grease
to prepare you for the operations of this wonderful instrument, which, I hope, will be exer-
cised this winter upon you and others at
Brambleton Hall." " I do no more than yuse
the words of my good lady who has got the
infectual calling ; and I trust that even myself,
though unworthy, shall find grease to be excepted." But, apart from this, it is impossible
not to help laughing at Mrs. Winifred's descriptions of places and things, which are irre-
sistibly comic.

" O Molly! what shall I say of London ? All
the towns that ever I beheld in my born-days
are no more than Welsh barrows and crum-
leeks to this wonderfully sitty ! Even Bath
itself is but a fillitch in the naam of God.
One would think there 's no end of the streets

but the land's end. Then there's such a power of people going hurry skurry! Such a racket of coxes! Such a noise and haliballoo! So many strange sites to be seen! O gracious! my poor Welsh brain has been spinning like a top ever since I came hither!" I have already quoted the rest of the description in which she tells her correspondent that she has seen "the Park and the pallass of Saint Gemses, ... and the hillyfents, and pyeball ass, and all the rest of the royal family."

A little misadventure that happened to Humphry Clinker is thus described by Mrs. Jenkins:—

"He was tuck up for a rubbery and had before gustass Bunhard, who made his mittamouse, and the pore youth was sent to prison upon the false oaf of a willain, that wanted to sware his life away for the looker of Cain."

And another that happened to herself—

"I went in the morning to a private place along with the house-maid, and we bathed in our birthday soot, after the fashion of the country (Scotland); and behold, whilst we dabbled in the loff, Sir George Coon started up with a gun; but we clapt our hands to our faces, and passed by him to the place where we had left our smocks.—A civil gentleman would have turned his head another way.—My comfit is, he knew not which was which ; and, as the saying is, *all cats in the dark are grey.*"

The description of the person of Miss Tabitha Bramble, as given by her nephew, is worth quoting :—

" She is tall, raw-boned, awkward, flat-chested, and stooping ; her complexion is sallow and freckled ; her eyes are not grey but greenish, like those of a cat, and generally inflamed ; her hair is of a sandy, or rather dusty hue ; her forehead low ; her nose long, sharp, and towards the extremity always red in cool weather ; her lips skinny ; her mouth extensive ; her teeth straggling and loose, of various colours and conformation ; and her long neck shrivelled into a thousand wrinkles."

Such was the beauteous spinster of forty-five who ensnared at last the immortal Lis-mahago—a tall meagre figure, with thighs like those of a grasshopper, very narrow in the shoulders and very thick in the calves of the legs, with a face half-a-yard in length, " brown and shrivelled, with projecting cheek-bones, little grey eyes of a greenish hue, a large hook nose, a pointed chin, a mouth from ear to ear, very ill-furnished with teeth, and a high, narrow forehead, well furnished with wrinkles." At this attractive cavalier Tabitha

makes a dead set, and she hooks her fish at
last.   " Who would have thought," asks
Winifred Jenkins, " that mistress, after all
the pains taken for the good of her prusias
sole, would go for to throw away her poor
body ?   That she would cast the heys of in-
fection upon such a carraying crow as Lishmi-
hago ! as old as Matthewsullin, as dry as a
red herring, and as pore as a starved veezel.
O Molly, hadst thou seen him come down the
ladder in a shurt so scanty that it could not
kiver his nakedness !"   And when they are
married they sit in state in the nuptial couch
while the benediction posset is drunk and a
cake is broken over the head of Mrs. Tabitha
Lismahago.

Although, upon the whole, the ' Expedition
of Humphry Clinker' is the most amusing of
Smollett's works, and we can never tire of laughing at such characters as Tabitha Bramble and
Winifred Jenkins and Lieutenant Lismahago, a
considerable part of the book is nothing more
than an itinerary through England and Scotland, which enables the author to give a sar-
castic description of the towns, and vent his
spleen upon the inhabitants.   Thus, the buildings at Bath " look like the wreck of streets
and squares disjointed by an earthquake, which

hath broken the ground into a variety of hills and hillocks, or as if some Gothic devil had stuffed them altogether in a bag, and left them to stand higgledy-piggledy, just as chance directed. . . . Every upstart of fortune, harnessed in the trappings of the mode, presents himself at Bath, as in the very focus of observation. Clerks and factors from the East Indies, loaded with the spoils of plundered provinces; planters, negro-drivers, and hucksters from our American plantations, enriched they know not how; agents, commissaries, and contractors, who have fattened in two successive wars on the blood of the nation; usurers, brokers, and jobbers of every kind; men of low birth and no breeding have found themselves suddenly translated into a state of affluence unknown to former ages; and no wonder that their brain should be intoxicated with pride, vanity, and presumption." And Mrs. Winifred Jenkins gives her view of the City of Waters. "O Molly! you that live in the country have no deception of our doings at Bath. . . . . Dear girl, I have seen all the fine shews: the Prades, the Squires and the Circlis, the Crashit, the Hottogon, and Bloody Buildings, and Harry King's Row, and I have been twice in the Bath with mistress, and ne'er a smoak upon our backs, hussy." As to 'Harrigate' (*sic*) Mr. Bramble says that it "is a wild common, bare and bleak, without tree or shrub or the least sign of cultivation ; and the people who come to drink the water are crowded together in paltry inns, where the few tolerable rooms are monopolised by the friends and favourites of the house, and all the rest of the lodgers are obliged to put up with dirty holes where there is neither space, air, nor convenience." The water was of course then as disagreeable as it is now. "Some people say it smells of rotten eggs ; and others compare it to the scouring of a foul gun." A visit to Scarborough furnishes an excuse for an elaborate description of a bathing-machine, which seems then to have been a thing unknown elsewhere. York Minster gives occasion for an attack upon Gothic architecture, which is called "proposterous in a country like England where the air is externally loaded with vapours, and where of consequence the builder's intention should be to keep the people dry and warm." And we have the following astounding description of a cathedral : "The external appearance of an old cathedral cannot but be displeasing to the eye of every man who has any idea of propriety and proportion, even

though he may be ignorant of architecture as a
science ; and the long slender spire puts one in
mind of a criminal impaled with a sharp stake
rising up through his shoulder !" We need not
wonder, therefore, that the cathedral of Durham is dismissed as " a huge, gloomy pile ;"
but it is undoubtedly true at the present day,
as when Mr. Matthew Bramble and his party
visited that city, that " the streets are generally
narrow, dark, and unpleasant." Edinburgh is
fairly dealt with, and praised for its romantic
site, its castle, and its palace. The Canongate
" would be undoubtedly one of the noblest
streets in Europe, if an ugly mass of mean
buildings, called the Lucken-booths, had not
thrust itself, by what accident I know not,
into the middle of the way, like Middle Row
in Holborn." But " the first thing that strikes
the nose of a stranger shall be nameless ;" and
the state of the stairs leading to the *flats* was
such that " a man must tread with great
circumspection to get safe housed with unpol-
luted shoes." It would not be possible to
quote the confidential letter of Winifred Jenkins to Mrs. Mary Jones at Brambleton Hall,
on the subject. It has all the vigour and
fidelity of a Dutch picture, but *tempora
mutantur*, and it must be read in private.

Linlithgow has " an elegant royal palace, which is now gone to decay, as well as the town itself;" but " Glasgow is the pride of Scotland," and, according to Mr. Bramble's opinion —or, in other words, the opinion of Dr. Smollett himself—it is " one of the prettiest towns in Europe." He thinks that its cathedral may be compared with York Minster or Westminster, and computes the number of inhabitants at 30,000 ;—they now amount to more than 400,000. But the journey is dull enough as a narrative, although it is enlivened by some ludicrous adventures ; as, for instance, that in which the kitchen chimney catches fire at night, and the women rush out in dishabille, when Tabitha Bramble, in her under-petticoat, endeavours to lay hold of Mr. Micklewhimmen, and he pushes her down, crying out, " Na, na, gude faith, charity begins at hame !" and Mrs. Winifred Jenkins falls from the ladder into the arms of Humphry Clinker.

The Brambles visit, in the course of their travels, the seat of a country gentleman in Argyleshire, where " the great hall, paved with flat stones, serves not only for a diningroom but also for a bed-chamber to gentlemen dependants and hangers-on of the family. At night half-a-dozen occasional beds are

ranged on each side along the wall. These
are made of fresh heath, pulled up by the roots,
and disposed in such manner as to make a very
agreeable couch, where they lie without any
covering but the plaid."

I have previously alluded to the mode in
which Smollett, in his 'Humphry Clinker,' attacked the doctrines of the new sect; and it
was to ridicule them that a clergyman named
Graves wrote his novel called 'The Spiritual
Quixote,' the hero of which is Geoffrey Wildgoose, a young man of a respectable family
and small estate, who having picked up some
old volumes of puritan divinity, such as
'Crumbs of Comfort,' 'Honeycombs for the
Elect,' the 'Marrow of Divinity,' the 'Spiritual
Eye Salve and Cordials for the Saints,' and
a book of Baxter with an unmentionable
name, resolves to sally forth and convert his
benighted fellow-countrymen in the highways
and byeways of England. He is accompanied
by Jeremiah Tugwell, a cobbler, who acts
as a sort of Sancho Panza, and they visit
Gloucester, Bath, and Bristol, where they are
involved in various adventures more creditable
to the zeal of Wildgoose than his discretion.

He holds such books as 'Tillotson's Sermons' and the 'Whole Duty of Man' in

sovereign contempt, and asserts that it would be as profitable to read the 'Seven Champions' or 'Jack the Giant Killer' as Tillotson, who, he says, quoting Whitfield himself, knew no more of Christianity than Mahomet.

It is, however, a stupid book; the attempts at satire are miserably poor, and the adventures of Wildgoose and his companion show neither wit nor invention.

CHAPTER X.

GOLDSMITH.—'THE VICAR OF WAKEFIELD.'—CHARACTER OF
LATER NOVELS AND ROMANCES.—MACKENZIE.—'THE MAN
OF FEELING,' 'THE MAN OF THE WORLD,' AND 'JULIA
DE ROUBIGNÉ.'—MISS BURNEY.—'EVELINA,' AND 'CECILIA.'
—MISS EDGEWORTH.—'BELINDA.'—JANE AUSTEN.—USES
OF NOVELS.—RESPONSIBILITY OF THE NOVELIST.

T is a sensible relief to turn from the
maudlin sentimentality of Richardson
and the coarseness of Fielding and
Smollett, to the purity of the pages of Goldsmith. We seem to breathe all at once

An ampler ether, a diviner air,

and have as sweet a picture as was ever drawn
of family life in a country parsonage, with its
joys and sorrows, its trials and rewards. One
great charm of the 'Vicar of Wakefield' is its
gentle irony—very different indeed from the
vicious *double entendre* of Swift or Sterne,
where the implied meaning is almost always
impure. With all the child-like simplicity of
Dr. Primrose, there is in him an under-current
of sound good sense, which makes him fully

sensible of the folly of his wife and daughters, while he indulges their vanity and smiles at their credulity. With what a soft touch of sarcasm he describes the good lady whom he chose, as she did her wedding gown, not for a fine glossy surface, but such qualities as would wear well. "She could read any English book without much spelling; but for pickling, preserving and cookery, none could excel her. She prided herself upon being an excellent contriver in housekeeping; though I could never find that we grew richer with all her contrivances." The key to his character is, I think, contained in the following sentence about his wife, when he tells us how she began to build castles in the air when Mr. Burchell had rescued their youngest daughter, Sophia, from drowning, and she said that if he had birth and fortune to entitle him to match into such a family as theirs, she knew no man she would sooner fix upon. "I could not but smile to hear her talk in this lofty strain; but I was never much displeased with those harmless delusions that tend to make us more happy." When, after the loss of his fortune, and the removal of his family to a humbler abode, his wife and daughters come down stairs on Sunday morning dressed out in all their former

finery, " their hair plastered up with pomatum,
their faces patched to taste, their trains bundled
up in a heap behind, and rustling at every
motion," the way in which Dr. Primrose re-
bukes their vanity is by ordering his son, with
an important air, to call their coach. " ' Surely,
my dear, you jest,' cried my wife, ' we can
walk perfectly well : we want no coach to carry
us now.' ' You mistake, child,' returned I,
' we do want a coach ; for if we walk to church
in this trim, the very children in the parish will
hoot after us ; ' " and he ends with the wise
apophthegm, " I do not know whether such
flouncing and shredding is becoming, even in
the rich, if we consider, upon a moderate calcu-
lation, that the nakedness of the indigent world
may be clothed from the trimmings of the vain."
When Squire Thornhill was expected to pay
them a visit, and Mrs. Primrose went to make
the venison pasty, the Vicar observed his
daughters busy cooking something over the
fire. He at first thought that they were as-
sisting their mother, but little Dick whispered
that they were making a *wash* for their faces.
Washes he abominated. " I therefore approached my chair by sly degrees to the fire,
and grasping the poker, as if it wanted mending,
seemingly, by accident, overturned the whole

composition, and it was too late to begin another."

The introduction into this scene of innocent happiness of the two town ladies—or rather ladies of the town—Lady Blarney, and Miss Carolina Wilhelmina Amelia Skeggs, is characteristic of the manners of the age; but it unpleasantly breaks in upon the harmony of the tale. Their attempt at personation is too gross, and no family, who were not all idiots, could have been deceived as to their real character. But Dr. Primrose only very gently hints his suspicions. " One of them, I thought, expressed her sentiments upon this occasion in a very coarse manner, when she observed that ' by the living jingo she was all of a muck of sweat.' " Possibly the family may have thought themselves disqualified by their rustic habits from appreciating the wit of conversation in fashionable life, as retailed by the two strangers, and may have fancied that something more was meant than met the ear, when they were informed by them that " the next morning my Lord Duke cried out three times to his *valet de chambre* ' Jernigan, Jernigan, Jernigan, bring me my garters.' "

How exquisitely the story is told of Moses and the colt and the gross of green spectacles !

Here, again, Dr. Primrose's good sense and temper are finely contrasted with his wife's impetuous anger. "' A fig for the silver rims,' said my wife in a passion : ' I dare swear they won't sell for above half the money at the rate of broken silver, five shillings the ounce.' ' You need be under no uneasiness,' cried I, ' about selling the rims ; for they are not worth sixpence, for I perceive they are only copper varnished over.' ' What !' cried my wife, ' not silver, the rims not silver !' ' No,' cried I, ' no more silver than your saucepan.' ' And so,' returned she, ' we have parted with the colt, and have only got a gross of green spectacles, with copper rims and shagreen cases ! A murrain take such trumpery ! The blockhead has been imposed upon, and should have known his company better.' ' There, my dear,' cried I, ' you are wrong ; he should not have known them at all.' ' Marry, hang the idiot,' returned she, ' to bring such stuff ! If I had them, I would throw them into the fire !' ' There, again, you are wrong, my dear,' cried I, ' for though they are copper, we will keep them by us, as copper spectacles, you know, are better than nothing.' "

But, however Dr. Primrose may have plumed himself on his worldly wisdom, he,

like his son Moses, was destined to be tricked
by the same sharper—and that, too, in the
matter of the sale of a horse. He takes him
to the fair, and puts him through his paces—
but the would-be purchasers find so many
faults in him — one declaring that he had a
spavin; another that he had a wind-gall;
others that he had the botts,—that at last his
owner begins to have a most hearty contempt
for the poor animal himself. At this juncture
the inimitable Ephraim Jenkinson appears on
the scene, " a venerable old man, wholly intent
over a book which he was reading; his locks
of silver gray venerably shaded his temples,
and his green old age seemed to be the result
of health and temperance." We all know how
the scoundrel swindled the Vicar out of his
horse, by palming off upon him a bill pay-
able at sight upon farmer Flamborough. But
who could doubt the honesty of a man who
could boast of his intimacy with honest Flamborough—and who could give such a con-
vincing proof of their friendship as to be able
to say, " I remember, I always beat him at
three jumps; but he could hop on one leg
farther than I." And this, too, after he had
disarmed all suspicion by asking the Doctor
if he was in any way related to the great

Primrose, that courageous monogamist, who
had been the bulwark of the Church. What
a flood of nonsensical learning he then poured
out upon him, quoting the opinions of San-
choniathon, Manetho, Berosus, and Ocellus
Lucanus, and ending with Greek. " ' But, sir,
I ask pardon ; I am straying from the question.' That he actually was ; nor could I for
my life see how the creation of the world
had anything to do with the business I was
talking of; but it was sufficient to show that
he was a man of letters, and I now reverenced
him the more."

The only fault in the plot of the ' Vicar of
Wakefield ' is the way in which the story is
huddled up at the close, and the lavish pro-
fusion with which, at the last, the favours of
fortune are showered down upon the family
which has so long been in the lowest depths
of adversity. " It never rains but it pours "
is an adage much more applicable to the evils
than to the blessings of life,—but it fully expresses the rapid succession of good-luck which
all of a sudden falls to the lot of the Primrose
family. When the Vicar and his son George
are beggars and in gaol, George is released
" from the incumbrances of justice," or, in
other words, set free, because the person he

was supposed to have wounded was detected to be an impostor; Sir William Thornhill is revealed in the person of Mr. Burchell, and offers his hand to Sophia. Olivia, who was thought to be dead after being vilely seduced, turns out to be alive, and the lawfully-married wife of her would-be betrayer—and this by the evidence of the quondam swindler, Ephraim Jenkinson,—and almost at the same moment news arrives that the merchant whose failure had caused Dr. Primrose the loss of his fortune, had been arrested, and given up property which was more than sufficient to pay all his creditors. And so the curtain falls upon a happy scene where the good Doctor has the pleasure of seeing all his family assembled once more by a cheerful fireside. " My two little girls sat upon each knee, the rest of the company by their partners. I had nothing now on this side of the grave to wish for; all my cares were over, my pleasure was unspeakable. It only remained that my gratitude in good fortune should exceed my former submission in adversity."

I have already alluded to the 'Simple Story,' by Mrs. Inchbald, 'The Female Quixote,' by Mrs. Lennox, the 'Spiritual Quixote,' by Graves, and the 'Fool of

Quality,' by Brooke,—and besides these I hardly know a novelist or a novel after the time of Goldsmith worth mentioning until we come to Mackenzie and Miss Burney. At all events, I know of no novels in the intermediate period which throw light upon the manners and opinions of the age, except in so far as their general worthlessness proves the low state of public taste. In a paper in the 'Microcosm' written by Canning, at Eton, in 1787, he describes the novels of his day as replete with "stories without invention, anecdotes without novelty, observations without aptness, and reflections without morality." To how many novels of the present day would the same criticism not apply? I say nothing of such romances as the 'Castle of Otranto' of Horace Walpole, which some think was intended as a burlesque, and the 'Old English Baron' of Clara Reeve, and the 'Romance of the Forest' and 'Mysteries of Udolpho' of Mrs. Radcliffe. They are too unreal to be of any service for my purpose, and it is enough to say that no young gentleman or young lady at the present day is likely to be frightened at night and disturbed in sleep by reading their shadowy horrors.

This style of romances is admirably parodied

by Miss Austen in her novel of 'Northanger
Abbey,' where Catherine Morland pays her first
visit to the Tilneys at the Abbey, a most com-
fortable house fitted up with all the appliances
of modern luxury; but which, misled by the
name, her imagination has painted as full of
trap-doors, sliding panels, secret passages, and
concealed mysteries.*   Henry Tilney tells her
that she will have to sleep in a bedroom apart
from the rest of the family, and asks, "Will not
your mind misgive you when you find yourself
in this gloomy chamber, too lofty and extensive for you, with only the feeble rays of a
single lamp to take in its size, its walls hung
with tapestry exhibiting figures as large as life,
and the bed, of dark green stuff or purple velvet, presenting even a funereal appearance?
Will not your heart sink within you? . . . You
will proceed into this small vaulted room, and
through this into several others, without perceiving anything very remarkable.   In one,
perhaps, there may be a dagger, in another a
few drops of blood, and in a third the remains
of some instrument of torture; but there being
nothing in all this out of the common way, and

* I am told by a friend, most competent to give an opinion,
that Barrett's 'Heroine' is one of the best parodies of these
romances, but I have not seen the book.

your lamp being nearly exhausted, you will return towards your own apartment. In repassing
through the small vaulted room, however, your
eyes will be attracted towards a large, old-
fashioned cabinet of ebony and gold, which,
though narrowly examining the furniture before, you had passed unnoticed. Impelled by
an irresistible presentiment, you will eagerly
advance to it, unlock its folding doors, and
search into every drawer; but for some time
without discovering anything of importance—
perhaps nothing but a considerable hoard of
diamonds. At last, however, by touching a
secret spring, an inner compartment will open,
a roll of paper appears, you seize it—it contains
many sheets of manuscript—you hasten with the
precious treasure into your own chamber; but
scarcely have you been able to decipher, 'Oh
thou, whosoever thou mayest be, into whose
hands these memorials of the wretched Matilda
may fall,' when your lamp suddenly expires in
the socket, and leaves you in total darkness."

After this pleasant description, Catherine retires to her bedroom to dress for dinner, and
she is about to unpack her trunk " when her
eye suddenly fell on a large high chest, standing back in a deep recess on one side of the
fire-place." She starts in wonder at the sight.

Here was the very realization of Henry's imaginary scene. " The lock was silver, though
tarnished from age ; at each end were the im-
perfect remains of handles also of silver, broken
perhaps prematurely by some strange violence ;
and in the centre of the lid was a mysterious
cipher in the same metal." The dinner-bell, however, rings, and Catherine has no time to satisfy
her eager curiosity. She must wait until bed-
time, and then when she goes to her apartment
her eyes are fascinated by the appearance of a
high, old-fashioned, black cabinet, which she had
not observed before. The key is in the door,
and with trembling eagerness she tries to unlock
it. After some difficulty she succeeds, and she
discovers a range of small drawers, which she
examines, and at last " her quick eyes fell on a
roll of paper pushed back into the further part
of the cavity, apparently for concealment, and
her feelings at that moment were indescribable.
Her heart fluttered, her knees trembled, and
her cheeks grew pale." She seizes the manuscript, and in her nervous anxiety snuffs out the
candle, and as the fire has died away she is
left in total darkness. She creeps into bed,
trembling from head to foot, while a howling
storm beats against the windows. In the morning she rushes to the cabinet and clutches the

manuscript. " Her greedy eye glanced rapidly over a page. She started at its import. Could it be possible, or did not her senses play her false ? An inventory of linen, in coarse and modern characters, seemed all that was before her ! If the evidence of sight might be trusted, she held a washing bill in her hand. She seized another sheet and saw the same articles, with little variation ; a third, a fourth, and a fifth presented nothing new. Shirts, stockings, cravats, and waistcoats faced her in each. Two others, penned by the same hand, marked an expenditure scarcely more interesting, in letters, hair-powder, shoe-string, and breeches-ball. And the larger sheet, which inclosed the rest, seemed, by its first cramp line, ' To poultice chestnut mare,' a farrier's bill ! "

From the description given by Canning of the novels of his youthful days must be excepted ' The Man of Feeling,' ' The Man of the World,' and ' Julia de Roubigné,' by Mackenzie. I do not know the exact dates when they were published, but I believe before the end of the century, and in point of style they deserve high praise. ' The Man of Feeling,' indeed, can hardly be called a novel, for it has no plot, and consists only of disjointed fragments ; the manuscript being assumed to have been used as wadding for his gun by a sporting curate. It reminds us in its tone of Sterne's 'Sentimental Journey,' and contains merely a few unconnected scenes in which the Man of Feeling alleviates distress and indulges in sentiments of pity. The hero is so shy and bashful that he cannot muster courage to declare his attachment to the lady whom he loves until he is on his death-bed, when she reciprocates the passion; but it is too late. He visits Bedlam, where the insane were treated more like wild beasts than men. " The clanking of chains, the wildness of their cries, and the imprecations which some of them uttered, formed a scene inexpressibly shocking." And such scenes might then, and for a long time afterwards, be witnessed in every lunatic-asylum in the kingdom. Terror, and not kind-ness, was the mode in which the poor afflicted creatures were treated, and the result, of course, was that few were restored to their senses."

'The Man of the World' is a regularly con-structed novel, and is much more interesting than the desultory sketches of 'The Man of Feeling,' although the chief incidents are rob-bery, seduction, and attempted incest. A country clergyman named Annesley has two children, a son and daughter, named William and Harriet. The squire of the parish where

he resides is a young baronet, Sir Thomas
Sindall, who is studying at Oxford, but in the
course of his vacations at home is smitten by
the beauty of Harriet, and determines if possible to seduce her. To effect this purpose he
thinks it necessary to undermine the principles
of her brother, and get him into his power.
He therefore persuades the father to send him
to Oxford, where, being introduced by the
baronet into a loose set of young men, he
becomes a gambler, and is extricated from his
debts by advances from Sir Thomas Sindall.
At last, on a pretended promise of being engaged as a travelling tutor, he is inveigled to
London, where he is again entrapped into play,
and stripped of his last shilling. Driven to
desperation, he possesses himself of a pistol,
attacks the " chair " of the man who had
won his money in the streets at night, and
succeeds in robbing him. He is, however,
tracked to his lodgings, arrested, and thrown
into Newgate to take his trial for the capital
felony. His sister Harriet comes to town to
visit him in prison, and there meets Sir Thomas,
who pretends the most sincere friendship and
pity. William Annesley is arraigned, and pleads
guilty. Sentence of death is passed, but the
punishment is commuted to transportation for

twelve years.   Harriet leaves London to return to her father's house, but on the road is
taken to a country inn, where Sir Thomas,
who, with her female attendant, had accompanied her, overpowers her reason by means
of drugs, and effects her ruin.   She reaches
home and conceals her shame from her father,
but in the course of time becomes a mother,
and the child is taken away under the care of
a woman.   Nothing further is heard of them,
and a cloak and other clothes found by the
side of a river lead to the supposition that they
have been drowned.   The father, who is in
weak health, hears the sad tale and dies, and
his wretched daughter dies also.   Years pass
on, Sir Thomas Sindall goes abroad, and when
he returns home brings with him a young lady
who, he says, had been confided to his care by
a friend when he was at the point of death.   She
grows up, and is beloved by a cousin of Sir
Thomas named Booth, whose affection she
returns.   But the infamous baronet wishes to
make her his victim, and when she fully under-
stands his designs, she escapes from the house,
but being betrayed by her attendant, is overtaken
and conveyed to the house of one of his creatures,
where she is on the point of being outraged by
Sir Thomas, when a woman—the person to

whom the care of Harriet's child had been entrusted—rushes into the room, and exclaims that
the young lady is Sir Thomas's own daughter,
the long lost child of Harriet. In the meantime her cries have brought upon the scene
Harriet's brother William, who had returned
from transportation, and Booth. A scuffle
ensues, swords are drawn, and Sir Thomas is
mortally wounded. I need not add that his
daughter and Booth are afterwards happily
married, and so the story, of which the above is
a mere outline, ends.

Although the incidents of this novel are very
much in unison with the incidents of the novels
of the century, with its profligate hero, its
ruined maiden, and its lone country inn as the
scene of villany, there is a marked improvement over most of them in tone and style.
There is no coarseness, and no vulgarity, nor,
unless my memory deceives me, does the book
contain a single oath. It betokens the dawn
of a period of more refined literary taste, which
was soon to brighten into day in the pages of
Miss Austen and Sir Walter Scott.

Julia de Roubigné has the uncommon fault
of being only too short. The story is told in a
series of letters, and the scenes are laid entirely
in France. The heroine is the daughter of a

French gentleman, reduced from affluence to poverty, whose hand is sought by a wealthy neighbour, M. Montauban, considerably older than herself. She at first refuses him, but is won over by his generosity to her father, whom he extricates from his difficulties, and she consents to marry him. But she does so in the belief that Savillon, the early object of her secret love, who had gone abroad, was married to another. This, however, was a mistake, and Savillon returns to France free to declare his passion, but learns that Julia is the wife of Montauban. He writes pressing for a secret interview, which she reluctantly and with perfect innocence of purpose consents to grant. But the suspicions of her husband are aroused, and when he has proof that the meeting has taken place, he determines to poison her. This he accomplishes by giving her a poisoned drink as a cordial, and when he finds from her dying avowal to him of all that had taken place, that she is perfectly innocent, he destroys himself with laudanum. The story is told in a charming style, and it is difficult to read parts of it without being affected to tears.

In one of his brilliant essays, Lord Macaulay says that " Miss Burney first showed that a tale might be written in which both the fashionable

and the vulgar life of London might be exhibited with great force and with broad comic
humour, and which yet should not contain a
single line inconsistent with rigid morality, or
even with virgin delicacy." But this is carrying
praise too far. There are scenes in ' Evelina '
which are certainly not such as virgin delicacy
now would imagine, and still less portray.

What are we to think of the scene in " Marybone Gardens," where Evelina, to protect herself from the insults of a young officer, throws
herself upon two courtesans, and walks with
them arm in arm ; and when she leaves them,
they get a gentleman between them and pinch
and pinion him to the great amusement of the
Miss Branghtons. This is certainly a situation
not very consistent with " virgin delicacy " of
mind, to say nothing of the extreme vulgarity
of the talk of such creatures as Captain Mirvan,
Madame Duval, and the whole family of
Branghtons. At the Pantheon a young lady,
the sister of Lord Orville, pretends to scold a
young nobleman for a profane allusion, and he
parries the attack by saying, " And how can one
sit by you and be good, when only to look at
you is enough to make one wicked, or wish to
be so ?" But it is impossible to read ' Evelina '
without seeing that a state of society existed

which was very different from that of the present day, and feeling thankful that our sisters and daughters can frequent public places, whether parks or gardens or ball-rooms, without being exposed to libertine advances, or offended by impertinent remarks.

What Lord Macaulay says of ' Evelina ' applies more truly to Miss Burney's 'Cecilia,' written at a later period; for this novel is really free from objectionable matter, so far as modesty is concerned. But it is not nearly so interesting a story, and is much more prosy. We respect ' Cecilia ' and all her well-meaning resolutions; but we fall in love with 'Evelina,' whose mistakes arise from the charming innocence of her heart.

It was for a long time believed that Miss Burney was only seventeen when she wrote 'Evelina.' If so, it was indeed an extraordinary book; but the question depended upon the exact period of her birth; and when Croker edited ' Boswell's Life of Johnson ' he took the pains, most properly and naturally one would think, to ascertain the fact by examining the parish register of the town where she was born, and it turned out that she was twenty-six when 'Evelina' was published. But this excited the ire of Macaulay, who hated Croker; and in an article on the 'Diary and Letters of Madame D'Arblay' he sneers at him, as if he had done an ungentlemanly action. He says that Miss Burney was too honest to confirm the report : *"probably she was too much a woman to contradict it:"* and that, although there was no want of low minds and bad hearts in the generation which witnessed· her first appearance as an authoress, "it did not however occur to them to search the parish register at Lynn in order that they might be able to twit a lady with having concealed her age. That truly chivalrous exploit was reserved for a bad writer of our own time, whose spite she had provoked by not furnishing him with materials for a worthless edition of 'Boswell's Life of Johnson,' some sheets of which our readers have doubtless seen round parcels of better books." I think it would be difficult in the annals of criticism to beat this. But when Lord Macaulay wrote that Miss Burney was too honest to confirm the report about her age, he forgot that in her preface to 'Evelina,' which was published anonymously, she speaks of herself "as a young female educated in the most secluded retirement," who "makes *at the age of seventeen her first appearance* on the great and busy stage of life." *

* In his edition of 'Boswell's Life of Johnson,' Croker took upon himself to omit, as he says, "in one or two instances, an

In his 'History of English Literature,' the late Mr. Shaw passes a rather severe criticism on this lady's works. "The chief defect of her novels," he says, "is vulgarity of feeling; not that falsely-called vulgarity which describes with congenial animation low scenes and humble personages, but the affectation of delicacy and refinement. The heroines are perpetually trembling at the thought of *impropriety*, and exhibit a nervous, restless dread of appearing indelicate, that absolutely renders them the very essence of vulgarity." I do not think that this is quite fair. Evelina and Cecilia are not vulgar, and the reason why they tremble at the thought of " impropriety " is that the manners of the age constantly exposed young women to contact with it both in conversation and conduct. They could not mix in society without hearing at times libertine language, from which they must have shrunk in proportion to their purity.

Miss Edgeworth's novel of ' Belinda ' was published in 1801, and belongs, therefore, to

indecent passage ; and to substitute in two or three others, for a coarse word, a more decorous equivalent." For this he was attacked by Macaulay, who called it capricious delicacy, and regretted the suppression of " a strong old-fashioned English word, familiar to all who read their Bibles." It is needless to determine which of the disputants was right—but at all events the controversy shows the difference between our free-spoken forefathers and ourselves.

the present century, but it describes a state of manners in *fashionable* life, which we may be certain is not worse than prevailed previously. In her preface, or advertisement, she called her story a Moral Tale, "not wishing to acknowledge a Novel," because "so much folly, error, and vice are disseminated in books classed under this denomination." * The heroine is a young lady who is sent by her aunt to London to pay a long visit to Lady Delacour, a fashionable dame, who is the victim of a disease which she supposes to be a cancer, and conceals from the knowledge of her husband and friends, putting herself in the hands of a quack doctor, with whom she has several interviews, in a small boudoir opening out of her bedroom; and these lead to the suspicion that she is engaged in some improper intrigue. The ailment from which she suffers was caused by a blow from a pistol, which she fired into the air when she met another lady with whom she had been engaged to fight a duel! She bears a brave front to the world, and assumes a gay appearance while she is consumed by inward

---

* Lord Jeffrey said, "A greater mass of trash and rubbish never disgraced the press of any country than the ordinary novels that filled and supported our circulating libraries, down nearly to the time of Miss Edgeworth's first appearance."

agony. The language which some of the young men admitted to the society of Lady Delacour and Belinda make use of in their presence is studded with oaths—and such as would be thought grossly improbable, if not impossible, now.   And Mrs. Freke is nearly as bad ; if she does not actually swear, she comes very near it in her talk, of which I have already in a previous page given a specimen.

Now, we must assume that Miss Edgeworth intended to represent the conversation and manners of society as she believed them to exist—although, no doubt, Mrs. Freke is, in some respects, a caricature ; and if her representation is true, we cannot but come to the conclusion that morality and good manners were at a very low ebb in fashionable life.

With the name of Jane Austen these references to the novels of the last century may fitly end.   But before saying a few words about her, I may, in passing, mention another authoress worthy of being placed beside her, and belonging to the same period,—I mean Miss Ferrier—whose three novels, ' Marriage,' ' Inheritance,' and ' Destiny,' especially the two former, I consider amongst the best in the English language. Sir Walter Scott speaks of her as a " gifted personage . . . . full of humour, and exceedingly ready at repartee; and all this without the least affectation of the blue-stocking." And Allan Cunningham says, " Edgeworth, Ferrier, and Austen, have all given portraits of real society far superior to anything man—vain man—has produced of the like nature."

But to return to Jane Austen. Strictly speaking, this charming writer belongs to the present century, for her first *publication* took place in 1811. But three of her novels were written several years before, and two of them had been offered in vain to the booksellers. Fully to appreciate the excellence of Miss Austen's works, one ought to have some acquaintance with the state of the literature of fiction at the time she began to write. Besides the gloomy horrors of the Radcliffe school, there was a flood of weak and vapid novels which deluged the libraries with trash.

In Hannah More's ' Cœlebs ' the hero questions two young ladies on the subject of books, and one of them says that she had read ' Tears of Sensibility,' and ' Rosa Matilda,' and ' Sympathy of Souls,' and ' Too Civil by Half,' and ' The Sorrows of Werter,' and ' The Stranger,' and ' The Orphans of Snowdon. ' " ' Yes, sir,' joined in the younger sister, who had not risen to so high a pitch of literature, 'and we have read 'Perfidy Punished,' and 'Jemmy and Jenny Jessamy,' and 'The Fortunate Footman,' and 'The Illustrious Chambermaid.'" I do not think that these were much worse, in point of morality, than many of the novels which now appear, and of which the incidents seem to be taken from the records of the Police Courts and the Divorce Courts; but the misfortune was, that at that time, a young lady had very little choice, and her mind must feed upon such garbage, or abstain from novel-reading altogether.

It is wonderful to think that Jane Austen, a young woman, the daughter of a country clergyman, brought up in absolute retirement, should, by the intuitive force of genius, have been able to produce a series of fictions which in a knowledge of the anatomy of the human heart, in purity and gracefulness of style, and in individuality of character, have never been surpassed.* We are introduced, at once, into the domestic life of England at the close of the century, and find that in her pages it does not much differ from that of the present day—the periwigs and swords have disappeared, and

---

* The late Sir George Lewis coupled the names of Defoe and Miss Austen together as writers of fiction, "which observes all the canons of probability."—See his 'Credibility of Early Roman History,' vol. ii. p. 489.

the habits of society are much the same as now. But still there are some differences which it is curious to observe, considering how short, in point of time, is the distance that separates us from the writer, and that there are still living persons who remember her. She is fond of introducing clergymen into her stories, and in some of them they are the heroes of the tale. But theology, and indeed religion, is kept entirely in the background. The type is rather secular than religious. But it is far higher and more refined than in the conceptions of the earlier novelists, although not so refined as it appears in the pages of a distinguished writer of the present day, I mean Anthony Trollope, who excels in the description of sleek Canons and polished Archdeacons, and courtly Bishops. The Reverend Josiah Crawley, perpetual curate of Hogglestock, would, in the hands of Fielding or Smollett, have been represented as smoking tobacco in the kitchen, drinking beer in the ale-house, and involved in very questionable scenes; but with all his poverty and obstinacy, he is a perfect gentleman and an accomplished scholar. The line which is now more strictly drawn as to the amusements in which the clergy allow themselves to indulge, was, in Miss Austen's time,

more flexible—and although in ' Mansfield
Park' the young clergyman, Edmund Bertram,
has some misgivings as to the propriety of
taking part in private theatricals, it is thought
quite a matter of course that clergymen should
dance at public balls, as the Rev. Mr. Tilney,
in ' Northanger Abbey,' does at Bath. And
the view taken of a clergyman's duties was
very superficial. With a snug parsonage and
decent income it seems to have been supposed
that nothing more was incumbent upon him
than to preach a few sermons, and he might
enjoy the pleasures of life with as little restric-
tion as if he were a layman.

In 'Persuasion' we have the following recom-
mendation of a living : " ' And a very good living
it was,' Charles added ; ' only five-and-twenty
miles from Uppercross, and in a very fine country—fine part of Dorsetshire. In the centre of
some of the best preserves in the kingdom, surrounded by three great proprietors, each more
careful and jealous than the other.' "

In 'Sense and Sensibility,' Robert Ferrars
laughs at the idea of his brother Edward becoming a clergyman. " The idea of Edward's
being a clergyman, and living in a small parsonage house, diverted him beyond measure ; and
when to that was added the fanciful imagery of

Edward reading prayers in a white surplice, and
publishing the banns of marriage between John
Smith and Mary Bacon, he could conceive nothing more ridiculous." And in 'Mansfield Park,'
the elder brother of Edmund Bertram says,
when Edmund is about to be ordained, " Seven
hundred a year is a fine thing for a younger
brother; and as, of course, he will live at
home, it will be all for his *menus plaisirs;* and
a sermon at Christmas and Easter, I suppose,
will be the sum total of all the sacrifice." It is,
however, only fair to state that Edmund has a
higher and more worthy conception of the
duties of a clergyman.

The vice of drunkenness hardly appears in
Miss Austen's novels; but she represents the
Rev. Mr. Elton as flustered with wine, if not
quite tipsy, when he surprises Emma by a de-
claration of his attachment as they drive home
together in a carriage after a dinner party.
And in another of her novels she speaks of a
clergyman "breathing of wine" as he passes
from the dining-room to the drawing-room to
join the ladies.

We are told by the Rev. Austen Leigh, in
the sketch he has lately published of Miss
Austen's life, that she was never in love. It is
difficult to believe this; but, if so, it is an

additional proof of her wonderful acquaintance with the human heart, that she was able
to write,

In maiden meditation fancy-free,

and yet to describe love in all its mysteries and
effects, with a subtlety of analysis and skill
which make her almost unapproachable amongst
novelists.   Where shall we find elsewhere such
touching pictures of concealed and aching attachment, where all hope seems to be struck dead,
as in Fanny Price in 'Mansfield Park,' in Elinor
Dashwood in 'Sense and Sensibility,' and in
Anne Elliot in 'Persuasion'?   The last heroine,
one of the most charming of Miss Austen's
characters, says to Captain Harville, " All the
privilege I claim for my own sex (it is not a
very enviable one, you need not covet it), is that
of loving longest, when existence or when hope
is gone."   And how finely contrasted with the
gnawing tooth of this " worm i' the bud " is the
half-formed love of Elizabeth Bennet for Mr.
Darcy in ' Pride and Prejudice,' and the un-
disguised and artless love of Catherine Morland
for Mr. Tilney in 'Northanger Abbey.'
    One thing, however, that strikes us in these
novels is the excessive and obtrusive eagerness
of all the minor heroines to get married.   Are

we to think that husband-hunting was the sole object in life of daughters, and the sole object for which mothers existed? 'Pride and Prejudice' opens with the sentence that when a single man of good fortune settles in a neighbourhood the maxim that he must be in want of a wife "is so well fixed in the minds of the surrounding families that he is considered as the rightful property of some one or other of their daughters." And when the Rev. Mr. Collins, who, it must be admitted, is intended as a fool, comes to visit his cousins with the intention of proposing to one of them, the first words he speaks in the presence of the young ladies, the Miss Bennets, is to assure them that he comes prepared to admire them. Here "he was interrupted by a summons to dinner; and the girls smiled on each other." As to Mrs. Bennet, she thinks and dreams and speaks of nothing else but getting her girls married. And the last chapter tells us that " happy for all her maternal feelings was the day on which Mrs. Bennet *got rid* of her two most deserving daughters " by marriage.

The story of 'Emma' is nothing but matchmaking from beginning to end, and a very charming story indeed it is. In 'Sense and Sensibility' Marianne Dashwood, who represents sensibility as opposed to her sister Elinor's sense, happens to fall and sprain her ancle, and is carried by a stranger to her mother's house. Sir John Middleton calls soon afterwards, and on being asked about the unknown by Elinor, answers, " Yes, yes, he is well worth catching, I can tell you, Miss Dashwood ; he has a pretty little estate of his own in Somersetshire besides; and if I were you I would not give him up to my younger sister, in spite of all this tumbling down hills." In ' Northanger Abbey,' the heroine, Catherine Morland, dances twice in the Lower Rooms at Bath with a young clergyman, whom she has never seen before ; and her friend Miss Thorpe, to whom she mentions the circumstance, immediately assumes that she has fallen desperately in love with him—exclaiming, when his sister is pointed out to her, " But where is her all-conquering brother ? Is he in the room ? Point him out to me this instant if he is. I die to see him." This is the speech of a silly girl, but from the general tone of the characters in these novels it would really seem as if it were thought that no man could look twice at a woman, or show her ordinary civility, without falling in love with her; or that, at all events, every woman was entitled to construe the commonest attentions as declarations of attachment.

I feel that I am treading on delicate ground, and my opinion on such a subject is perhaps worth little; but I cannot believe that, except amongst those who are known by the *sobriquet* of "Belgravian mothers," young women at the present day are so brought up. That they should desire to be happily married is most reasonable, and that they should fall in love is most natural; but this is something very different from the constant husband-hunting which we see displayed in Miss Austen's novels. For the change that has taken place in this respect several reasons may be assigned. In the first place, there is generally now-a-days amongst gentlewomen a greater degree of modesty and reserve; they are also better educated, and do not feed their minds with such trash as the old circulating libraries supplied. In the next, their resources are greatly multiplied, and they can find in works of charity and benevolence, in visiting the sick and ministering to the wants of the poor, means of occupation and outlets for their affections, which were practically unknown to young women of a former generation.

It is happily no part of my plan to discuss the novels of the present century, for their number would render the task one of appalling magnitude. In no department of literature has

authorship been so prolific as the Literature of
Fiction.   And, taking it as a whole, we have
good reason to be proud of it.   No nation can
produce the names of novelists which can stand
a comparison—I speak only of writers who are
deceased—with those of Scott, Thackeray, and
Dickens.*   So far as my knowledge of them
extends, German novels are heavy and uninteresting, and overloaded with minute details of
family *ménage ;* while those of France, with
a few brilliant exceptions—amongst which I
cannot refrain from mentioning the names of
Louis Reybaud and the dual-authors Erckmann-
Chatrian—are defiled by impurity.   Since the
beginning of the reign of Louis Philippe,
the French press has been deluged with
novels of what I may call the Cyprian School,
the staple incidents of which are crime, seduction and adultery.   If we may take these
as any indication of the state of morals in
France, it is difficult not to believe that it was
corrupt to the very core.   And whatever exception may be made for the provinces, where
domestic purity was less exposed to attack, I

---

* When I visited, in Paris, the prison called *Maison des Con-
damnés,* or *La Roquette,* and was in the library there, I asked
what books were most read by the prisoners, and I was told
that they were translations of the novels of Sir Walter Scott.

fear that this may be said with too much truth of the luxurious capital. If there had not been a demand for such a literature the supply would soon have ceased ; but the supply went on increasing, and betokened that

> ——increase of appetite
> Had grown by what it fed upon.

In **our own** country there have of late been novels—and some of them from female pens—which if not quite so unreserved in their details of profligacy, have been quite as bad in their tone and tendency. But the difference is this. In England they have been rather the exception than the rule ; whereas in France they have been the rule and not the exception. Would, however, that all novelists bore in mind the responsibility of their vocation ! There is no literature so fascinating, and none which is perused with more avidity by the young. The old prejudice which condemned novel-reading as dangerous and improper has almost worn away, and people have the sense to see that lessons of purity and truth may be taught most attractively when dressed in the garb of fiction, whether that fiction assume the form of parable or novel. What Bacon says of Poetry applies equally to Prose Fiction. " Therefore, because the acts or wants of true history have not that magnitude which satisfieth the mind of man, poesy feigneth acts and events greater and more heroical ; because true history propound- eth the successes and issues of actions not so agreeable to the merits of virtue and vice, there- fore poesy feigns them more just in retribution, and more according to revealed Providence ; because true history representeth actions and events more ordinary and less interchanged, therefore poesy indueth them with more rare- ness, and more unexpected and alternative variations ; so it appeareth that poesy serveth and conformeth to magnanimity, morality, and delectation." *

And even if the story has no moral, it is enough if it supplies the means of innocent re- creation ; and it need not be like ' Cœlebs in search of a Wife,' which has been called a "dra- matic sermon." Youth is the season of imagina- tion, and the imagination requires its proper aliment as much as any other of our faculties. But what shall we say of the writer who feeds it with the poison of impurity, and having the power to range at will over the whole realm of fancy, chooses for his subject the prurient details of vice and crime ? The coarseness of the

* ' Advancement of Learning,' Book ii.

novels of the last century may, to a certain extent, have acted as an antidote to the harm which they would otherwise have done, for often in them

> Vice is a monster of so frightful mien,
> As to be hated needs but to be seen ;

—although the age was so coarse that I doubt whether these lines were quite applicable then. But now a thin veil of decency is thrown over incidents which in themselves are as immoral as any of the adventures of 'Peregrine Pickle' or 'Tom Jones,' and the only antidote to their insidious mischief is their silliness and stupidity. Indeed, the veil of decency makes some of the modern novels more dangerous than the old ; just as, to use the illustration which Bacon has drawn from the Hebrew law regarding leprosy, "*If the whiteness have overspread the flesh, the patient may go abroad for clean ; but if there be any whole flesh remaining, he is to be shut up for unclean,*" which "noteth a position of moral philosophy, that men, abandoned to vice, do not so much corrupt manners as those that are half-good and half-evil." Again, I say, let novelists remember the responsibility they incur in the creation of their fictions. It would be well if they would lay to heart the words of an American writer, with which I will conclude this volume :—

" If they (*i.e.*, the ideals we set before us) are consistent with the conditions of our human nature and our human life, if they are conformed to the physical and moral laws of our nature, and the government and will of God, they are healthful and ennobling.   Such ideals can scarcely be too high or too ardently and stead-fastly adhered to.   But if they are false in their theory of life and happiness, if they are untrue to the conditions of our actual existence, if they involve the disappointment of our hopes, and discontent with real life, they are the bane of all enjoyments, and fatal to true happiness.   The brief excitement which these unreal dreams oc-casion, however highly wrought this excitement may be, is a poor offset to the painful contrasts which they necessarily involve." *   The author is here speaking of the day-dreams of our waking thoughts; but what he says applies equally to the fictions of the Novelist.

* Porter on ' The Human Intellect,' pp. 371-2. New York, 1869.

INDEX.

A.

ABDUCTION, 246
Addison, 14, 20, 40, 68, 118
'Adventures of Count Fathom,' 144, 278
'Amelia,' 9, 63, 86, 92, 103, 107, 274—277
'Amorous Widow,' 32
Astræa, 174, 176
'Atalantis,' New, 152, 196
Athenæus, 17, 66
Austen, Miss Jane, 39, 82, 99, 314, 328—337

B.

Bacon, 339, 341
Bambridge, Trial of, 90
Bate, Rev. Henry, 104
Bath, 28, 299
Bathing in public, 28
Beau Nash, 22, 83
Beaux, 64
Behn, Mrs., 52, 174—178
'Belinda,' 97, 102, 104, 130, 326
Bracegirdle, Mrs., 77
Bradshaigh, Lady, 33, 35, 252—254, 260
Brooke, Henry, 12, 21, 48, 93, 165
Buck-parson, 130
Bucks, 64
Burney, Miss, 28, 33, 324

C.

'Cœlebs,' 329, 340
Calderwood, Mrs., 84
Cameron, Dr., 59
Canning, 100, 266, 313, 317
Capital punishment, 46
Caricature, 49, 102
Carlyle, 7
Cassock, 133
'Cecilia,' 62
'Chances, The,' 33
Chesterfield, Lord, 27
'Chrysal, or the Adventures of Guinea,' 164, 165
Cibber, Colley, 247—249
'Clarissa Harlowe,' 132, 169, 215 218
Clergy, the, 121—134, 331—333
— distinction between Tow and Country, 129
Clubs, 66
Coaches, 79
Coffee Houses, 66
Coleridge, 18, 172, 260, 263
'Connoisseur,' 8, 23, 65, 73, 112
'Contempt of the Clergy,' 121, 12
'Conversation, Essay on,' 162
Country Squires, 111—113, 119
Coverley, Sir Roger de, 78, 113—1
Cowper's (Lady) Diary, 32, 59, 83 96
Croker and Lord Macaulay, 324—

D.

Debtors, law against, 93
Defoe, 3, 15, 213, 266
Delany, Mrs., 56, 80, 96, 103, 246, 259
De Quincey, 20
Derwentwater, Lord, 59
Dickens, 49, 244
Dinner hour, 210
Dress of Gentlemen, 58
— of Ladies, 55
Drunkenness, 86, 94—98
Drums, 63
Duelling, 103—109

E.

Edgeworth, Miss, 326—328
Edinburgh, 301
'Emma,' 335
'English Humourists,' 42
Ephraim the Quaker, 29
Essayists, 36—40
'Evelina,' 28, 33, 169, 323
Executions, 85, 87
Extravagance of conduct, 23

F.

'Fair Hypocrite,' 197—202
Faro's Daughters, 102
'Female Quixote,' 26, 152—154
Fielding, 9, 16, 85, 242, 259—277, 279
Fleet marriages, 134—148
Fleet Prison, 89
Fleet Registers, 144
Flying Coach, The, 79
'Fool of Quality,' 12, 21, 48, 93, 165—169
French Novels, 338

G.

Gambling, 101
Gay's 'Trivia,' 78, 123
Gent, Thomas, 88, 155
Godwin, 94, 113
Goldsmith, 22, 44, 58, 305—312
'Grandison, Sir Charles,' 22, 2 70, 107, 169, 219—241
Greeks, love as described by, 17
Grub St. Journal, 138
Gunnings, Miss, 65, 146

H.

Harrogate, 300
Hell Fire Club, 8
Herschel, Sir John, 214
Heywood, Mrs., 174, 203
Highwaymen, 83—87
Hill, Captain, 77
Hogarth, 42
Hoop-petticoats, 57
House rents, 76
Huggins, Trial of, 91
'Humphry Clinker,' 28, 55, 7 76, 104, 293—303
Husband-hunting, 335

I.

'Idler, The,' 38, 94
Imprisonment for debt, 93
Insults to women, 29

J.

Jeffrey, Lord, 327
Johnson, Dr., 5, 16, 38, 59, 68, 7 103, 106, 114, 219, 325

Jokes, practical, 65
'Joseph Andrews,' 126, 133, 271—274
'Julia de Roubigné,' 321
Justice of the Peace, 109

K.

Kingsley, Rev. Charles, 12, 48, 165
Kingston, Duchess of, 62

L.

Labourer, Condition of, 11
Lecky's 'History of Rationalism,' 40, 45, 47
Letters, Novels under form of, 170—1
Lewis, Sir George, 330
London, 76, 77, 295
Love, 17—24
'Love and Madness,' 27
'Love for Love,' 33

M.

Macaulay, Lord, 39, 124, 214, 322, 324—5
Maccaronies, 64
Mackenzie, 317
Malmesbury, Earl of, Letters, 85
Manley, Mrs., 195
'Man of Feeling,' The, 317
'Man of the World,' The, 318
'Mansfield Park,' 332
Marriage, 68—70, 237
Marriage of the Clergy, 124
'Marybone Gardens,' 71, 323
Masquerades, 62
Matrimony, 68—71
'Memoirs of a Lady of Quality,' 27, 291

'Microcosm,' 100, 266, 313
'Miss Betsy Thoughtless,' 28, 107, 203—212
Modesty, want of, 27
Mohock Club, 78
Molière, 153, 154
Montague, Lady Mary Wortl 125

N.

'New Atalantis,' 152, 196
Newspapers, Modern, 41
'Northanger Abbey,' 39, 314, 33
Novelists, responsibility of, 341

O.

Oldham's Poem on the Clergy, 12
'Oroonoko,' 179—184

P.

Painting, 42
'Pamela,' 126, 214, 218
Parson, 121—134, 331—3
'Peregrine Pickle,' 27, 59, 134, 2 —292
Periwigs, 60
Peter Pindar, 131
Petticoats, 57
'Persuasion,' 334
'Polly Honeycomb,' 156, 157
'Pompey, or the Adventures of Lap Dog,' 165
Porter on 'The Human Intellec 342
Pretty fellows, 64
'Pride and Prejudice,' 334
Prisons, 89
Puritans, 47

R.

Radcliffe, Mrs., 313
' Ranelagh,' 71—75
Refinement, Want of, 9
Religion, 13—16
Richardson, 21, 33, 35, 65, 81, 148,
        152, 160, 217, 238,
        265, 272, 276
  —   his style, 242
  —   correspondence, 247—
    257
  —   portrait of, 255—257
Roads, State of, 79
Robberies, 83—87
Romances, the old, 149—151
  —   parodied, 314—317
Romans, love as described by, 17
Rosamond's Pond, 210
' Roxana,' 266

S.

Satire, 49
Scott, Sir Walter, 52, 338
Sermons of Swift, 15
' Sense and Sensibility,' 332, 335
Settlement, Law of, 10
Shaw's ' History of English Litera-
  ture,' 10, 325
' Simple Story,' 104, 170
Smollett, 278—280
Social aspects, 7, 39, 68
Society, State of, 51
' Spectator,' 29, 31, 39, 54, 78, 99,
  116, 118, 132
' Spiritual Quixote,' 26, 61, 128,
  158, 303—304
Squire, Country, 111—113, 119
Squire Western, 112
Stage, 31—33
Steele, 16, 22, 30, 68, 97, 124

Stella, 24
Sterne, 16, 161
Streets, 78
Swearing, 98, 112
Swift, Dean, 14, 15, 25, 121, 124

T.

Taine's ' Hist. de la Littératu
  Anglaise,' 172, 245, 274, 279
' Tatler,' 22, 30, 56, 97, 100, 123
Thackeray, 2, 42, 75, 261—263
Thoresby's Diary, 83, 95
' Tom Jones,' 179, 258—271
Travelling, 79
Trees, punishment for cutting dow
  110
' Tristram Shandy,' 160
' Trivia,' 78, 123

U.

' Unfortunate Bride,' 194
' Unfortunate Happy Lady,' 188
  193
' Unhappy Mistake,' 194

V.

Vane, Lady, 27
' Vanity Fair,' 74
Vauxhall, 71—75
' Vicar of Wakefield,' 305—312

W.

Walpole, Horace, 11, 62, 72,
  84, 85, 101
' Wandering Beauty,' 185—188

' Wanton Wife,' 32
Watches, size of, 59
Watchmen, 86
Wesley, 62, 168
Wig-makers, petition of, 60
Wigs, 61
Women, insults to, 29
— and the Stage, 31
— influence of the Age upon, 24—28

Wray, Daniel, 64

Y.

York Cathedral, 300
Young, Dr., 158, 249

THE END.

BRADBURY, EVANS, AND CO., PRINTERS, WHITEFRIARS.

50A, ALBEMARLE STREET, LONDON

January, 1871.

MR. MURRAY'S
LIST OF STANDARD WORKS.

AIDS TO FAITH; a Series of Theological Essays. By various Writers. *Seventh Edition.* 8vo. 9s.

CONTENTS :

Miracles.—DEAN MANSEL.
Evidences of Christianity.—BISHOP OF KILLALOE.
Prophecy—and the Mosaic Record of Creation.—Rev. Dr. M'CAUL.
Ideology and Subscription.—Canon F. C. COOK.
The Pentateuch.—Rev. GEORGE RAWLINSON.
Inspiration.—BISHOP OF ELY.
Death of Christ.—ARCHBISHOP OF YORK.
Scripture and its Interpretation.—BISHOP OF GLOUCESTER AND BRISTOL.

AUSTIN'S (JOHN) LECTURES ON JURISPRUDENCE; or, The PHILOSOPHY OF POSITIVE LAW. *Third Edition.* Revised by ROBERT CAMPBELL. 2 vols. 8vo. 32s.

———— (SARAH) POLITICAL AND ECCLESIASTICAL HISTORY OF THE POPES OF ROME. Translated from the German of Leopold Ranke. *Fourth Edition.* With a Preface by DEAN MILMAN. 3 vols. 8vo. 30s.

BARROW'S (SIR JOHN) AUTOBIOGRAPHICAL MEMOIR, including Reflections, Observations, and Reminiscences at Home and Abroad. From Early Life to Advanced Age. Portrait. 8vo. 15s.

———— VOYAGES OF DISCOVERY AND RESEARCH WITHIN THE ARCTIC REGIONS, since 1818. Abridged and Arranged from the Official Narratives. 8vo. 15s.

BARRY'S (ALFRED, D.D.) MEMOIR OF THE LIFE AND WORKS OF SIR CHARLES BARRY, R.A. *Second Edition.* With Portrait and 40 Illustrations. Medium 8vo. 15s.

BELCHER'S (LADY) MUTINEERS OF THE 'BOUNTY,' AND THEIR DESCENDANTS; in PITCAIRN and NORFOLK ISLANDS. With Illustrations. Post 8vo. 12s.

BELL'S (SIR CHAS.) FAMILIAR LETTERS. With Portrait. Crown 8vo. 12s.

BERTRAM'S (JAS. G.) HARVEST OF THE SEA; A CONTRIBUTION TO THE NATURAL AND ECONOMIC HISTORY OF THE BRITISH FOOD FISHES. *Second Edition.* With 50 Illustrations. 12s.

BIBLE COMMENTARY; THE HOLY BIBLE, according to the AUTHORIZED VERSION, A.D. 1611. With an EXPLANATORY and CRITICAL COMMENTARY and a REVISION of the TRANSLATION. By BISHOPS and other CLERGY of the ANGLICAN CHURCH. Edited by F. C. COOK, M.A., Canon of Exeter. Vol. I. The PENTATEUCH. PARTS 1 & 2. Medium 8vo. 30s.

BIRCH'S (SAMUEL) HISTORY OF ANCIENT POTTERY AND PORCELAIN. Egyptian, Assyrian, Greek, Etruscan, and Roman. With coloured Plates and 200 Woodcuts. 2 vols. Medium 8vo. 42s.

BANKES' (George) STORY OF CORFE CASTLE, including the Private Memoirs of a Family resident there in the time of the Civil Wars, together with Unpublished Correspondence of the Ministers and Court of Charles I. at York and Oxford. With Woodcuts. Post 8vo. 10s. 6d.

BISSET'S (Andrew) HISTORY OF THE COMMONWEALTH OF ENGLAND, from the Death of Charles the First to the Expulsion of the Long Parliament by Cromwell. From MSS. in the State Paper Office, &c. 2 vols. 8vo. 30s.

BYRON'S (Lord) POETICAL WORKS. Edited with Notes. *Library Edition.* With Portrait. 6 vols. 8vo. 45s.

———————————————————— With Notes and Illustrations. *Cabinet Edition.* With Plates. 10 vols. Fcap. 8vo. 30s.

———————————————————— With Portrait and Illustrations. One Volume. Royal 8vo. 9s.

————————— LIFE. With his Letters and Journals. By THOMAS MOORE. With Notes and Illustrations. *Cabinet Edition.* With Plates. 6 vols. Fcap. 8vo. 18s.

————————————— With Portraits. One Volume. Royal 8vo. 9s.

BLUNT'S (Rev. J. J.) LECTURES ON THE RIGHT USE OF THE EARLY FATHERS. *Third Edition.* 8vo. 9s.

————————— UNDESIGNED COINCIDENCES IN THE OLD AND NEW TESTAMENTS: an Argument of their Veracity. With an Appendix, containing Undesigned Coincidences between the Gospels, Acts, and Josephus. *Ninth Edition.* Post 8vo. 6s.

————————— CHRISTIAN CHURCH DURING THE FIRST THREE CENTURIES. *Fourth Edition.* Post 8vo. 6s.

————————— PARISH PRIEST: His Duties, Acquirements, and Obligations. *Fifth Edition.* Post 8vo. 6s.

————————— PLAIN SERMONS PREACHED TO A COUNTRY CONGREGATION. *Fifth Edition.* 2 vols. Post 8vo. 12s.

BONAPARTE'S (Napoleon) CONFIDENTIAL CORRE-SPONDENCE WITH HIS BROTHER JOSEPH, KING OF SPAIN. Selected and Translated with Explanatory Notes. 2 vols. 8vo. 26s.

BORROW'S (George) GYPSIES OF SPAIN; their Manners, Customs, Religion and Language. *Third Edition.* 2 vols. Post 8vo. 18s.

————————— BIBLE IN SPAIN ; or, The Journeys, Adventures, and Imprisonments of an Englishman in an attempt to circulate the Scriptures in the Peninsula. *Fourth Edition.* 3 vols. Post 8vo. 27s.

————————— LAVENGRO ; The Scholar—The Gipsy—and The Priest. With Portrait. 3 vols. Post 8vo. 30s.

————————— ROMANY RYE ; A Sequel to Lavengro. 2 vols. Post 8vo. 21s.

BOSWELL'S (James) LIFE OF SAMUEL JOHNSON, LL.D.; including the TOUR to the HEBRIDES. By the Rt. Hon. J. W. CROKER. With Portraits. Royal 8vo. 10s.

BRAY'S (Mrs.) REVOLT OF THE PROTESTANTS IN THE CEVENNES. With some Account of the Huguenots in the Seventeenth Century. Post 8vo. 10s. 6d.

————— LIFE OF THOMAS STOTHARD, R.A. With Personal Reminiscences. With Portrait and Illustrations. 8vo. 21s.

BROGDEN'S (Rev. Jas.) ILLUSTRATIONS OF THE LITURGY AND RITUAL OF THE CHURCH OF ENGLAND AND IRELAND; selected from the Works of eminent Divines of the 17th Century. 3 vols. Post 8vo. 27s.

———————— CATHOLIC SAFEGUARDS AGAINST THE ERRORS, CORRUPTIONS, AND NOVELTIES OF THE CHURCH OF ROME. 3 vols. 8vo. 42s.

BULGARIA; NOTES on the RESOURCES and ADMINISTRATION of TURKEY—the CONDITION, CHARACTER, MANNERS, CUSTOMS, and LANGUAGE of the CHRISTIAN and MUSSULMAN POPULATIONS, &c. By S. G. B. ST. CLAIR and CHARLES A. BROPHY. 8vo. 12s.

CAMPBELL'S (LORD) LIVES OF THE LORD CHANCELLORS AND KEEPERS OF THE GREAT SEAL OF ENGLAND, from the Earliest Times to the Reign of George the Fourth. 10 vols. Post 8vo. 60s.

———————————— LIVES OF LORDS LYNDHURST AND BROUGHAM. 8vo. 16s.

——————— (SIR NEIL) JOURNAL OF OCCURRENCES, and Notes of Conversations with Napoleon at Fontainbleau and Elba in 1814–15. With a Memoir of that Officer. By his Nephew, REV. A. N. C. MACLACHLAN. With Portrait. 8vo. 15s.

——————— (GEORGE) MODERN INDIA. A Sketch of the System of Civil Government. With some Account of the Natives and Native Institutions. *Second Edition.* 8vo. 16s.

——————— INDIA AS IT MAY BE. An Outline of a Proposed Government and Policy. 8vo. 12s.

CASTLEREAGH'S (VISCOUNT) MEMOIRS, CORRESPONDENCE, AND DESPATCHES. Edited by THE MARQUIS OF LONDONDERRY. 12 vols. 8vo. 14s. each.

CATHCART'S (SIR GEORGE) COMMENTARIES ON THE WAR IN RUSSIA AND GERMANY, 1812–13. With Plans. 8vo. 14s.

———————— MILITARY OPERATIONS IN KAFFRARIA. *Second Edition.* 8vo. 12s.

CHALMERS' (GEORGE) POETICAL REMAINS OF SOME OF THE SCOTTISH KINGS. Post 8vo. 10s. 6d.

CHURCH AND THE AGE. Essays on the Principles and Present Position of the Anglican Church. By various Writers. *Second Edition.* 8vo. 14s.

CONTENTS :

Anglican Principles.—DEAN HOOK.
Modern Religious Thought.—BISHOP OF GLOUCESTER AND BRISTOL.
The State, The Church, and Synods.—Rev. Dr. IRONS.
Religious Use of Taste.—Rev. R. ST. JOHN TYRWHITT.
Place of the Laity.—Professor BURROWS.
The Parish Priest.—Rev. WALSHAM HOW.
Divines of 16th and 17th Centuries.—Rev. A. W. HADDAN.
Liturgies and Ritual.—Rev M. F. SADLER.
The Church and Education.—Rev. Dr. BARRY.
Indian Missions.—SIR BARTLE FRERE.
The Church and the People.—Rev. W. D. MACLAGAN.
Conciliation and Comprehension.—Rev. A. WEIR.

CHURTON AND JONES' (ARCHDEACON) NEW TESTAMENT. With a Plain Explanatory Commentary for Families and General Readers; with more than 100 Illustrations of Scripture Scenes, from Photographs and Sketches taken on the Spot. 2 vols. 8vo. 21s.

CICERO'S LIFE and TIMES, with his CHARACTER as a STATES-
MAN, ORATOR, and FRIEND; and a Selection from his Correspondence and
Orations. By WILLIAM FORSYTH. *Third Edition.* With 40 Illus-
trations. 8vo. 10s. 6d.

CLODE'S (C. M.) HISTORY OF THE ADMINISTRATION
AND GOVERNMENT OF THE BRITISH ARMY FROM THE REVO-
LUTION, 1688. 2 vols. 8vo. 42s.

COLCHESTER'S (LORD) DIARY AND CORRESPONDENCE
WHILE SPEAKER OF THE HOUSE OF COMMONS, 1802-1817. Edited
by HIS SON. With Portrait. 3 vols. 8vo. 42s.

CORNWALLIS'S (MARQUIS) CORRESPONDENCE DURING
THE AMERICAN WAR: Administrations in India,—Union with Ireland,
and Peace of Amiens. Edited by CHARLES ROSS. *Second Edition.* With
Portrait. 3 vols. 8vo. 63s.

COWPER'S (COUNTESS) DIARY WHILE LADY OF THE
BEDCHAMBER TO CAROLINE, PRINCESS OF WALES, 1714-20.
Edited by Hon. SPENCER COWPER. *Second Edition.* Portrait. 8vo. 10s. 6d.

CRABBE'S (REV. GEORGE) POETICAL WORKS; with his Life,
Letters, and Journals. By HIS SON. With Notes and Illustrations.
Cabinet Edition. With Plates, 8 vols., Fcap. 8vo, 24s.; or, with Illustrations,
one volume, Royal 8vo, 7s.

CROKER'S (RT. HON. J. W.) WORKS OF ALEXANDER
POPE. With Introductions and Notes by REV. WHITWELL ELWIN. Vols. I.
to III. With Portraits. 8vo. 10s. 6d. each.

———— BOSWELL'S LIFE OF SAMUEL JOHNSON, D.D.,
including their Tour to the Hebrides. Edited with Notes. With Portraits.
1 vol. Royal 8vo. 10s.

———— ESSAYS ON THE FRENCH REVOLUTION.
8vo. 16s.

CROWE AND CAVALCASELLE'S HISTORY OF PAINTING
IN ITALY, from the Second to the Sixteenth Century. With 100
Illustrations. 3 vols. 8vo. 63s.

———————— HISTORY OF PAINTING IN NORTH
ITALY. With Illustrations. 2 vols. 8vo.

———————— EARLY FLEMISH PAINTERS. With
Illustrations. Post 8vo. 12s.

CUNNINGHAM'S (PETER) GOLDSMITH'S WORKS. Printed
from the last Edition, revised by the Author, and edited, with Notes. With
Vignettes. 4 vols. 8vo. 30s.

———————— JOHNSON'S LIVES OF THE MOST
EMINENT ENGLISH POETS. With Critical Observations on their Works.
Edited, with Notes. 3 vols. 8vo. 22s. 6d.

———————— (J. D.) HISTORY OF THE SIKHS, from
the Origin of the Nation to the Battles of the Sutlej. *Second Edition.* With
Maps. 8vo. 15s.

CUST'S (SIR EDWARD) ANNALS OF THE WARS OF THE
18TH AND 19TH CENTURIES, 1700-1815. With Maps. 9 vols. Fcap. 8vo.
5s. each.

———— LIVES OF THE WARRIORS OF THE 17TH CEN-
TURY—The Thirty Years' War—The Civil Wars of France and England—
The Commanders of Fleets and Armies before the Enemy. 1604-1704. 6 vols.
Post 8vo. 50s.

DARWIN'S (CHARLES) Journal of Researches into the Natural History of the Countries visited during a Voyage round the World. *Tenth Edition*. Post 8vo. 9s.

———— ORIGIN OF SPECIES BY MEANS OF NATURAL SELECTION; or, the Preservation of Favoured Races in the Struggle for Life. *Fifth Edition*. Post 8vo. 14s.

———— FERTILIZATION OF ORCHIDS THROUGH INSECT AGENCY, and as to the good of Intercrossing. With Woodcuts. Post 8vo. 9s.

———— VARIATION OF ANIMALS AND PLANTS UNDER DOMESTICATION. With Illustrations. 2 vols. 8vo. 28s.

———— DESCENT OF MAN, and on SELECTION in RELATION to SEX. With Illustrations. 2 vols. Crown 8vo. 24s

DELEPIERRE'S (OCTAVE) HISTORY OF FLEMISH LITERA- TURE FROM THE TWELFTH CENTURY. 8vo. 9s.

DENISON'S (E. B.) LIFE OF BISHOP LONSDALE. With Portrait. Crown 8vo. 10s. 6d.

DERBY'S (EARL OF) HOMER'S ILIAD RENDERED INTO ENGLISH BLANK VERSE *Seventh Edition*. 2 vols. Post 8vo. 10s.

DE ROS' (LORD) MEMORIALS OF THE TOWER OF LON- DON. *Second Edition*. With Illustrations. Crown 8vo. 12s.

DEVEREUX'S (W. B.) LIVES OF THE EARLS OF ESSEX IN THE REIGNS OF ELIZABETH, JAMES I., AND CHARLES I. Portraits. 2 vols. 8vo. 30s.

DOUGLAS' (SIR HOWARD) LIFE AND ADVENTURES. By S. W. FULLOM. 8vo. 14s.

———— TREATISE ON GUNNERY. *Fifth Edition*. Woodcuts. 8vo. 21s.

———— CONSTRUCTION OF MILITARY BRIDGES AND THE PASSAGE OF RIVERS IN MILITARY OPERATIONS. Plates. 8vo. 21s.

DUCANGE'S MEDIÆVAL LATIN-ENGLISH DICTIONARY. Illustrated and enlarged by numerous additions, derived from patristic and scholastic authors, the works of the Record Commission, Mediæval Histories, Charters, Glossaries, &c., &c. By E. A. DAYMAN, B.D. 4to. [*In Preparation.*

DUDLEY'S (EARL OF) LETTERS TO BISHOP COPLESTONE. *Second Edition*. Portrait. 8vo. 10s. 6d.

DYER'S (THOS. H.) HISTORY OF MODERN EUROPE, from the Taking of Constantinople by the Turks to the Close of the War in the Crimea, 1453–1857. With an Index. 4 vols. 8vo. 42s.

———— LIFE AND LETTERS OF JOHN CALVIN. Com- piled from authentic Sources. With Portrait. 8vo. 15s.

EASTLAKE'S (SIR CHARLES) CONTRIBUTIONS TO THE LITERATURE OF THE FINE ARTS. *Second Edition*. 8vo. 12s.

———— MEMOIR; WITH SELECTIONS FROM HIS CORRE- SPONDENCE, and Additional Contributions to the Literature of the Fine Arts. By LADY EASTLAKE. 8vo 12s.

———— ITALIAN SCHOOLS OF PAINTING. From the German of KUGLER. Edited, with Notes. *Sixth Edition*. With 100 Illustrations. 2 vols. Post 8vo. 30s.

EGYPTIANS (ANCIENT): Their Manners and Customs. By SIR J. GARDNER WILKINSON. *Fourth Edition.* With Illustrations. 2 vols. Post 8vo. 12s.

———————— **(MODERN): Their MANNERS and CUSTOMS. By** E. W. LANE. *Fifth Edition.* With Illustrations. 2 vols. Post 8vo. 12s.

ELLESMERE'S (LORD) ESSAYS ON HISTORY, BIOGRAPHY, GEOGRAPHY, and ENGINEERING. 8vo. 12s.

ELPHINSTONE'S (MOUNT STUART) HISTORY OF INDIA. The Hindu and Mahometan Periods. *Fifth Edition.* With Notes and Additions by PROFESSOR COWELL. With Map. 8vo. 18s.

ELWIN'S (REV. WHITWELL) WORKS OF ALEXANDER POPE. With Introductions and Notes, and many original Letters now for the first time published. With Portrait Vols. I. to III. 8vo. 10s. 6d. each.

ENGEL'S (CARL) MUSIC OF THE MOST ANCIENT NATIONS; particularly of the Assyrians, Egyptians, and Hebrews; with Special Reference to the Discoveries in Western Asia and in Egypt. *Second Edition.* With 100 Illustrations. 8vo. 10s. 6d.

FARRAR'S (REV. A. S.) CRITICAL HISTORY OF FREE THOUGHT IN REFERENCE TO THE CHRISTIAN RELIGION. 8vo. 16s.

FEATHERSTONHAUGH'S (G. W.) TOUR THROUGH THE SLAVE STATES OF NORTH AMERICA, from the River Potomac, to Texas and the Frontiers of Mexico. 2 vols. 8vo. 26s.

FERGUSSON'S (JAMES) HISTORY OF ARCHITECTURE IN ALL COUNTRIES. From the Earliest Times. With 1200 Illustrations. VOLS. I. & II. 8vo. 42s. each.

———————— Vol. III. The Modern Styles. With 312 Illustrations. 8vo. 31s. 6d.

FERRIER'S (T. P.) CARAVAN JOURNEYS IN PERSIA, AFFGHANISTAN, HERAT, TURKISTAN, AND BELOOCHISTAN, with Descriptions of Meshed, Balk, and Candahar, and Sketches of the Nomade Tribes of Central Asia. *Second Edition.* With Map. 8vo. 21s.

———————— HISTORY OF THE AFFGHANS. With Map. 8vo. 21s.

FORSTER'S (JOHN) HISTORY OF THE GRAND REMON- STRANCE, 1641. With an Introductory Essay on English Freedom under Plantagenet and Tudor Sovereigns. *Second Edition.* 8vo. 12s.

———————— LIFE OF SIR JOHN ELIOT, 1590–1632. With Portrait. 2 vols. 8vo. 30s.

———————— CROMWELL, DEFOE, STEELE, CHURCHILL, FOOTE.—Biographies. Post 8vo. 12s.

FORSYTH'S (WILLIAM) LIFE AND TIMES OF CICERO. With Selections from his Correspondence and Orations. *Third Edition.* With Illustrations. 8vo. 10s. 6d.

FOSS' (EDWARD) JUDGES OF ENGLAND. With Sketches of their Lives, and Notices of the Courts at Westminster, from the Conquest to the Present Time. 9 vols. 8vo. 126s.

——— **BIOGRAPHICAL DICTIONARY OF THE JUDGES** OF ENGLAND, FROM THE CONQUEST TO THE PRESENT TIME, 1066-1870. Condensed from the above work. Medium 8vo. 21s.

GEORGE THE THIRD'S CORRESPONDENCE WITH LORD
NORTH, 1769-82. Edited, with Notes and Introduction, by W. BODHAM DONNE. 2 vols. 8vo. 32s.

GIBBON'S (EDWARD) HISTORY OF THE DECLINE AND
FALL OF THE ROMAN EMPIRE. With Notes by DEAN MILMAN and M. GUIZOT. A new Edition. Edited, with additional Notes incorporating the Researches of recent writers, by WM. SMITH, D.C.L. With Portrait and Maps. 8 vols. 8vo. 60s.

GOLDSMITH'S (OLIVER) WORKS. Edited, with Notes, by
PETER CUNNINGHAM, F.S.A. With Portrait and Vignettes. 4 vols. 8vo. 30s.

GRENVILLE'S (GEORGE) PUBLIC AND PRIVATE COR-
RESPONDENCE WITH HIS FRIENDS AND CONTEMPORARIES, during a period of Thirty Years. Including his Diary of Political Events while First Lord of the Treasury. Edited, with Notes, by W. J. SMITH. 4 vols. 8vo. 16s. each.

GREY'S (EARL) CORRESPONDENCE WITH KING WILLIAM
IV. and SIR HERBERT TAYLOR, from November, 1830, to the Passing of the Reform Act in 1832. Edited by HIS SON. 2 vols. 8vo. 30s.

GROTE'S (GEORGE) HISTORY of GREECE, from the Earliest
Period to the Close of the Generation contemporary with Alexander the Great. *Fourth Edition.* With Portrait, Maps, and Plans. 8 vols. 8vo. 112s.

———————————— *Cabinet Edition.* With Portrait an
Plans. 12 vols. Post 8vo. 6s. each.

———— PLATO AND THE OTHER COMPANIONS OF
SOCRATES. *Second Edition.* 3 vols. 8vo. 45s. *** An Index, 8vo. 2s. 6d.

GRUNER'S (LEWIS) TERRA-COTTA ARCHITECTURE OF
NORTH ITALY. From careful Drawings and Restorations. With Illustrations, engraved and printed in Colours. Small folio. 5l. 5s.

GUIZOT'S (M) MEDITATIONS ON CHRISTIANITY, AND
ON THE RELIGIOUS QUESTIONS OF THE DAY. 2 vols. Post 8vo. 20s.

GURWOOD'S (COL.) SELECTIONS FROM THE WELLING-
TON DESPATCHES AND GENERAL ORDERS. Intended as a convenient Manual for Officers while Travelling or on Service. 8vo. 18s.

GUSTAVUS VASA (LIFE OF). His Exploits and Adventures.
With Extracts from his Correspondence. With Portrait. 8vo. 10s. 6d.

HALLAM'S (HENRY) CONSTITUTIONAL HISTORY OF
ENGLAND, from the Accession of Henry VII. to the Death of George II. *Eighth Edition.* 3 vols. 8vo. 30s.

———————— HISTORY OF THE STATE OF EUROPE
DURING THE MIDDLE AGES. *Eleventh Edition.* 3 vols. 8vo. 30s.

———————— LITERARY HISTORY OF EUROPE. *Fourth
Edition.* 3 vols. 8vo. 36s.

———————— HISTORICAL WORKS. With the Author's latest
Corrections and Additions. Containing HISTORY OF ENGLAND—EUROPE DURING THE MIDDLE AGES—LITERARY HISTORY OF EUROPE. *Cabinet Edition.* 10 vols. Post 8vo. 6s. each.

*** The public are cautioned against editions of Hallam's Histories recently advertised, which are merely reprints of old editions, *which the author himself declared to be full of errors,* and do not contain the additional notes, &c.

The only correct editions are published by JOHN MURRAY.

HAMILTON'S (JAMES) WANDERINGS IN NORTHERN
AFRICA, BENGHAZI, CYRENE, THE OASIS OF SIWAH, &c. *Second Edition.* With Woodcuts. Post 8vo. 12*s.*

———————— **(W. J.) RESEARCHES IN ASIA MINOR,**
PONTUS, AND ARMENIA; with some Account of the Antiquities and Geology of those Countries. With Map and Plates. 2 vols. 8vo. 38*s.*

HANDBOOK TO THE CATHEDRALS OF ENGLAND; a
Concise History of each See, with Biographical Notices of the Bishops. By RICHARD J. KING, B.A. With 300 Illustrations. 6 vols. Post 8vo. Containing:—

Southern Division; WINCHESTER, SALISBURY, EXETER, WELLS, ROCHESTER, CANTERBURY, AND CHICHESTER. With 110 Illustrations. 2 vols. Crown 8vo. 24*s.*

Eastern Division; OXFORD, PETERBOROUGH, ELY, NORWICH, AND LINCOLN. With 90 Illustrations. Crown 8vo. 18*s.*

Western Division; BRISTOL, GLOUCESTER, HEREFORD, WORCES-TER, AND LITCHFIELD With 60 Illustrations. Crown 8vo. 16*s.*

Northern Division; YORK, RIPON, DURHAM, CARLISLE, CHESTER, AND MANCHESTER. With 60 Illustrations. Crown 8vo. 2 vols. 21*s.*

HANNAH'S (REV. DR.) DIVINE AND HUMAN ELEMENTS
IN HOLY SCRIPTURE. 8vo. 10*s.* 6*d.*

HATHERLEY'S (LORD) CONTINUITY OF SCRIPTURE, as
declared by the Testimony of our Lord and of the Evangelists and Apostles. *Fourth Edition.* Crown 8vo. 6*s.*

HEAD'S (SIR F. B.) ROYAL ENGINEER, AND THE ROYAL
ESTABLISHMENTS AT WOOLWICH AND CHATHAM. With Illustrations. 8vo. 12*s.*

———————— **DEFENCELESS STATE OF GREAT BRITAIN.**
Contents—1. Military Warfare. 2. Naval Warfare. 3. The Invasion o England. 4. The Capture of London by a French Army. 5. The Treatmen of Women in War. 6. How to Defend Great Britain. Post 8vo. 12*s.*

———————— **FAGGOT OF FRENCH STICKS; or, Description of**
Paris in 1851. *2nd Edition.* 2 vols. Post 8vo. 12*s.*

———————— **DESCRIPTIVE ESSAYS.** Contributed to the 'Quar-terly Review.' 2 vols. Post 8vo. 18*s.*

HERODOTUS: A New English Version. Edited, with copious
Notes, from the most Recent Sources of Information. By GEORGE RAWLINSON, M.A. Assisted by Sir HENRY RAWLINSON and Sir GARDNER WILKINSON. *Second Edition.* With Maps and Woodcuts. 4 vols. 8vo. 48*s.*

HESSEY'S (REV. DR.) SUNDAY: its Origin, History, and
Present Obligations. *Second Edition.* Post 8vo. 9*s.*

HILL (FREDERICK) ON CRIME: its Amount, Causes, and
Remedies. 8vo. 12*s.*

HOMER'S ILIAD, rendered into English Blank Verse. By the
EARL OF DERBY. *Seventh Edition.* 2 vols. Small 8vo. 10*s.*

HOOK'S (DEAN) CHURCH DICTIONARY: a Manual of Reference
for the Clergy—Students—and General Readers. *Tenth Edition.* 8vo. 16*s.*

HORACE. A New Edition of the Text. Edited by DEAN
MILMAN. With 100 Illustrations. Small 8vo. 7*s.* 6*d.*

———————— **LIFE.** By DEAN MILMAN. With Illustrations. 8vo. 9*s.*

JAMESON'S (Mrs.)· LIVES OF THE EARLY ITALIAN
PAINTERS—and the Progress of Painting in Italy from Cimabue to Bassano.
Tenth Edition. With 50 Portraits. Post 8vo. 12s.

JOHNSON'S (Samuel) LIFE. By JAMES BOSWELL. In-
cluding the Tour to the Hebrides. Edited by the Rt. Hon. J. W. Croker.
With Portraits. Royal 8vo. 10s.

———— LIVES OF THE MOST EMINENT ENGLISH
POETS, with Critical Observations on their Works. Edited, with Notes,
by Peter Cunningham, F.S.A. With Portrait. 3 vols. 8vo. 22s. 6d.

JOHNSTON'S (Wm.) ENGLAND AS IT IS: Political, Social,
and Industrial, in the Nineteenth Century. 2 vols. Post 8vo. 18s.

JONES AND CHURTON'S (Archdeacon) NEW TESTA-
MENT. Edited, with a Plain Practical Commentary for the use of
Families and General Readers. With 100 Panoramic and other Views
from Sketches and Photographs made on the Spot. 2 vols. Crown 8vo. 21s.

JUNIUS; the Handwriting of Junius professionally investigated.
By Mr. CHABOT, Expert. With Preface and Collateral Evidence, by the
Hon. Edward Twisleton. With Facsimiles, Woodcuts, &c. 4to.

KEN'S (Bishop) LIFE. *Second Edition.* With Portrait. 2 vols.
8vo. 18s.

KERR'S (Robert) GENTLEMAN'S HOUSE; or, How to Plan
English Residences, from the Parsonage to the Palace. *Third Edition.*
With Views and Plans. 8vo. 24s.

———— (R. Malcolm) BLACKSTONE'S COMMENTARIES,
adapted to the present state of the Law. *Fourth Edition.* 4 vols. 8vo.
[*In the Press.*

KING'S (Rev. C. W.) ANTIQUE GEMS; their Origin, Use, and
Value, as Interpreters of Ancient History, and as illustrative of Ancient Art.
Second Edition. With Illustrations. 8vo. 24s.

KIRK'S (J. Foster) HISTORY OF CHARLES THE BOLD,
DUKE OF BURGUNDY. With Portraits. 3 vols. 8vo. 45s.

KORFF'S (Baron) ACCESSION OF NICHOLAS I., compiled
by special command of the Emperor Alexander II. Translated from the
Russian. 8vo. 10s. 6d.

KUGLER'S (Franz) HISTORY OF PAINTING (The Italian
Schools). Edited, with Notes, by SIR CHARLES EASTLAKE. *Sixth
Edition.* With Illustrations. 2 vols. Post 8vo. 30s.

———————————— (German, Dutch, and Flemish Schools).
Edited, with Notes, by Dr. WAAGEN. *Second Edition.* With Illustrations,
2 vols. Post 8vo. 24s.

LANE'S (Edw. W.) ACCOUNT OF THE MANNERS AND
CUSTOMS OF THE MODERN EGYPTIANS. *Fifth Edition.* With Woodcuts. 2 vols. Post 8vo. 12s.

LAYARD'S (A. H.) TRAVELS AND RESEARCHES AT
NINEVEH AND BABYLON. With an Account of the Manners and Arts
of the Ancient Assyrians; being the Narrative of a First and Second Expedition to the Ruins of Assyria. With Maps and Illustrations. 3 vols. 8vo.
57s.

LENNEP'S (H. Van) TRAVELS IN ASIA MINOR. With
Illustrations of Biblical Literature and Archæology. With Maps and Illustrations. 2 vols. Post 8vo. 24s.

LEWIS' (Sir G. C.) ESSAY ON THE GOVERNMENT OF
DEPENDENCIES. 8vo. 12s.

LEXINGTON (The) PAPERS; or, Some Account of the Courts
of London and Vienna at the end of the 17th Century. Edited by HON. H.
MANNERS SUTTON. 8vo. 14s.

LIDDELL'S (Dean) HISTORY OF ROME: from the Earliest
Times to the Establishment of the Empire. With Chapters on the History
of Literature and Art. 2 vols. 8vo. 28s.

LINDSAY'S (Lord) LIVES OF THE LINDSAYS; or, a
Memoir of the Houses of Crawford and Balcarres. 3 vols. 8vo. 24s.

LOWE'S (Sir Hudson) HISTORY OF THE CAPTIVITY OF
NAPOLEON AT ST. HELENA. Edited by WILLIAM FORSYTH. With
Portrait. 3 vols. 8vo. 45s.

LYELL'S (Sir Charles) PRINCIPLES OF GEOLOGY; or,
the Ancient Changes of the Earth and its Inhabitants, as illustrated by Geological Monuments. *Tenth Edition.* With Illustrations. 2 vols   8vo.   32s.

—————— **ANTIQUITY OF MAN FROM GEOLOGICAL**
EVIDENCES. With Remarks on Theories of the Origin of Species by
Variation. *Third Edition.* With Illustrations. 8vo. 14s.

LYTTON'S (Lord) LOST TALES OF MILETUS. *Second*
Edition. Post 8vo. 7s. 6d.

—————— **POEMS.** *A New Edition.* Post 8vo. 10s. 6d.

MACDOUGALL'S (Col.) MODERN WARFARE AS IN-
FLUENCED BY MODERN ARTILLERY. With Plans and Woodcuts.
Post 8vo. 12s.

MACGREGOR'S (John) CRUISE IN THE 'ROB ROY'
CANOE ON THE JORDAN, THE NILE, THE RED SEA, LAKE OF
GENNESARETH, &c. *Third Edition.* With Maps and Illustrations. Crown
8vo. 12s.

MAETZNER'S (Professor) COPIOUS ENGLISH GRAMMAR.
A Methodical, Analytical, and Historical Treatise on the Orthography,
Prosody, Inflections, and Syntax of the English Tongue. With numerous
authorities, cited in the order of historical development. 3 vols. 8vo.
[In the Press.

MAHON (Lord). See STANHOPE (Earl of).

MAINE'S (H. Sumner) ANCIENT LAW; its Connection with
the Early History of Society, and its relation to Modern Ideas. *Fourth*
Edition. 8vo. 12s.

MANSEL'S (Dean) LIMITS OF RELIGIOUS THOUGHT
EXAMINED. *Fifth Edition.* Post 8vo. 8s. 6d.

MARCO POLO'S TRAVELS. A New English Version. Illus-
trated by the Light of Modern Travels and Oriental Writers. By COL.
YULE, C.B. With Maps and Illustrations. 2 vols. Medium 8vo.

MARRYAT'S (Joseph) HISTORY OF MEDIÆVAL AND
MODERN POTTERY AND PORCELAIN *Third Edition.* With Coloured
Plates and 240 Woodcuts. Medium 8vo. 42s.

MILMAN'S (DEAN) HISTORY OF THE JEWS, from the
EARLIEST PERIOD, continued to MODERN TIMES, with a new Preface and
Notes. 3 vols. Post 8vo. 18s.

———————————————— OF CHRISTIANITY, from the
BIRTH OF CHRIST to the ABOLITION of PAGANISM in the ROMAN EMPIRE.
3 vols. Post 8vo. 18s.

————————————— LATIN CHRISTIANITY;
and of the POPES down to NICHOLAS V. 9 vols. Post 8vo. 54s.

————— CHARACTER AND CONDUCT OF THE APOS-
TLES CONSIDERED AS AN EVIDENCE OF CHRISTIANITY. 8vo.
10s. 6d.

————— ANNALS OF ST. PAUL'S CATHEDRAL. Second
Edition. With Portrait and Illustrations. 8vo. 18s.

————— SAVONAROLA, ERASMUS, and other LITERARY
ESSAYS. 8vo. 15s.

—————— HISTORICAL WORKS; containing the 'HISTORY
OF THE JEWS,' 'EARLY CHRISTIANITY,' and 'LATIN CHRISTIANITY.' With
the Author's latest Additions and Corrections. Cabinet Edition. 15 vols.
Post 8vo. 6s. each.

————— POETICAL WORKS; containing 'Samor,' 'Fall of
Jerusalem,' 'Belshazzar,' 'Martyr of Antioch,' 'Anne Boleyn,' &c. With Plates.
3 vols. Fcap. 8vo. 18s.

—————— AGAMEMNON OF ÆSCHYLUS AND THE
BACCHANALS OF EURIPIDES. With Passages from the Lyric and Later
Poets of Greece. With Illustrations. Crown 8vo. 12s.

————— HORACE; a New Edition of the Text. With 100
Woodcuts. Small 8vo. 7s. 6d.

————————————— LIFE OF. With Illustrations. 8vo. 9s.

MOLTKE'S (BARON) RUSSIAN CAMPAIGNS ON THE
DANUBE AND THE PASSAGE OF THE BALKAN, 1828-9. With Plans.
8vo. 14s.

MONGREDIEN'S (A.) TREES AND SHRUBS FOR ENGLISH
PLANTATION. A Selection and Description of the most Ornamental
which will flourish in the open air. With Classified Lists. With 30 Illustrations. 8vo. 16s.

MOORE'S (THOMAS) LIFE OF LORD BYRON; his Letters
and Journals. With Notes and Illustrations. Cabinet Edition. With Plates.
6 vols. Fcap. 8vo. 18s.

—————————————————— With Portraits.
One Volume. Royal 8vo. 9s.

MOTLEY'S (J. L.) HISTORY OF THE UNITED NETHER-
LANDS, from the Death of William the Silent to the Twelve Years' Truce:
with a full view of the English-Dutch struggle against Spain, and of the origin
and destruction of the Spanish Armada. Fourth Edition. With Portraits.
4 vols. 8vo. 60s.; or, Cabinet Edition, 4 vols., Post 8vo, 6s. each.

MOZLEY'S (REV. J. B.) TREATISE ON THE AUGUSTINIAN
DOCTRINE OF PREDESTINATION. 8vo. 14s.

————— PRIMITIVE DOCTRINE OF BAPTISMAL RE-
GENERATION. 8vo. 7s. 6d.

MURCHISON'S (SIR RODERICK) SILURIA: a History of the
Oldest Rocks in the British Isles and other Countries. With a Sketch of
the Distribution of Native Gold. Fourth Edition. With Plates and Woodcuts. 8vo. 30s.

NAPIER'S (Sir Charles) LIFE AND OPINIONS : chiefly
derived from his Journals and Letters. *Second Edition.* With Portraits.
4 vols. Post 8vo. 48s.

———————— **(Sir William) ENGLISH BATTLES AND SIEGES**
IN THE PENINSULA. Extracted from his History of the Peninsular
War. *Fifth Edition.* With Portrait. Post 8vo. 9s.

———————— **LIFE.** With Portraits. 2 vols. Post 8vo. 30s.

NELSON'S (Robert) LIFE AND TIMES. By Rev. C. T.
SECRETAN, M.A. With Portrait. 8vo. 12s.

NEWBOLD'S (Lieut.) STRAITS OF MALACCA, PENANG,
AND SINGAPORE. 2 vols. 8vo. 26s.

NEW TESTAMENT. With a Plain Explanatory Commentary
for General Readers. By ARCHDEACON CHURTON, M.A., and
ARCHDEACON BASIL JONES, M A. With 110 authentic Views of
Scripture Sites, &c., from Sketches and Photographs taken on the Spot.
2 vols. 8vo. 21s.

NICHOLAS' (Sir Harris) HISTORIC PEERAGE OF ENG-
LAND. Exhibiting the Origin, Descent, and Present State of every Title of
Peerage which has existed in this Country since the Conquest. *A New
Edition.* Edited by W. COURTHOPE. 8vo. 30s.

NICHOLLS' (Sir George) HISTORY OF THE ENGLISH,
—IRISH,—AND SCOTCH POOR LAWS. 4 vols. 8vo. 54s.

NORTH'S (Lord) CORRESPONDENCE with KING GEORGE
THE THIRD, 1769–82. Edited, with Notes and Introduction, by W. BOD-
HAM DONNE. 2 vols. 8vo. 32s.

OLD LONDON; its Archæology and Antiquities; A Series
of Papers read at the Meeting of the Archæological Institute, July, 1866. By
VARIOUS WRITERS. 8vo. 12s.

CONTENTS :

Archæology in its Religious Aspect.—DEAN STANLEY.
An Address.—A. J. BERESFORD HOPE, M.P.
Chapter House of Westminster Abbey —G. G. SCOTT, R.A.
Sculpture in Westminster Abbey.—R. WESTMACOTT, R.A.
Westminster Hall.—E. FOSS, F.S.A.
Architectural History of the Tower.—G. T. CLARK.
Public Record Office.—JOSEPH BURTT.
London and her Election of Stephen.—Rev. J. R. GREEN.
Royal Picture Galleries.—G. SCHARF, F.S.A.

OWEN'S (Lieut.-Col.) PRINCIPLES AND PRACTICE OF
MODERN ARTILLERY, including ARTILLERY MATERIAL, GUNNERY, and
ORGANIZATION AND USE OF ARTILLERY IN WARFARE. With Illustrations.
8vo.

PARKMAN'S (Fras.) DISCOVERY OF THE GREAT WEST ;
or, The Valleys of the Mississippi and the Lakes of North America. An
Historical Narrative. With Map. 8vo. 10s. 6d.

PEEL'S (Sir Robert) MEMOIRS. I. ROMAN CATHOLIC RELIEF
BILL, 1828–9. II. FORMATION OF THE NEW GOVERNMENT IN 1834–5.
III. REPEAL OF THE CORN LAWS IN 1845-6. Edited by EARL STANHOPE
and RT. HON. EDWARD CARDWELL. 2 vols. Post 8vo. 15s.

PERCY'S (John) METALLURGY: or, The Art of Extracting
Metals from their Ores, and Adapting them to Various Purposes
of Manufacture. With numerous Illustrations. 5 vols. 8vo.

    I.—Fuel, Wood, Peat. Coal, Charcoal, Coke. Fire-Clays. Copper,
    Zinc, and Brass. 30s.
    II.—Iron and Steel. 42s.
    III.—Lead, including Desilverization and Cupellation. 30s.
    IV.—Gold, Silver. and Mercury.   [In the Press.
    V.—Platinum, Tin, Nickel, Cobalt, Antimony, Bismuth, Arsenic,
    &c.   [In the Press.

PHILLIP'S (John) RIVERS, MOUNTAINS, AND SEA-
COAST OF YORKSHIRE; with Essays on the Climate, Scenery, and
Ancient Inhabitants. With 36 Plates. 8vo. 15s.

POPE'S (Alexander) WORKS. Collected in part by the late
Rt. Hon. J. W. Croker. Edited, with Introductions and Notes, by Rev.
Whitwell Elwin. With Portraits. Vol. 1. to III. 8vo. 10s. 6d. each.

POTTERY (ANCIENT): Egyptian, Assyrian, Greek, Etruscan,
and Roman. By SAMUEL BIRCH, F.S.A. With Coloured Plates and 200
Woodcuts. 2 vols. Medium 8vo. 42s.

———— (MEDIÆVAL AND MODERN). By JOSEPH
MARRYAT. Third Edition. With Coloured Plates and 300 Woodcuts.
Medium 8vo. 42s.

———— NOTES ON VENETIAN CERAMICS. By W. R.
DRAKE, F.S.A. A Supplement to ' Marryat's Pottery.' Medium 8vo. 4s.

PRINCIPLES AT STAKE. Essays on Church Questions of the
Present Day. By various Writers. Second Edition. 8vo. 12s.

CONTENTS :

Ritualism and Uniformity.—Benjamin Shaw, M.A.
Increase of the Episcopate.—Bishop of Bath and Wells.
Powers and Duties of the Priesthood.—Canon Payne Smith.
National Education.—Rev. Alex. R. Grant.
Doctrine of the Eucharist.—Rev. G. H. Sumner.
Scripture and Ritual.—Canon T. D. Bernard.
The Church in South Africa.—Arthur Mills, M.A.
Schismatical Tendency of Ritualism.—Rev. Dr. Salmon.
Revisions of the Liturgy—Rev. W. G. Humphry.
Parties and Party Spirit.—Dean of Chester.

RANKE'S (Leopold) HISTORY OF THE POPES OF ROME:
Political and Ecclesiastical. Translated from the German, by MRS. AUSTIN.
Fourth Edition. With a Preface by Dean Milman. 3 vols. 8vo. 30s.

RASSAM'S (Hormuzd) NARRATIVE OF THE BRITISH
MISSION TO ABYSSINIA. With Notices of the Countries from Mas-
sowah, through the Soodan, and back to Annesley Bay, from Magdala.
With Map and Illustrations. 2 vols. 8vo. 28s.

RAWLINSON'S (Rev. George) MONARCHIES OF THE
ANCIENT WORLD; or, The History, Geography, and Antiquities of
Chaldæa, Media, Assyria, Babylonia, and Persia. With Maps and Illus-
trations. 3 vols. 8vo. 42s.

———— HERODOTUS. A New English Version.
Edited, with Notes and Essays, Historical, Ethnographical, and Geogra-
phical. By SIR GARDNER WILKINSON and SIR HENRY RAWLIN-
SON. *Second Edition.* With Maps and Woodcuts. 4 vols. 8vo. 48s.

REED'S (E. J.) SHIPBUILDING IN IRON AND STEEL; a Practical Treatise, giving full details of Construction, Processes of Manufacture, and Building Arrangements. With Plans and Woodcuts. 8vo. 30s.

———— **IRON-CLAD SHIPS; their Qualities, Performances,** and Cost. With Chapters on Turret Ships, Iron-clad Rams, &c. With Illustrations. 8vo. 12s.

REYNOLDS' (Sir Joshua) LIFE. With Notices of Hogarth, Wilson, Gainsborough, and other Artists, his Contemporaries. Commenced by C. R. LESLIE, R.A., and continued by TOM TAYLOR. With Portraits. 2 vols. 8vo. 42s.

ROBERTSON'S (Canon) HISTORY OF THE CHRISTIAN CHURCH, from the Apostolic Age to the End of the Fifth Council of the Lateran. 4 vols 8vo.

Vol. I., A.D 64–590. 18s.	Vol. III., A.D. 1122–1303. 18s.
Vol. II., A.D. 590–1122. 20s.	Vol. IV., A.D. 1303–1517. [In the Press.

ROBINSON'S (Rev. Edward) BIBLICAL RESEARCHES IN PALESTINE AND THE ADJACENT REGIONS; a Journal of Travels in 1838 and 1852. *Third Edition.* Maps. 3 vols. 8vo. 42s.

———————— **PHYSICAL GEOGRAPHY OF THE HOLY** LAND. Post 8vo. 10s. 6d.

SCOTT'S (Gilbert) REMARKS ON GOTHIC ARCHITEC- TURE, SECULAR AND DOMESTIC, PRESENT AND FUTURE. 8vo. 9s.

SIMMONS (Capt. T. F.) ON THE CONSTITUTION AND PRACTICE OF COURTS MARTIAL; with a Summary of the Law of Evidence, &c. *Sixth Edition*, revised and corrected. 8vo. [*In the Press.*

SMILES'S (Samuel) LIVES OF BRITISH ENGINEERS. From the Earliest Times down to the Death of Robert Stephenson, with an Account of their Principal Works, a History of Inland Communication in Britain, and the Introduction and Invention of the Steam Engine. With Portraits and Illustrations. 4 vols 8vo. 21s. each.

SMITH'S (Dr. Wm.) DICTIONARY OF THE BIBLE: its Antiquities, Biography, Geography, and Natural History. By various Writers. With Illustrations. 3 vols. Medium 8vo. 5l. 5s.

———— **CONCISE BIBLE DICTIONARY, condensed from** the above work. With Maps and 300 Illustrations. Medium 8vo. 21s.

———— **DICTIONARY OF CHRISTIAN BIOGRAPHY AND** ANTIQUITIES: from the times of the Apostles to the age of Charlemagne. With Illustrations. 2 vols. Medium 8vo. [*In the Press.*

———————————— **GREEK AND ROMAN ANTI-** QUITIES. With Woodcuts. Royal 8vo. 21s.

———— ———————— **GREEK AND ROMAN BIO-** GRAPHY AND MYTHOLOGY. With Woodcuts. 3 vols. Royal 8vo. 63s.

———————————— **GREEK AND ROMAN GEO-** GRAPHY. With Woodcuts. 2 vols. Royal 8vo. 42s.

———— **LATIN-ENGLISH DICTIONARY. With Tables** of the Roman Calendar, Measures, Weights, and Money. *Eighth Edition* (1250 pp.). Medium 8vo. 21s.

———— **ENGLISH-LATIN DICTIONARY. Compiled from** Original Sources. By WM. SMITH, D.C.L., and THEOPHILUS D. HALL, M.A. (964 pp.) Medium 8vo. 21s.

SOMERVILLE'S (MARY) PHYSICAL GEOGRAPHY. *Sixth Edition, revised.* By H. W. BATES. With Portrait. Post 8vo. 9s.

———————— SCIENCES. *Ninth Edition.* With Portrait and Woodcuts. Post 8vo. 9s.

————————MOLECULAR AND MICROSCOPIC SCIENCE. With Illustrations. 2 vols. Post 8vo. 21s.

STANHOPE'S (EARL) HISTORY OF ENGLAND, from the Peace of Utrecht to the Peace of Versailles, 1713-83. *Library Edition.* 7 vols. 8vo. 93s. Or, *Cabinet Edition*, 7 vols., Post 8vo, 35s.

———————— REIGN OF QUEEN ANNE UNTIL THE PEACE OF UTRECHT, 1701-1713. 8vo. 16s.

———————— SPAIN UNDER CHARLES THE SECOND. *Second Edition.* 8vo. 6s. 6d.

———————— LIFE OF BELISARIUS. 8vo. 10s. 6d.

———————— WILLIAM PITT. With Portraits. 4 vols. 8vo. 24s

———————— MISCELLANIES. 8vo. 5s. 6d.

STANLEY'S (DEAN) SINAI AND PALESTINE IN CON-NECTION WITH THEIR HISTORY. *Eleventh Edition.* With Map. 8vo 14s.

———————— EPISTLES OF ST. PAUL TO THE CORIN-THIANS. With Dissertations and Notes. *Third Edition.* 8vo. 18s.

———————— HISTORY OF THE EASTERN CHURCH. *Fourth Edition.* Plans 8vo. 12s.

———————— JEWISH CHURCH. From Abraham to the Captivity. *Third Edition.* 2 vols. 8vo. 24s.

———————— MEMORIALS OF CANTERBURY. *Fourth Edition.* With Woodcuts. Post 8vo. 7s. 6d.

———————— WESTMINSTER ABBEY. *Third Edition.* With Illustrations. 8vo. 21s.

———————— ESSAYS ON CHURCH AND STATE. 8vo. 16s.

———————— SERMONS PREACHED IN THE EAST DURING A TOUR WITH H.R.H. THE PRINCE OF WALES. With Notices of the Localities Visited. 8vo. 9s.

———————— ADDRESSES AND CHARGES OF BISHOP STANLEY. With Memoir. 8vo. 10s. 6d.

STREET'S (G. E.) GOTHIC ARCHITECTURE IN SPAIN. *Second Edition.* With Illustrations. Medium 8vo. 30s.

STYFFE (KNUT) ON THE STRENGTH OF IRON AND STEEL. Translated from the Swedish. By CHRISTER P. SANDBERG. With Preface, by DR. PERCY. With Lithographic Plates. 8vo. 12s.

SYBEL'S (VON) HISTORY OF EUROPE DURING THE FRENCH REVOLUTION, 1789-1795. From Secret Papers and Documents in the Archives of Germany, &c. Translated by W. C. PERRY. 4 vols. 8vo. 48s.

TAIT'S (ARCHBISHOP) DANGERS AND SAFEGUARDS; or, Suggestions to the Theological Student under present Difficulties. *2nd Edition.* 8vo. 12s.

THOMSON'S (A. S.) STORY OF NEW ZEALAND: PAST AND PRESENT—SAVAGE AND CIVILIZED. With Map and Illus-trations. 2 vols. Post 8vo. 24s.

THOMSON'S (ARCHBISHOP) LIFE IN THE LIGHT OF GOD'S
WORD. 2nd Edition. Post 8vo. 5s.

TOZER'S (H. F.) RESEARCHES IN THE ISLANDS OF
TURKEY, ALBANIA, MONTENEGRO, &c. With Notes on the Classical
Superstitions of the Modern Greek. With Map and Illustrations. 2 vols.
Crown 8vo. 24s.

TYLOR'S (E. B.) RESEARCHES INTO THE EARLY HIS-
TORY OF MANKIND, and the DEVELOPMENT OF CIVILIZATION. Second
Edition. With Illustrations. 8vo 12s.

———————— PRIMITIVE CULTURE ; Researches into the Development of Mythology, Philosophy, Religion, Art, and Custom. 2 vols. 8vo.

UBICINI'S (M. A.) TURKEY AND ITS INHABITANTS.
The Moslems, Greeks, Armenians, &c.—The Reformed Institutions, Army,
&c., described. 2 vols. Post 8vo. 21s.

WAAGEN'S (DR.) TREASURES OF ART IN GREAT
BRITAIN. Being an Account of the Chief Collections of Paintings,
Sculptures, Drawings, MSS., Miniatures, &c. 4 vols. 8vo. 54s.

WELLINGTON'S (DUKE OF) DESPATCHES DURING HIS
VARIOUS CAMPAIGNS. Edited by COL. GURWOOD. 8 vols. 8vo. 8l. 8s.

——————— SUPPLEMENTARY DESPATCHES. Edited
by HIS SON. 12 vols. 8vo. 20s. each.

——————— CIVIL AND POLITICAL CORRESPOND-
ENCE. Edited by HIS SON. Vols. I. to III. 8vo. 20s. each.

——————— SPEECHES ON VARIOUS OCCASIONS.
2 vols. 8vo. 42s

WHYMPER'S (EDWARD) SCRAMBLES AMONG THE ALPS,
1860-9. Including the First Ascent of the Matterhorn. With Observations
on GLACIER PHENOMENA in the Alps and in Greenland. With 100 Maps
and Illustrations. Medium 8vo. 21s.

WILKINSON'S (SIR GARDNER) ANCIENT EGYPTIANS;
their Private Life, Manners, and Customs. Fourth Edition. With Illustrations. 2 vols. Post 8vo. 12s.

WILLIAM THE FOURTH'S CORRESPONDENCE WITH
SIR HERBERT TAYLOR AND EARL GREY, from Nov., 1830, to the
Passing of the Reform Act in 1832. 2 vols. 8vo. 30s.

WILSON'S (SIR ROBERT) SECRET HISTORY OF EVENTS
DURING THE INVASION OF RUSSIA AND RETREAT OF THE
FRENCH ARMY, 1812. Second Edition. With Map and Plans. 8vo. 15s.

WORDSWORTH'S (BISHOP) GREECE — Pictorial, Historical,
and Descriptive. With an Essay on Greek Art, by GEORGE SCHARF, F.S.A.
Fourth Edition. With 600 Illustrations. Royal 8vo. 21s.

——————— TOUR IN ATHENS AND ATTICA.
Fourth Edition. With Plates. Post 8vo. 5s.

YULE'S (COL. HENRY) MARCO POLOS TRAVELS. Illus-
trated by the light of Modern Travels and Oriental Writers. With Maps
and Illustrations. 2 vols. Medium 8vo. 42s.

JOHN MURRAY, 50A, ALBEMARLE STREET.

LONDON : PRINTED BY WILLIAM CLOWES AND SONS, STAMFORD STREET,
AND CHARING CROSS.

50A, ALBEMARLE STREET, LONDON,
January, 1871.

MR. MURRAY'S
LIST OF POPULAR WORKS.

One Shilling.

THE PRINCIPAL SPEECHES AND ADDRESSES OF
H.R.H THE PRINCE CONSORT, with an Introduction giving some Out-
lines of his Character. With Portrait.

MUSIC AN THE ART OF DRESS. Two Essays. By A
LADY. D

THE FALL OF JERUSALEM. A Dramatic Poem. By DEAN
MILMAN.

THEODORE HOOK. A Sketch. By J. G. LOCKHART.

HISTORY OF THE GUILLOTINE. By RT. HON. J. W.
CROKER. Woodcuts.

THE CHACE. A Descriptive Essay. By C. J. APPERLEY
(NIMROD). With Woodcuts.

REJECTED ADDRESSES; or, The New Theatrum Poetarum.
By HORACE and JAMES SMITH. With Woodcuts.

THE ROAD. A Descriptive Essay. By C. J. APPERLEY
(NIMROD). With Woodcuts.

MAXIMS AND HINTS ON ANGLING, CHESS, SHOOTING,
AND OTHER MATTERS; also, the Miseries of Fishing. By RICHARD
PENN. With Woodcuts.

THE STORY OF JOAN OF ARC. By LORD MAHON.

THE PROGRESS OF LITERATURE AND SCIENCE—
THE STUDY OF HISTORY—AND ANTIQUITIES AND ART IN
ROME. By EARL STANHOPE.

CHILDE HAROLD'S PILGRIMAGE. A Romaunt. By LORD
BYRON. With Woodcuts.

HISTORY AND ANTIQUITIES OF NORTHAMPTONSHIRE.
By REV. THOMAS JAMES.

THE HONEY BEE. By REV. THOMAS JAMES.

THE FLOWER GARDEN, with an Essay on the Poetry of
Gardening. By REV. THOMAS JAMES.

One Shilling and Sixpence.

THE ART OF DINING; or, GASTRONOMY AND GASTRONOMERS. By A. HAYWARD.

WELLINGTON;—HIS CHARACTER,—ACTIONS, — AND WRITINGS. By JULES MAUREL. With Preface by LORD ELLESMERE.

WORKMEN'S EARNINGS—STRIKES—AND SAVINGS. By SAMUEL SMILES.

THE TURF. A Descriptive Essay. By C. J. APPERLEY (NIMROD). With Woodcuts.

THE STORY OF PUSS IN BOOTS. With 12 Illustrations. By OTTO SPECKTER.

PROGRESSIVE GEOGRAPHY FOR CHILDREN. By RT. HON. J. W. CROKER.

HYMNS, written and adapted to the Weekly Church Service of the Year. By BISHOP HEBER.

Two Shillings.

THE AMBER WITCH: the most interesting Trial for Witchcraft. From the German. By LADY DUFF GORDON.

OLIVER CROMWELL AND JOHN BUNYAN: Biographies. By ROBERT SOUTHEY.

LIFE OF SIR FRANCIS DRAKE. With his Voyages and Exploits by Sea and Land. By JOHN BARROW.

CAMPAIGNS OF THE BRITISH ARMY AT WASHINGTON AND NEW ORLEANS. By REV. G. R. GLEIG.

THE FRENCH IN ALGIERS; the Soldier of the Foreign Legion and Prisoners of Abd-el-Kadir. Translated by LADY DUFF GORDON.

HISTORY OF THE FALL OF THE JESUITS IN THE 18TH CENTURY. By COUNT ALEXIS DE ST. PRIEST.

LIVONIAN TALES; the Disponent—the Wolves—the Jewess. By A LADY.

NOTES FROM LIFE. MONEY — Humility — Independence — WISDOM — Choice in Marriage — CHILDREN — Life Poetic. By HENRY TAYLOR.

THE SIEGE OF GIBRALTAR, 1779–83. With a Description and Account of that Garrison from the Earliest Periods. By JOHN DRINKWATER.

SIR ROBERT SALE'S BRIGADE IN AFFGHANISTAN AND THE DEFENCE OF JELLALABAD. By REV. G. R. GLEIG.

THE TWO SIEGES OF VIENNA BY THE TURKS. Translated from the German. By LORD ELLESMERE.

THE WAYSIDE CROSS ; or, The Raid of Gomez: a Tale of the Carlist War. By CAPT. MILMAN.

ADVENTURES ON THE ROAD TO PARIS DURING THE CAMPAIGNS OF 1813-14. From the Autobiography of HENRY STEFFENS.

STOKERS AND POKERS ; or, The North-Western Railway.—The Electric Telegraph—and Railway Clearing House. By SIR FRANCIS HEAD.

TRAVELS IN EGYPT, NUBIA, SYRIA, AND THE HOLY LAND, with a Journey round the Dead Sea, and through the Country East of the Jordan. By IRBY and MANGLES.

WESTERN BARBARY; An Account of the Wild Tribes and Savage Animals. By JOHN H. DRUMMOND HAY.

LETTERS FROM THE SHORES OF THE BALTIC. By A LADY.

NOTES AND SKETCHES OF NEW SOUTH WALES DURING A RESIDENCE OF MANY YEARS IN THAT COLONY. By MRS. CHARLES MEREDITH.

RECOLLECTIONS OF BUSH LIFE IN AUSTRALIA, during a Residence of Eight Years in the Interior. By REV. H. W. HAYGARTH.

JOURNAL OF A RESIDENCE AMONG THE NEGROES IN THE WEST INDIES. By M. G. LEWIS.

MEMOIRS OF FATHER RIPA DURING THIRTEEN YEARS' RESIDENCE AT THE COURT OF PEKIN, in the Service of the Emperor of China, with an Account of the Foundation of the College for the Education of Young Chinese in Naples. From the Italian. By FORTUNATO PRANDI.

PHILIP MUSGRAVE; or, Memoirs of a Church of England Missionary in the North American Colonies. By REV. J. ABBOTT.

A MONTH IN NORWAY. By JOHN G. HOLLWAY.

LETTERS FROM MADRAS ; or, First Impressions of Life and Manners in India. By A LADY.

ROUGH NOTES TAKEN DURING SOME RAPID RIDES ACROSS THE PAMPAS AND AMONG THE ANDES. By SIR FRANCIS HEAD.

A VOYAGE UP THE RIVER AMAZON, including a Visit to PARA. By WILLIAM H. EDWARDS.

A POPULAR ACCOUNT of the MANNERS and CUSTOMS
OF INDIA. By REV. CHARLES ACLAND.

ADVENTURES IN THE LIBYAN DESERT AND THE
OASIS OF JUPITER AMMON. By BAYLE ST. JOHN.

LIFE OF SIR FOWELL BUXTON. By his Son, CHARLES
BUXTON. With an Inquiry into the Results of Emancipation.

Two Shillings and Sixpence.

THE CONTINUITY OF SCRIPTURE, as declared by the
Testimony of our Lord and of the Evangelists and Apostles. By LORD
HATHERLEY.

LIFE OF LORD BACON. By LORD CAMPBELL.

CHILDE HAROLD'S PILGRIMAGE. A Romaunt. By LORD
BYRON.

TALES AND POEMS. By LORD BYRON.

LITTLE ARTHUR'S HISTORY OF ENGLAND. By LADY
CALLCOTT. With 28 Woodcuts.

THE EMIGRANT. By SIR FRANCIS HEAD.

THE FABLES OF ÆSOP; A New Version, chiefly from
Original Sources. By REV. THOMAS JAMES. With 100 Woodcuts.

STORIES FOR CHILDREN SELECTED FROM THE HIS-
TORY OF ENGLAND. By Rt. Hon. J. W. CROKER. With 24 Woodcuts.

THE COMPLETE POETICAL WORKS OF LORD BYRON.

THE PHILOSOPHY OF THE MORAL FEELINGS. By
JOHN ABERCROMBIE.

POEMS AND SONGS. By ALLAN CUNNINGHAM. With
Biographical Notice.

THE FRANCHISE; a Privilege and not a Right. Proved by the
Political Experience of the Ancients. By H. S. TREMENHEERE.

Three Shillings.

"THE FORTY-FIVE;" A Narrative of the Insurrection of
1745 in Scotland. To which are added Letters of Prince Charles Stuart.
By LORD MAHON.

Three Shillings and Sixpence.

THE BIBLE IN SPAIN; or, The Adventures and Imprisonment of an Englishman in attempting to Circulate the Scriptures in the Peninsula. By GEORGE BORROW.

THE GYPSIES OF SPAIN; their Manners, Customs, Religion, and Language By GEORGE BORROW.

THE BEAUTIES OF LORD BYRON'S WRITINGS; POETRY AND PROSE. With Portrait.

LIFE OF LOUIS PRINCE OF CONDÉ, SURNAMED THE GREAT. By LORD MAHON.

SKETCHES OF GERMAN LIFE AND SCENES FROM THE WAR OF LIBERATION IN GERMANY. By VARNHAGEN VON ERESE. Translated by SIR ALEXANDER DUFF GORDON.

THE TRUE STORY OF THE BATTLE OF WATERLOO. By REV. G. R. GLEIG.

DEEDS OF NAVAL DARING; or, ANECDOTES OF THE BRITISH NAVY. By EDWARD GIFFARD.

TYPEE; or, The Marquesas Islanders. By HERMAN MELVILLE.

OMOO : A Narrative of Adventures in the South Seas; a Sequel to 'Typee.' By HERMAN MELVILLE.

THE BIBLE IN THE HOLY LAND; being Extracts from Dean Stanley's 'Sinai and Palestine.' With Woodcuts.

AN ESSAY ON ENGLISH POETRY. With Short Notices of the British Poets. By THOMAS CAMPBELL.

HISTORICAL AND CRITICAL ESSAYS. By LORD MAHON.

LIFE OF LORD CLIVE. By REV. G. R. GLEIG.

LIFE OF SIR THOMAS MUNRO. With Selections from his Correspondence. By REV. G. R. GLEIG.

THE RISE OF OUR INDIAN EMPIRE : being a History of British India from its Origin till the Peace of 1783. By LORD MAHON.

A NARRATIVE OF THE SIEGE OF KARS, and of the Six
Months' Resistance by the Turkish Garrison under General Williams. With
Travels and Adventures in Armenia, &c. By HUMPHREY SANDWITH,
M.D.

SKETCHES OF PERSIA. By SIR JOHN MALCOLM.

THE WILD SPORTS AND NATURAL HISTORY OF THE
HIGHLANDS. By CHARLES ST. JOHN.

GATHERINGS FROM SPAIN. By RICHARD FORD.

TRAVELS IN MEXICO AND THE ROCKY MOUNTAINS.
By G. F. RUXTON.

PORTUGAL AND GALLICIA; with an Account of the
Social and Political state of the Basque Provinces. By LORD
CARNARVON.

A RESIDENCE AT SIERRA LEONE. Described from a
Journal kept on the Spot, and Letters written to Friends at Home. By
A LADY.

THE REMAINS IN VERSE AND PROSE OF ARTHUR
HENRY HALLAM. With Preface, Memoir, and Portrait.

THE POETICAL WORKS OF BISHOP HEBER; containing
Palestine, Europe, the Red Sea, Hymns, &c. With Portrait.

GLEANINGS IN NATURAL HISTORY. By EDWARD
JESSE. With Woodcuts.

THE REJECTED ADDRESSES; or, The New Theatrum
Poetarum. By HORACE and JAMES SMITH. With Portrait and
Woodcuts.

CONSOLATIONS IN TRAVEL; or, The Last Days of a Philosopher. By SIR HUMPHRY DAVY. With Woodcuts.

SALMONIA; or, Days of Fly-fishing. By SIR HUMPHRY
DAVY. With Woodcuts.

THE INTELLECTUAL POWERS AND THE INVESTIGA-
TION OF TRUTH. By JOHN ABERCROMBIE.

SPECIMENS OF THE TABLE-TALK OF THE LATE
SAMUEL TAYLOR COLERIDGE. With Portrait.

PRACTICAL INSTRUCTIONS IN GARDENING, for every
Month in the Year. By MRS. LOUDON. With Woodcuts.

A SMALLER HISTORY OF ENGLAND. Edited by DR. WM. SMITH. With Woodcuts.

A SMALLER HISTORY OF GREECE. Edited by DR. WM. SMITH. With Woodcuts.

A SMALLER HISTORY OF ROME. Edited by DR. WM. SMITH. With Woodcuts.

A SMALLER CLASSICAL MYTHOLOGY. With Translations from the Ancient Poets. Edited by DR. WM. SMITH. With Woodcuts.

A SMALLER ANCIENT HISTORY, from the Earliest Times to the Conquest of Alexander the Great. Edited by DR. WM. SMITH. With Woodcuts.

A SMALLER HISTORY OF ENGLISH LITERATURE, from the earliest period to the Georgian Era. Edited by DR. WM. SMITH.

SPECIMENS OF THE CHIEF WRITERS IN ENGLISH LITERATURE. Chronologically arranged. Edited by DR. WM. SMITH.

A SMALLER SCRIPTURE HISTORY.—I. Old Testament History; II. Connection of Old and New Testaments; III. New Testament History to A.D. 70. Edited by DR. WM. SMITH. With Woodcuts.

Four Shillings.

HISTORY OF ENGLAND, from the FIRST INVASION by the ROMANS, continued down to 1865. With CONVERSATIONS at the end of each CHAPTER. By MRS. MARKHAM. With 100 Woodcuts.

HISTORY OF FRANCE, from the CONQUEST by the GAULS, continued down to 1867. With CONVERSATIONS at the end of each CHAPTER. By MRS. MARKHAM. With 70 Woodcuts.

HISTORY OF GERMANY, from the INVASION of the KINGDOM by the ROMANS under MARIUS, continued down to 1867. On the Plan of MRS. MARKHAM. With 50 Woodcuts.

SHALL AND WILL; or, the Future Auxiliary Verb. By SIR EDMUND HEAD.

Four Shillings and Sixpence.

CHILDREN OF THE LAKE. A Poem. By EDWARD SALLESBURY.

A LADY'S DIARY OF THE SIEGE OF LUCKNOW.

HOUSEHOLD SURGERY; or, Hints on Emergencies. By JOHN F. SOUTH. With Woodcuts.

Five Shillings.

ANCIENT SPANISH BALLADS; HISTORICAL AND ROMANTIC. Translated with Notes by J. G. LOCKHART. With Portrait and Illustrations.

MISCELLANIES. By LORD BYRON. 2 vols.

INTRODUCTIONS TO THE STUDY OF THE GREEK CLASSIC POETS. By HENRY NELSON COLERIDGE.

HYMNS IN PROSE FOR CHILDREN. By MRS. BARBAULD. With 112 Illustrations.

RECOLLECTIONS OF THE DRUSES, AND SOME NOTES ON THEIR RELIGION. By LORD CARNARVON.

THE ORIGIN OF LANGUAGE. BASED ON MODERN RE-SEARCHES. By REV. F. W FARRAR.

MODERN DOMESTIC COOKERY. Founded on Principles of Economy and Practical Knowledge, and adapted for Private Families. With Woodcuts.

DRAMAS AND PLAYS. By LORD BYRON. 2 vols.

THE HORSE AND HIS RIDER. By SIR FRANCIS HEAD. With Woodcuts.

HANDBOOK OF FAMILIAR QUOTATIONS, chiefly from English Authors.

THE CHACE—THE TURF—AND THE ROAD. A Series of Popular Essays. By C. J. APPERLEY (NIMROD). With Portrait and Illustrations.

AUNT IDA'S WALKS AND TALKS. A Story Book for Children. By A LADY.

STORIES FOR DARLINGS. A Book for Boys and Girls. With Illustrations.

THE CHARMED ROE. A Story Book for Young People. Illustrated by OTTO SPECKTER.

DON JUAN AND BEPPO. By LORD BYRON. 2 vols.

LIFE IN THE LIGHT OF GOD'S WORD. By ARCHBISHOP THOMSON, D.D.

ATHENS AND ATTICA; Notes of a Tour. By BISHOP WORDSWORTH, D.D. With Illustrations.

ANNALS OF THE WARS—XVIIITH CENTURY, 1700–1799. Compiled from the most Authentic Sources. By SIR EDWARD CUST, D.C.L. With Maps. 5 vols. Post 8vo. 5s. each.

ANNALS OF THE WARS — XIXTH CENTURY, 1800–15. Compiled from the most Authentic Sources. By SIR EDWARD CUST. 4 vols. Fcap. 8vo. 5s. each.

Six Shillings.

BENEDICITE; or, THE SONG of the THREE CHILDREN. Being ILLUSTRATIONS of the POWER, BENEFICENCE, and DESIGN manifested by the CREATOR in HIS WORKS. By DR. CHAPLIN CHILD.

OLD DECCAN DAYS; or, HINDOO FAIRY LEGENDS current in Southern India. By M. FRERE. With Introduction by SIR BARTLE FRERE. With Illustrations.

THE WILD GARDEN; or, OUR GROVES AND SHRUBBERIES MADE BEAUTIFUL BY THE NATURALIZATION OF HARDY EXOTIC PLANTS. By WILLIAM ROBINSON. With Frontispiece.

MISSIONARY TRAVELS AND RESEARCHES IN SOUTH AFRICA. By DAVID LIVINGSTONE, M.D. With Map and Illustrations.

FIVE YEARS OF A HUNTER'S LIFE IN SOUTH AFRICA; By GORDON CUMMING. With Illustrations.

THOUGHTS ON ANIMALCULES; or, The Invisible World, as revealed by the Microscope. By GIDEON A. MANTELL. With Plates.

LIVES OF BRINDLEY AND THE EARLY ENGINEERS. By SAMUEL SMILES. With Woodcuts.

LIFE OF TELFORD. With a History of Roads and Travelling in England. By SAMUEL SMILES. With Woodcuts.

LIVES OF GEORGE AND ROBERT STEPHENSON. By SAMUEL SMILES. With Woodcuts.

SELF-HELP. With Illustrations of Character and Conduct. By SAMUEL SMILES.

INDUSTRIAL BIOGRAPHY: Iron-workers and Toolmakers. A Sequel to 'Self-help.' By SAMUEL SMILES.

THE HUGUENOTS IN ENGLAND AND IRELAND: their Settlements, Churches, and Industries. By SAMUEL SMILES.

WILD WALES; its People, Language, and Scenery. With Introductory Remarks. By GEORGE BORROW.

A MANUAL OF ETHNOLOGY; or, A POPULAR HISTORY of the RACES of the OLD WORLD. By CHARLES L. BRACE.

Seven Shillings.

JOURNALS OF A TOUR IN INDIA. By BISHOP HEBER. 2 vols.

ADVENTURES AMONG THE MARQUESAS AND SOUTH SEA ISLANDERS. By HERMAN MELVILLE. 2 vols.

CONSTITUTIONAL PROGRESS. By MONTAGU BURROWS, M.A.

LIFE AND POETICAL WORKS OF REV. GEORGE CRABBE. Edited by HIS SON. With Notes, Portrait, and Illustrations.

Seven Shillings and Sixpence.

THE ART OF TRAVEL; or, Hints on the Shifts and Contrivances available in Wild Countries. By FRANCIS GALTON. With Woodcuts.

VISITS TO THE MONASTERIES OF THE LEVANT. By HON. R. CURZON. With Illustrations.

LETTERS FROM HIGH LATITUDES; an Account of a Yacht Voyage to Iceland, Jan Mayen, and Spitzbergen, &c. By LORD DUFFERIN. With Illustrations.

BUBBLES FROM THE BRUNNEN OF NASSAU. By an Old Man (SIR FRANCIS HEAD). With Illustrations.

NINEVEH AND ITS REMAINS; a Narrative of an Expedition to Assyria in 1845-47. By A. H. LAYARD. With Illustrations.

NINEVEH AND BABYLON; a Narrative of a Second Expedition to Assyria in 1849-51. By A. H. LAYARD. With Illustrations.

THREE YEARS' RESIDENCE IN ABYSSINIA, with Travels in that Country. By MANSFIELD PARKYNS. With Illustrations.

FIVE YEARS IN DAMASCUS, with TRAVELS in PALMYRA, LEBANON, and among the GIANT CITIES OF BASHAN and THE HAURAN. By REV. J. L. PORTER. With Illustrations.

THE VOYAGE OF THE 'FOX' IN THE ARCTIC SEAS, and the Discovery of the Fate of Sir John Franklin and his Companions. By SIR LEOPOLD McCLINTOCK. With Illustrations.

REMINISCENCES OF ATHENS AND THE MOREA, during Travels in Greece. By LORD CARNARVON. With Map.

PEN AND PENCIL SKETCHES IN INDIA. By GENERAL MUNDY. With Illustrations.

PHILOSOPHY IN SPORT, MADE SCIENCE IN EARNEST: or, The First Principles of Natural Philosophy explained by the Toys and Sports of Youth. By DR. PARIS. With Woodcuts.

BLIND PEOPLE; their Works and Ways. With Lives of some famous Blind Men. By REV. B. G. JOHNS. With Illustrations.

HORACE: A New Edition of the Text. Edited by DEAN MILMAN. With 100 Woodcuts.

THE BOOK OF THE CHURCH. By ROBERT SOUTHEY.

A HANDBOOK FOR YOUNG PAINTERS. By C. R. LESLIE, R.A. With 24 Illustrations.

A GEOGRAPHICAL HANDBOOK OF FERNS, with Tables to show their Distribution. By K. M. LYELL. With a Frontispiece.

THE STORY OF THE LIFE OF LORD BACON. By W. HEPWORTH DIXON.

A SMALLER DICTIONARY OF THE BIBLE ; Its Antiquities,
Geography, Biography, and Natural History. By DR. WM. SMITH. With
Maps and Illustrations.

A SMALLER CLASSICAL DICTIONARY OF MYTHOLOGY,
BIOGRAPHY, AND GEOGRAPHY. By DR. WM. SMITH. With
200 Woodcuts.

A SMALLER DICTIONARY OF GREEK AND ROMAN
ANTIQUITIES. By DR. WM. SMITH. With 200 Woodcuts.

A SMALLER LATIN - ENGLISH DICTIONARY. With a
Dictionary of Proper Names, and Tables of the Roman Calendar, Measures,
Weights, and Moneys. By DR. WM. SMITH.

A SMALLER ENGLISH-LATIN DICTIONARY. By DR. WM.
SMITH.

THE STUDENT'S HUME; An Epitome of the History of
England. By DAVID HUME. Corrected and continued to 1868. With
Woodcuts.

THE STUDENT'S CONSTITUTIONAL HISTORY OF ENG-
LAND. By HENRY HALLAM. With the Author's latest Additions.
Edited by DR. WM. SMITH. [In the Press.

THE STUDENT'S HISTORY OF THE MIDDLE AGES OF
EUROPE. By HENRY HALLAM. With the Author's Supplemental
Notes. Edited by DR. WM. SMITH. [In the Press.

THE STUDENT'S HISTORY OF FRANCE. From the
Earliest Times to the Establishment of the Second Empire, 1852.
With Woodcuts.

THE STUDENT'S HISTORY OF ROME. From the Earliest
Times to the Establishment of the Empire. With Chapters on the
History of Literature and Art. By DEAN LIDDELL. With Woodcuts.

THE STUDENT'S GIBBON; An Epitome of the History of
the Decline and Fall of the Roman Empire. By EDWARD GIBBON.
With Woodcuts.

THE STUDENT'S HISTORY OF GREECE. From the
Earliest Times to the Roman Conquest. With Chapters on the
History of Literature and Art. By DR. WM. SMITH. With Woodcuts.

THE STUDENT'S ANCIENT HISTORY OF THE EAST.
From the Earliest Times to the Conquests of Alexander the Great, including
Egypt, Assyria, Babylonia, Media, Persia, Asia Minor, and Phœnicia. By
PHILIP SMITH, B.A. With Woodcuts.

THE STUDENT'S OLD TESTAMENT HISTORY. From the
Creation to the Return of the Jews from Captivity. With Maps and
Woodcuts.

THE STUDENT'S NEW TESTAMENT HISTORY. With an
Introduction, containing the connection of the Old and New Testaments.
With Maps and Woodcuts.

THE STUDENT'S MANUAL OF THE ENGLISH LAN-
GUAGE. By GEORGE P. MARSH. Edited, with additional Chapters and
Notes.

HANDBOOK — GLOUCESTER, HEREFORD, AND
WORCESTER — CIRENCESTER, CHELTENHAM, STROUD, TEWKESBURY, LEO-
MINSTER, ROSS, MALVERN, KIDDERMINSTER, DUDLEY, BROMSGROVE, EVESHAM.
With Map. 6s. 6d.

HANDBOOK — NORTH WALES — BANGOR, CARNARVON,
BEAUMARIS, SNOWDON, CONWAY, &c. With Map. 6s. 6d.

HANDBOOK — SOUTH WALES — MONMOUTH, CARMARTHEN,
TENBY, SWANSEA, AND THE WYE, &c. With Map. 7s.

HANDBOOK — DERBY, NOTTS, LEICESTER, AND
STAFFORD — MATLOCK, BAKEWELL, CHATSWORTH, THE PEAK, BUXTON,
HARDWICK, DOVE DALE, ASHBORNE, SOUTHWELL, MANSFIELD, RETFORD,
BURTON, BELVOIR, MELTON MOWBRAY, WOLVERHAMPTON, LITCHFIELD,
WALSALL, TAMWORTH. With Map. 7s. 6d.

HANDBOOK — SHROPSHIRE, CHESHIRE, AND LANCA-
SHIRE — SHREWSBURY, LUDLOW, BRIDGNORTH, OSWESTRY, CHESTER, CREWE,
ALDERLEY, STOCKPORT, BIRKENHEAD, WARRINGTON, BURY, MANCHESTER,
LIVERPOOL, BURNLEY, CLITHEROE, BOLTON, BLACKBURN, WIGAN, PRESTON,
ROCHDALE, LANCASTER, SOUTHPORT, BLACKPOOL, &c. With Map. 10s.

HANDBOOK — YORKSHIRE — DONCASTER, HULL, SELBY,
BEVERLEY, SCARBOROUGH, WHITBY, HARROGATE, RIPON, LEEDS, WAKEFIELD,
BRADFORD, HALIFAX, HUDDERSFIELD, SHEFFIELD. With Map. 12s.

HANDBOOK — DURHAM AND NORTHUMBERLAND —
NEWCASTLE, DARLINGTON, BISHOP AUCKLAND, STOCKTON, HARTLEPOOL, SUN-
DERLAND, SHIELDS, BERWICK, TYNEMOUTH, ALNWICK. With Map. 9s.

HANDBOOK — WESTMORLAND AND CUMBERLAND —
LANCASTER, FURNESS ABBEY, AMBLESIDE, KENDAL, WINDERMERE, CONISTON,
KESWICK, GRASMERE, CARLISLE, COCKERMOUTH, PENRITH, APPLEBY. With
Map. 6s.

  ₊ MURRAY'S MAP OF THE LAKE DISTRICT, 3s. 6d.

HANDBOOK — SCOTLAND — EDINBURGH, MELROSE, KELSO,
GLASGOW, DUMFRIES, AYR, STIRLING, ARRAN, THE CLYDE, OBAN, INVERARY,
LOCH LOMOND, LOCH KATRINE AND TROSACHS, CALEDONIAN CANAL, INVER-
NESS, PERTH, DUNDEE, ABERDEEN, BRAEMAR, SKYE, CAITHNESS, ROSS, AND
SUTHERLAND. With Maps and Plans. 9s.

HANDBOOK — IRELAND — DUBLIN, BELFAST, DONEGAL, GAL-
WAY, WEXFORD, CORK, LIMERICK, WATERFORD, KILLARNEY, MUNSTER.
With Map. 12s.

JOHN MURRAY, 50A, ALBEMARLE STREET.

LONDON: PRINTED BY WILLIAM CLOWES AND SONS, STAMFORD STREET,
AND CHARING CROSS.

Lightning Source UK Ltd.
Milton Keynes UK
UKHW021854191218
334260UK00013B/1334/P